Sarah Goldman has spent most of her life as a journalist. Initially working for newspapers in Sydney and London, she later transferred to television with the BBC. Back in Australia, Sarah continued as a producer for both commercial and ABC television news in Sydney and Melbourne. Much of Sarah's journalistic work has involved international news. *Caroline Chisholm: An Irresistible Force* is Sarah's first book. She and her partner, Steven, have two sons and a dog. They live in Sydney.

Caroline Chisholm

AN IRRESISTIBLE FORCE

SARAH GOLDMAN

HarperCollinsPublishers

HarperCollins*Publishers*

First published in Australia in 2017
This edition published in 2019
by HarperCollins*Publishers* Australia Pty Limited
ABN 36 009 913 517
harpercollins.com.au

HarperCollins*Publishers*
Level 13, 201 Elizabeth Street, Sydney NSW 2000, Australia
Unit D1, 63 Apollo Drive, Rosedale, Auckland 0632, New Zealand
A 53, Sector 57, Noida, UP, India
1 London Bridge Street, London SE1 9GF, United Kingdom
Bay Adelaide Centre, East Tower, 22 Adelaide Street West, 41st floor,
  Toronto, Ontario M5H 4E3, Canada
195 Broadway, New York NY 10007, USA

A catalogue record for this book is available from the National Library of Australia.

ISBN: 978 1 4607 5344 6 (paperback)
ISBN: 978 1 4607 0800 2 (ebook)

Cover design by Darren Holt, HarperCollins Design Studio
Cover image: Caroline Chisholm, Famous Australians stamp series, 1968;
designer: Alfred Cook, engraver: Lyell Dolan; © Australian Postal Corporation

Typeset in Bembo Std by Kirby Jones
Printed and bound in Australia by McPhersons Printing Group
The papers used by HarperCollins in the manufacture of this book are a natural,
recyclable product made from wood grown in sustainable plantation forests. The
fibre source and manufacturing processes meet recognised international
environmental standards, and carry certification

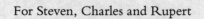

For Steven, Charles and Rupert

CONTENTS

Introduction

Sydney 1841

"Madam, what would you have me do?" The voice was elegant, indifferent, giving no hint of the speaker's irritation, though his raven eyebrows bushed together ominously above his chalk white face, his lips pale and dry as parchment. Sir George Gipps, Governor of New South Wales, had little time to waste on do-gooders, even one as attractive as this woman.

Indeed, he had been surprised when Caroline Chisholm had been ushered into the room, even wondered if he had misheard the name. Instead of the frumpy, bespectacled matron in plain gown and white cap that he had expected, he had been confronted by a handsome, even stately young matron, fashionably dressed and wearing a very fetching bonnet. He was no connoisseur of female attire, but he liked the way she looked.[1]

She was smiling at him now, and he couldn't for the life of him resist smiling back. It put him at a disadvantage. That was the trouble when dealing with women. With a man you could be curt, even dismissive. It was easily done: a nod or handshake and they were gone. But how did you get rid of a lady who looked more suited to your wife's drawing room than your office? His own wife, Elizabeth, was part of the problem: she had plagued him to meet Mrs Chisholm. And now

1

look what had come of it. He had to invite her to sit down and listen to her concerns about the bounty women. They were needed, of course, as workers and wives, and his government paid boat captains a fair price for each woman of good character brought to the colony. But he had little interest in them.

Mrs Chisholm, though, had made it her business to haunt Sydney's wharves, meeting the boats, giving advice to these immigrant girls, the debris of Britain's overcrowded towns, now looking for a toehold in the New World. Times were difficult, respectable jobs scarce; some females, destitute, resorted to immoral activities just to survive. This woman, this Mrs Chisholm, wanted to start a home for them. He was told that not everyone was on her side: strangely, churchmen, both Anglican and Catholic, were suspicious of her. So even if he agreed to help her, there was no guarantee of success. He had imagined that Mrs Chisholm would talk to him about goodness and his soul and being in God's grace, but there was little of that. She was dealing in practicalities, as though, he realised with some amazement, she imagined her reason and experience were worth as much as his own.[2]

Now she was answering his question. Had she not the wit to realise that it had been rhetorical?

"Sir George," she said, "what I would have you do is let me have the old Immigration Barracks, the one up near the Domain on the corner of Bent Street. It stands empty. It could provide shelter for the girls."

It was an audacious request, too expensive a proposition for the Colonial Government. He would have no truck with it, and said so.

"What if I raised the funds to support the costs, Your Excellency?" she countered.

She spoke with poise, her voice soft, pleasing. But he would not be outwitted by a female. Did she really expect to go through with this outrageous plan? To work as though she were a man in need of employment? If he remembered aright, she was the wife of a military *captain; she ought to have been at home looking after her children.*[3] *He would finish this now.*

Deliberately pulling out his watch, Sir George stood up to indicate that the interview was over, while softening the blow with an indulgent smile. "Mrs Chisholm, I understand that your motives are of the purest. There is, however, very little that you can do by yourself. I suggest that you consider joining the Ladies' Committee, or some such thing." He put out his hand. "It has been a pleasure having this little chat."

She stood also, but refrained from taking his hand; instead, delving into her reticule, she pulled out a package of letters tied together with blue ribbon. "Before I go, Your Excellency, would you be willing to frank these letters for me?[4] *I wish to write to farmers, churchmen and police magistrates in the bush to find out what prospects and wages are available for the girls outside Sydney Town."*

"By Jove, you would try the patience of a saint, madam!" he exclaimed, exasperation and amusement warring within. She stood perfectly still like a graceful figurine, an almost penitent smile hovering about her lips. She reminded him of one of his nieces caught in some mischief. The humour won out; unable to contain a bark of laughter, he requested the letters.

Completing the task, he once more held out his hand to her. "Mrs Chisholm, I am glad that I was able to assist you with something, but you are not to harbour expectations of me changing my mind. That is a bird that will not fly, madam."

She put her gloved hand into his. "Sir, I do not easily give up hope."

She curtsied and withdrew as his secretary entered the room with a sheaf of papers. However comely she was, he hoped it would be the last he saw of Mrs Chisholm, about this matter at least. He had an uneasy suspicion, though, that he was being challenged by an unusually adept general. She might wear petticoats and overrate the powers of her own mind, but as a military man he recognised that this could be just the first skirmish in a long campaign.[5]

S ydney in 1838 was fifty years old: a violent, unequal, racist town slowly developing a conscience. It was a time of fluidity: the Myall Creek massacre trials were dividing society between supporters of the stockmen accused of butchering defenceless Aborigines and the relatively few determined to see justice prevail; the economy was brittle; transportation was ending; and thousands of poor new settlers — free bounty immigrants whose passage was paid by the Colonial Government — were pouring into Sydney. The white settlement camped on the eastern edge of the continent was an eclectic mix of peoples, whose only commonality was a shared language. Half a century had not been enough time to put down roots, create traditions or meld social cohesion. Each disparate group, be it convicts, emancipists, poor immigrants, wealthy free settlers or the military, was striving for survival and some measure of success. Few had even registered the growing humanitarian crisis in front of them. If a measure of a society is how it treats its most vulnerable, then the penal colony of Terra Australis was just beginning to discover its character. This is the world that Caroline Chisholm had entered. Confronted by the desperation of the poorest and most vulnerable immigrants, she sought help from the pinnacle of colonial authority.

We can only speculate on the details of Caroline's first meeting with the most powerful person in the Colony of New South Wales. She deemed it a success, believing that ultimately Sir George would not refuse her request, even if he would *rather not* grant it.[6] The governor's initial opinion of Caroline, though, comes down to us loud and clear: he was bemused that a female had the temerity to argue her case on equal terms; he also found her undeniably attractive and was not the only man in Sydney to describe her so.[7] There is other evidence too that she possessed considerable personal charm and congeniality, without which she would have floundered in polite colonial society.[8]

What is most remarkable is that Caroline, emerging from the lowly strata of British society, had the self-confidence and determination to take on the governor, the church and the establishment and ultimately win. It was not the first time, and it would not be the last, that she successfully pitted her resolve against the authority of the opposite sex. In India in the 1830s, she had founded a school for the daughters of ordinary soldiers and in doing so convinced one of the most formidable heroes of the Battle of Waterloo, Sir Frederick Adam, then the Governor of Madras, not only to support the school but also to contribute to its establishment. Years later, in London, she would persuade the Secretary of State for the Colonies, Earl Grey, to comply with her request to help reunite convicts and adult immigrants with wives and children they had been forced to leave behind.

Even more surprising was the ultimatum Caroline had given the man she loved. Displaying a bold disregard for social custom, she had refused to marry Archibald Chisholm unless he agreed to let her lead a public life. For an Englishwoman in 1830, that was an extraordinary bid for freedom.

Born into the flux of the nascent rural middle class, and uncertain of her actual parentage and legitimacy, Caroline faced the same prospects as most women: marriage, child-bearing and governing the minutiae of domestic trivialities. "The first object of every woman in married life should be the happiness of her husband," wrote a respected woman author of the era.[9] The man held all legal, financial and social power in the relationship. Indeed, a nineteenth-century wife was a ghostly being without any lawful entity: her money and possessions, owned or earned, belonged to her husband, who also had indisputable conjugal rights and ultimate authority over his wife and children. Women of all standings were conditioned from birth to believe fathers, brothers, husbands and even sons superior, both cerebrally and emotionally. "As Women, then, the first thing of importance is to be content to be inferior to men — inferior in mental power, in the same proportion that you are inferior in bodily strength," wrote Sarah Stickney Ellis, advising young women on their preparation for marriage.[10]

The few female contemporaries who dared to challenge the system came mainly from the upper-class intelligentsia, for example the French author Amantine-Lucile-Aurore Dupin (George Sand), who scandalously revelled in cross-dressing and extramarital affairs, and English writer Mary Ann Evans (George Eliot), who, just as shockingly, lived openly with a married man. As a young woman, Caroline was no revolutionary. Boldly negotiating her own future put her directly at odds with her conservative roots, yet she was morally and socially conventional. Her radicalism developed from her profound desire to help the poor and distressed and, amazingly, given her background, from her inherent belief in her own abilities. That overarching confidence is more typical of a woman of the twenty-first century than one of the 1800s.

Caroline Chisholm's position in Australian history has been subject to fashion and fancy. Among her contemporaries and for about ninety years after her death in 1877, she was lauded as "the Emigrant's Friend".[11] Her conversion to Catholicism following her marriage in 1830 and her deep-seated religious faith led ardent admirers to suggest that she was a candidate for canonisation — at least one biography appears to have been written in support of this aim.[12] By the late 1960s and early 1970s, however, sentiment was turning against her. She was belittled by some writers who claimed that her reputation and achievements had been exaggerated by the Catholic Church.[13] Others decried her "anti-feminist" stance: notably, the prominent journalist and feminist Anne Summers accused her of providing "the ideological underpinnings for more than a century of domestic servitude by Australian women".[14]

More recently, Caroline's name has remained vaguely familiar through its association with many places and institutions. She was the first woman, apart from the Queen, to feature on our currency, adorning the five-dollar note from 1967 to 1992, and in 1968 she was pictured on a five-cent stamp. A federal electorate named Chisholm, a suburb of Canberra, a hill in the New South Wales Southern Highlands, parks, buildings, and streets too numerous to mention, various aged care homes, schools and an anti-abortion pregnancy counselling society all bear her name.

Despite this and at least one new biography this century, Caroline has now all but faded from our national consciousness.[15] Only a few schoolchildren today know her name or what she achieved for our infant colony; indeed, it was my own sons' lack of knowledge of Caroline that drew me to her. I found previous biographies fulsome with facts and figures relating to her path through the politics of the day, but, frustratingly, what I couldn't discover in these otherwise excellent accounts was a sense of the woman herself, the flesh and blood creature.

What she did and where she went has been well documented. Who she was, much less so. The first biographies of Caroline were written in 1852, 165 years ago, by contemporaries, men who eulogised her work but had little or no interest in her personal life or her motivation. Eneas Mackenzie, for instance, said that he would not gratify "a mere morbid taste by rudely peering behind the veil of domestic life" whilst describing her work as "God-like ... in fervid devotion to the Christian duties of charity and mercy. Her zeal has been apostolic."[16] This was a theme continued by most subsequent biographers, with her religious beliefs taking precedence over any investigation into her true character or personality. The result was the creation of a Caroline Chisholm too perfect to be true. Even Mary Hoban's extensively researched book of more than four hundred pages published in 1973, *Fifty-One Pieces of Wedding Cake,* offers a Caroline without any human frailty. Anyone who did criticise Caroline, and there were a few, were in Hoban's opinion themselves at fault rather than the other way around. There were two exceptions to this biographical whitewash approach. The first was Margaret Kiddle's *Caroline Chisholm,* initially published in 1950. It was very well researched, but Kiddle noted in her preface, "This is not the personal biography of Caroline Chisholm ... I have been unable to trace her private papers."[17] The second was Carole Walker's *A Saviour of Living Cargoes,* based on her PhD thesis and published in 2009. Walker's excellent investigations discovered a few of Caroline's letters and other details not known to previous biographers. However, whilst both Kiddle and Walker have placed Caroline within the political world and temperament of the times, they have ignored both the social and emotional sides of Caroline, leaving a character, who, although admirable, is at best two-dimensional.

My approach has been different. I have adhered to the evidence and facts of Caroline's life, but have tried to focus more on Caroline as a woman. For instance, I have considered what it might have been like for Caroline, a nineteenth-century woman, to give birth, to lose a child and to be separated from her husband for years at a time — particularly when an attractive and eligible bachelor made her the centre of his attention. Just as salient, how did she manage the work–life balance of a working mother, recognised today as a major challenge for women, but almost unknown to the females of Caroline's era? In a similar vein, and partly in response to the attacks of the feminists of last century, I wanted to determine her true attitude towards the role of women in society.

I also wanted to reveal Caroline as a living, breathing person in a real world, not just a historical figure from a bygone age. I have therefore, at the start of most chapters, imagined scenes that relate directly to incidents covered within the subsequent pages. In creating these scenes, particularly when writing about Caroline's interaction with named people, I drew on historical records. For example, the short piece, including most of the dialogue, at the start of Chapter 6, "Flora's Story", comes directly from Caroline's own pen. Her meeting and interaction with Charles Dickens at the start of Chapter 12 is based on what Dickens subsequently wrote about Caroline and their ensuing collaboration. Elsewhere, I have used evidence from both Caroline and other sources to convey a sense of the world she was entering, whether it was India, Sydney or the bush. The endnotes provide further details on the sources.

Delving into the environments Caroline inhabited, in Britain, India and Australia, I learnt something of how she dealt with the challenges of both her physical and social surroundings. Reading her few private and many public letters, pamphlets and other writings, along with newspaper reports and accounts from people who knew her and others who inhabited the same or similar space, provided further revelations. Caroline was not perfect. Some contemporaries found her "unreasonable and indiscreet".[18] She also displayed a fair measure of hubris and sarcasm.

On balance, though, the Caroline that I discovered was surprisingly modern in her approach to ethnicity, religion and women; she was also charitable, humane and immensely self-confident. I came to know a charismatic, pragmatic, political reformer with a large vision of her world, a lively sense of humour, great intelligence and an unexpectedly active imagination, all of which gave her the scope to conceive what could be done and accomplish it.

Caroline has been my constant companion for the past six years. What has fascinated me most about her is that she was a woman so far ahead of her time that many of her ideas fit easily into our era. She believed essentially in the rights of women and a fair go for all. Her influence is still being felt in modern Australia today.

CHAPTER 1

Love Child

1808–28

Spring slipping into summer in the English Midlands at the end of May 1808 was most likely a dulcet time, a world of sensual delights: the spicy sweetness of crab-apple flowers, bees humming over lilac bushes, clumps of buttercups raising their yolky heads against a soft breeze smelling of sunshine. The town of Northampton, though on the verge of massive expansion, was then home to only seven thousand souls. The shoe trade, whilst dominant, was still cottage-based and although there was a busy market square and a cathedral, nowhere in the town was far from the farming culture that had sustained it for centuries.

Two days before the start of summer, Caroline, a red-headed baby with an evidently fierce will to live, was born into the prosperous Jones family of the Mayorhold district of the town. For Sarah Jones, a matron of some thirty-seven years, the little girl was to be her seventh and last child. The father, William Jones, was already sixty-four years old and would not live to see this latest infant reach adolescence.

An early nineteenth-century view of the town of Northampton, England *(Alamy)*

Born just before the midway point of the previous century, William Jones typified not only the upward mobility of the Industrial Revolution but also the relaxed morals of the eighteenth century. There are no pictures of William Jones nor any writings apart from his will, which was transcribed in the legalese of the day by his lawyers. It is probable that he was not even literate, as the document bears his mark, rather than his signature.[1] Nonetheless, more than two hundred years later we see a shrewd man with a big heart and a certain *joie de vivre*, determined on success and with an appetite to enjoy it. He married four times (three wives died in childbed or shortly afterwards; only Sarah survived him), sired sixteen children (at least three died in infancy) and lived seventy years — considerably more than the forty-one years' average life expectancy of the time.[2] There is little doubt that Caroline inherited much of her initiative and vim from her father.

William was just eighteen years old when his first child was born in 1762. He married the mother about six months later. To have a child out of wedlock was not unusual for the working class in the sexually relaxed 1700s. For one thing, it proved the woman's fertility in a world that considered children both a blessing and a bane.[3] If they survived, youngsters were put to work by the age of six, but their birth could also rob a family of its mother, as William could attest.

William began his working life as a farm labourer, occupying the lowest rung of rustic society. Such employment was itinerant, seasonal and paid by the day; a bad harvest or foul weather would mean no work and no money. William was not prepared to accept the poverty of such an existence, and so was constantly on the move, changing jobs almost as often as wives during the next thirty years as he climbed the financial and social ladder. From toiling in the fields, he graduated to shoemaking and then inn-keeping. By the time he married twenty-year-old Sarah Allum in 1791, he was forty-seven years old, owned a number of properties and had become a hog jobber, or pig trader, in Northampton.

Times had changed too, particularly attitudes to women and sex. When William was growing up, the Industrial Revolution was just starting. Of equal importance, the Age of Enlightenment was also shaping society; even in the bucolic backwaters of England there was a ripple-down effect. For much of the 1700s, what was natural was considered veracious, and what is more natural than sex? In the eighteenth century it was widely regarded as a central pleasure, to be enjoyed rather than hidden away. It was also taken for granted that women were less able to bridle their desire and were often responsible for leading men astray.[4] The literature of the time, predominantly written by men, backs up these beliefs. "Every woman is at heart a rake," wrote one serious-minded man in 1739, intent on explaining the cause of unhappy marriages, adding that "As of lewdness, women when they are wicked, generally exceed the men."[5]

William, no doubt, would have been little troubled by sexual morality — until, that is, he married Caroline's mother, Sarah Allum, in 1791. At the end of the eighteenth century, a rolling back of carnal freedom became central to the new evangelical movement within the Christian Church and this in turn gave rise to the Victorians' more prudish attitude towards sex.[6] Little is known about Sarah, except that she was of an evangelical persuasion and very possibly a member of the early Wesleyan Church.[7] The flexibility that allowed William to change careers and build his fortune apparently also equipped him to negotiate shifting values.

So, what was there in Sarah to attract a man like William, particularly when she is described by one early biographer as "a clever woman, of quite Quaker-like simplicity in her mode of dressing"? The answer must lie in the rest of the description: "but whose face was dimpled and roguish".[8] It was presumably a happy union, producing seven children in sixteen years, the first three born within just three years, which suggests that the family was wealthy enough to employ a wet nurse.

In the language of the day, William Jones was a "warm man", a person of wealth, by the time Caroline was born. Maybe more importantly, he was also a very generous one, possibly of his own volition or maybe Sarah's. Evangelists placed huge importance on charity.[9] The leading evangelical minister of the day, John Wesley, had warned his followers that they must help the poor if they wished "to escape everlasting fire, and to inherit the everlasting kingdom".[10] One suspects that Sarah and William did escape the inferno because both were considerable philanthropists. So, it's likely that from an early age Caroline understood the plight of the poor and that it was within her power to help alleviate it.

William's mode of charity was far from passive: he was not the sort of man to throw a bit of coinage at a needy individual and walk away, preferring to intervene in a person's life to some material effect. Indeed, it seems that he was unable to pass a downtrodden waif or stray without interceding — another trait his daughter would inherit. Caroline was still very young when William encountered a broken old soldier and took him home to be nursed.[11] The man had lost a leg in the Napoleonic Wars and would most likely have starved without support. In the early 1800s, state-sponsored social welfare, even for maimed veterans, was a concept not yet understood: the deformed, damaged and diseased depended on the goodwill of the community and the church for their survival.

The aged warrior apparently repaid the family in one of the honeyed currencies of the day: storytelling. Having lived and travelled in foreign climes, endured the terrors of battle and witnessed macabre scenes of death and violence, he was able to describe a world unimaginable for a sedate rural family of little education. As well as scenes of combat and privation in Europe, the soldier related tales of the exotic Americas and how Britain had attempted to clone its culture in alien lands. This was probably the first time that Caroline heard of colonisation.

Not long after the soldier departed, William took in another outcast, one who had been harried through the streets of Northampton by crowds pelting him with stones and mud.[12] An elderly Catholic priest, a Frenchman escaping the revolution across the Channel, he had been leading a vaguely itinerant life, shifting from one recusant community to another.

In an age when new Protestant religions were emerging in England, Catholicism was still vilified by the government and many citizens. It was therefore a small but highly unusual act for William, a member of the Church of England, to show such compassion to a Catholic priest. The chasm between Catholics and the Anglican English establishment dated back almost three hundred years to Henry VIII's Reformation. Although never actually stopped in England, Catholic worship — along with basic civil rights for Catholics, such as freedom of occupation, voting and holding public office — was severely curtailed and only grudgingly allowed following a series of Roman Catholic Relief Acts introduced during the late eighteenth and early nineteenth centuries. When William went out of his way to save the old priest from the angry mob, there was still bad blood and considerable prejudice between the two religions. William, apparently, had seen enough of life to be interested in the man and not the style of his beliefs; possibly more importantly, William's standing in the local community was substantial enough to withstand any backlash. The story, told by the essayist Edith Pearson and attributed to one of Caroline's daughters, suggests that the priest stayed with the family for a number of weeks, again revealing a world outside their restricted view.[13] On his departure he blessed the household, making special mention of Caroline, the youngest child and probably his most constant companion during his convalescence.

It is significant that the few stories we know of Caroline's childhood marry together philanthropy and religion. As these became her major obsessions, it is reasonable to suppose that they were also what she remembered most of her youthful days and later shared with her children and friends. It is also curious that these stories centre around William rather than Sarah — normally a young girl would have spent much more time with her mother than her father.

The other pertinent memory from her early childhood was an entertainment she devised for herself, a colonisation game, which also addressed themes of charity and religion, with a bit of a twist.

She made up the game before she was six years old — about the time her father took in the two wanderers. She described it in detail years later, in a letter she wrote to a friend in Sydney:

> I made boats of broad beans; expended all my money in
> touchwood dolls; removed families, located them in the
> bed-quilt, and sent the boats, filled with wheat, back to their
> friends, of which I kept a store in a thimble case. At length I
> upset the basin, which I judged to be a facsimile of the sea,
> spoiled a new bed, got punished, and afterwards carried out
> my plan in a dark cellar, with a rushlight stuck upon a tin
> kettle ... I had a Wesleyan minister and a Catholic priest in
> the same boat. Two of my dolls were very refractory, and
> would not be obedient; this made me name them after two
> persons I knew who were always quarrelling ... at length
> I put the two into a boat, and told them if they were not
> careful they would be drowned; and having landed them
> *alive*, I knelt to pray to God to make them love each other.[14]

Caroline's description of her game provides a wealth of insight into her circumstances and her developing personality. Clearly, she had access to money at a very young age and was allowed to buy herself toys. Similarly, it appears she had considerable leisure time and, unlike her much older step-brothers and sisters at the same age, was not expected to work to supplement the family coffers. Her nearest siblings, Harriet and Robert, four and eight years older respectively, were probably too impatient to befriend the baby of the family. Was Caroline lonely? Possibly, but she wasn't bored. She delighted in imagining a new world, devising endless possibilities with a mix of religions and a bevy of characters, some based on humorous, cantankerous personalities she already knew, others probably garnered from stories told by the old soldier and the French priest. She doesn't appear to have picked up any prejudices about different faiths, happily ascribing roles in her game to both Wesleyan and Catholic clerics, with the impartiality of a child who has not been taught to denigrate any other creed. Like so many other little girls down the ages, Caroline was playing dolls; instead of amusing herself with "house" or "dress-ups", though, she was designing her own domain, establishing rules and settling disputes. It was an early harbinger of what was to follow.

*

Caroline's father, William Jones, retired from life in early April 1814, just five days after his seventieth birthday. He was survived by Sarah, then aged forty-three, and twelve living children ranging in age from fifty-two down to Caroline, just a few weeks' shy of six years old. William's death was the catalyst for Caroline to progress even further from the humble beginnings of her parents and grandparents and would thrust her onto an entirely different trajectory from that of her siblings. It also revealed a conundrum about her background that has never successfully been explained.

Was Caroline the love child of William and a mistress — in all likelihood, forty-one-year-old Sarah Laws, who conveniently lodged just down the road from the Jones family in the Mayorhold in Northampton?[15] It may be that, after all, William was loath to forgo the sexual freedoms of his youth for the more restricted ethos of the new century. Possibly confirming the suspicion are records from many years later that show that a Sarah Laws was residing in London with Caroline on the night of the 1851 census, and was described as her "Mother"; that same evening William's widow, Sarah Jones, was to be found at her home in

Northampton.[16] If Caroline was actually the bastard child of William and his mistress, then presumably William's strictly evangelical wife forgave his philandering and accepted the new chick into her brood, like a slightly confused bird nurturing an alien cuckoo hatchling — at least, while William was alive.

Following William's death, the fledgling was tossed from the nest.[17] Without ever apparently repudiating Caroline as her daughter, Sarah Jones sent the child to reside with an older woman in Northampton, possibly even Sarah Laws. The widow may have been aping upper-class families, who quite often sent their children to live elsewhere if the house was overcrowded, or for education. However, given Sarah Jones's evangelical nature, it is more likely that she was exorcising the misbegotten daughter from her home — particularly because that daughter had been provided for so unusually and so handsomely.

Caroline (as well as her brother Robert) received a substantial individual bequest in William's will.[18] Dated the day he died, the document was remarkably concise for the patriarch of such a diverse, blended family. It proved that he was extremely wealthy: he left £500 cash — equivalent to more than £400,000 today — to be paid to his wife, Sarah, "immediately after my demise". The oddity in the will, however, was that before any mention of Sarah, or anyone else, it stipulated that thirteen-year-old Robert and Caroline, the fifth and seventh children from his marriage with Sarah, were each to be given a significant property. In Caroline's case it was a house on Bearward Street (no longer in existence) in Northampton, including all buildings, improvements and rents. At the time Caroline's thirty-eight-year-old step-brother, also called William, lived and worked on this estate, so Caroline effectively became his landlady. (For his part, the younger William was forgiven all monies that his father had "in the past advanced to or for him".) There is no evidence of what the younger William thought of becoming his little step-sister's tenant. One imagines it may have made for some awkwardness at family gatherings.

Apart from various small bequests to Caroline's other half-siblings, the rest of William's personal effects and assets and all income went to Sarah, to support herself and the remaining five children from their marriage. Sarah and William Snr's brother, Plowman Jones, were appointed joint trustees and executors.

It's still possible that Caroline was simply William's favourite daughter rather than his illegitimate progeny, and that he just wanted to ensure that she would be financially secure if her mother remarried, in which case her uncle rather than her step-father would control her inheritance until she came of age (in the early 1800s, only a single woman of legal age or a widow could hold and use income and assets). The bequest would also provide a considerable dowry for Caroline when she married. This, however, immediately begs the question why he didn't do the same for the other daughters who were also under age when he died — Mary, eighteen; Sarah, sixteen; and Harriet, ten. It is difficult to imagine that William would take such pains to safeguard Caroline's future, and ignore the claims of the older three. For one daughter, and that the youngest, to be so favoured must have placed great strain on family unity. No wonder she was sent away.

At six years of age, though, what a confusing transformation it must have been. The life that she had known vanished with her father; she was exiled from all that was familiar, and abandoned by the family she had always called her own. One can only imagine the child deserted and heartbroken. Yet she already had some understanding of a solitary existence — it was not so long since she had hidden away down in the cellar to play her made-up colonisation game.

There is only one story that survives from her time with the "older woman" and it is something of an adventure. Caroline and her hostess were sitting in an upstairs room one dark night in the nadir of winter when they were startled by a suspicious creaking from the floor below. Creeping onto the landing they spied an unkempt villain with his foot on the stairs. Caroline and the lady seized large lumps of coal and flung them down onto the intruder's head until he ran in panic from the house.[19] No doubt her hostess led the way, but the story suggests clear thought and steely resolve on Caroline's part rather than nerves or hysterics: she was acting on necessity rather than emotion. It's a dramatic and funny tale that she shared with her daughter many years later.

After living with the unknown lady for a time, it's likely that Caroline was sent to a girls' boarding school — once more uprooted and hurled amongst strangers. It's not known which school she might have attended, but there were numerous ladies' academies in Northampton of varying quality; most were expensive.[20] The rent from Caroline's Bearward property would no doubt have paid the fees and, in all likelihood, a number of extras as well, such as dancing and French lessons. Whilst her siblings and stepsiblings received more basic tuition, Caroline's superior education would enable her to climb the social ladder and, ultimately, build a remarkable career.

Caroline's days in school would, however, have been ordered and constrained. Female education in the nineteenth century was almost an oxymoron. The upper and middle classes paid some lip service to tutoring young women, but few girls received more than rudimentary instruction. Some authorities even referenced the Bible to justify keeping women in a state of semi-ignorance: "When Eve, the mother of the human race, sinned through a vain desire of knowledge, the most holy God was pleased to punish that vanity," wrote the Reverend Henry Venn in 1829.[21] Reading, writing and basic arithmetic were considered enough to run a household; other lessons focused unashamedly on nurturing those attributes required to successfully ensnare a husband. As one commentator wrote, "There are some exceptions ... [but] ... they learn chiefly to dress, to dance, to speak bad French, to prattle much nonsense."[22] Caroline's prestigious schooling may have been Sarah Jones's idea, but again it raises the question of why her other daughters did not receive anything close to a similar level of tuition. It may be that boarding school was just another way to keep the child at a distance, and the quality of the education Caroline gained may have been more a matter of luck than design.

Whatever the case, Caroline proved to be an apt student. Her daughter later described her as "an immensely clever woman ... an accomplished linguist, mathematician and scientist".[23] There is ample evidence of Caroline's scholarship in the wide-ranging collection of letters, pamphlets, diaries and notes she eventually left behind, and when she wrote *Little Joe,* a children's novelette, in 1859, even Charles Dickens was enthusiastic, saying that Caroline had "expressed herself well".[24]

What is missing from the record of Caroline's early years, though, is any reference to companions of her own age. Once she left Northampton, Caroline stayed in touch with her nearest sister, Harriet, but there was never any mention of other friendships. Clearly, Caroline learnt to be her own companion, to reject loneliness and put her faith in her own abilities to persist and succeed. The lessons of youth become the character of the adult. Time and again throughout her life, and often in times of pain and stress, with little love or support, Caroline would be thrown back on her own devices. Her internal strength may have come from her religious belief, and that certainly played its part, but undeniably her fierce determination and extraordinary self-confidence were what helped her survive.

Whilst Caroline's education would supply the skills for her future work, it would also enable her to achieve what was then considered the prime objective of every young woman: marriage. As one contemporary commentator noted, "Marriage was the life plan of most women, and the single state a fate to be avoided like the plague."[25] By the time she reached twenty-two, Caroline had emerged as a sanguine creature ready to engage with the world. The boarding school had done its job well: her voice was musical and she spoke without the slightest provincialism.[26] She was described as beautiful with slender grace and a happy character — she was certainly no Puritan, no fanatic bent on rejecting the sweets of life.[27] She was passionate, inquisitive and determined to lead a useful, purposeful life. All she lacked was a soul mate to augment the adventure. As in all good romances, one was then just coming into view, though, as in the nature of such narratives, true love would not run smoothly.

CHAPTER 2

Marriage and Faith

1828–31

A chance decision by a lieutenant of the East India Company was to transform Caroline's life. It was mid-1828 and thirty-year-old Archibald Chisholm, who served with the 30th Madras Native Infantry Regiment, was returning from the Indian subcontinent on two years' furlough. He was making his way north to visit family in Scotland when he broke his journey in Northampton, perhaps to stay with friends. It was then that he encountered Caroline Jones. The precise date and circumstances are unknown. The town had a healthy social calendar; the two may have been introduced at a private party, but more likely at a public ball or similar event.

Archibald was the younger son of a gentleman farmer, by then deceased, who had been one of the principal cadets of the Laird, Colin of Knockfin, in Inverness-shire in the Scottish Highlands.[1] The Clan Chisholm had a long and impressive history, being first mentioned in a letter from the Pope in 1252.[2] The family had produced its share of rebels and radicals over the years, culminating in brother fighting brother in the ferocious battle of Culloden, which saw Bonnie Prince Charlie finally defeated as pretender to the British throne, in 1745. Clan history reports that after the bloodshed, three Chisholms aided the prince's escape into exile.

Almost a century later, Archibald's family was still proudly Roman Catholic; one of his half-brothers was a priest, and two of his close cousins were bishops. This impeccable Catholic lineage, though, did not translate into wealth. Archibald's father married twice and sired six sons.[3] Fortified with an excellent classical education and little else, the five younger boys were sent into the world to find their own way; three of them joined the East India Company. By 1828 one had been killed in battle, one had been promoted to captain and Archibald, after ten years' active service, was taking a well-earned break.

An early painting of Archibald reveals his character: an attractive man, especially in uniform. We see a boyish, open face framed by a mass of well-ordered, wavy dark hair and long, curly sideburns. His clear, piercing eyes, classic Roman nose and cleft

Portrait of Captain Archibald Chisholm (courtesy of Don Chisholm)

chin suggest strength and seriousness, whereas his bow-shaped mouth hints at both sensuality and a certain weakness. Dressed in his regimental red uniform with gold buttons and epaulettes, a sword sash lending a hint of danger, Archibald creates a highly favourable impression. One wonders why, in 1828, at the age of thirty, he was still single.

Caroline and Archibald soon fell in love. Who can say what sparked the flames of affection? On her side the attraction was obvious: here was a handsome man of elegant lineage who could give her the life that she had dreamt about since she was a little girl. With the lieutenant, not only would she move up in the world but she would also *see* the world. He was, in effect, her passport out of the myopic confines of rural England. He was also a man, she soon realised, with a kind heart, whom she believed would support her good works.

On the other hand, what was there in Caroline to excite Archibald's admiration? She was certainly a lovely looking young woman, but, even allowing for a paucity of candidates during Archibald's years in India, she would not have been the only eligible female to cross his path. For a mature, cultured, serious-minded man, the answer could not just be Caroline's pretty face and lively character; there had to be something more that encouraged him to partner with a woman of inferior social status. No doubt her superior education would have helped convince him of her suitability, along with her evident compassion and, in all likelihood, her dowry also.

In 1830, marriage was offered — and rejected.

Why did Caroline rebuff such an attractive offer from a man she apparently loved? At twenty-two, she had been mistress of herself and her fortune for at least twelve months — long enough to understand and enjoy her independence. She was not about to conform to the claustrophobic expectations of nineteenth-century womanhood. As Caroline was to explain many years later in a letter to a friend, the Bishop of Birmingham, she had decided two or three years before she met Archibald that she would pursue a charitable career. She wrote: "I consulted a friend ... who knew my mind ... and told me that to carry out my views I must have more of public support and confidence than I could ever expect to gain, that wealth, that influence were needed." She went on: "I did not marry until I told Captain Chisholm to what my whole mind was devoted."[4]

When Archibald proposed, Caroline had still not decided which cause to champion or how to do it, but she was determined to maintain the freedom she felt she needed to achieve her goals. The autonomy she insisted upon was virtually unheard of amongst her peers. Mary Wollstonecraft would have been proud of Caroline's resolution to break the mould; so too should have been the feminists of the 1960s.[5]

Having explained her intentions to Archibald, Caroline softened the blow by making a counter-proposition: she asked him to withdraw from her for one month to consider whether he would "accept a wife who would make all sacrifices to carry into effect her public duties".[6] If he was unable to accept her conditions, they would part; if, on the other hand, he would agree, she would marry him.

Such an unconventional wife could have been difficult for a man toeing the line of the East India Company and seeking promotion. Furthermore, Caroline's negotiation ran directly counter to just about every piece of eighteenth- and nineteenth-century commentary on marriage, from either sex: "Married life is woman's profession: and to this life her training — that of dependence — is modelled," wrote a female author of the era, condemning women to a life of servitude and banality.[7] Was Caroline gambling that Archibald could be brought to heel? Or did she already realise that his affectionate nature and softer character meant that she could, with relative impunity, have the best of both worlds? He was a clever man who, atypically for the time, apparently sought a well-educated woman for a wife. Caroline, it seems, rated her intelligence as equal to if not greater than his. Mary Wollstonecraft could have been speaking to Caroline directly when she wrote: "Some women govern their husbands without degrading themselves, because intellect will always govern."[8]

Archibald kept his distance from Caroline for a full month before proposing again. He agreed to her terms and this time she accepted him. From the very start of their life together, he was submissive to her rule and totally loyal. It is doubtful, indeed, whether she ever questioned that he would return to her.

The Catholic clergy were still not legally allowed to conduct or register wedding services, so the pair were married by special licence two days after Christmas in 1830, at the Anglican Church of the Holy Sepulchre in Northampton. It was the same church where Caroline had been christened and where her father lay buried.

As was the custom generally, only a small group of well-wishers witnessed the ceremony on that frosty morning. Within the splendid old church, candlelight dispelled the frigidity of winter, casting warm light on sombre tombs of stone and marble and creating an aura of sacred mystery. Outside, weak sunshine perhaps filtered through forbidding grey clouds, its rays illuminating fragile wisps of snow upon skeletal trees, and welcoming the newly married couple into a glistening world of wedded bliss. Caroline had now committed her life to a partnership with Archibald, but what did she know about the practicalities of marriage and its effects? What, one wonders, did she know about sex?

*

For their honeymoon, Archibald and Caroline chose Brighton, situated about two hundred kilometres south of Northampton on the Channel coast. The incurably flamboyant monarch George IV's fifty-year love affair with this small seaside town had transformed it into a fashionable and glamorous holiday destination, complete with its extravagant quasi-Eastern-style Royal Pavilion. No doubt this exotic building would have piqued Caroline's interest, but one suspects, given her practical nature, that she would have disapproved of it as a folly.

There was more to Brighton though than just that lavish palace, and as the second most important business of a honeymoon was sightseeing, there was much to investigate. The promenade along Marine Parade passed above the pebbly beach and onto Chain Pier, jutting out precariously over the water. It was probably the first time that Caroline had seen the sea, and, walking above its salty breaths, watching its rhythmic undulations, she may have started to understand the power that controlled both the sailing ships and the new steamboats that were to become so germane to her future life. Possibly she was even a little fearful as she watched, in wild, windy weather, the vessels rolling and pitching on heaving waves, and she may have wondered what it would be like to have such untamed monsters beneath her feet.

Most likely, the newlyweds visited the lending library and the stylish shops in North Lane. Maybe Caroline bought a gown or trinkets to wear to an evening concert. Perhaps Archibald, sporting a new cravat, outlaid five shillings on a box at the theatre. There was always something to do and to see.

The honeymoon gave Caroline and Archibald the opportunity to gradually develop a better understanding of each other. Victims of stringent middle-class mores, they would barely have spent any time alone together before their wedding day; now, however, each moved wholly in the other's realm. The sudden intensity of the relationship, even allowing for the obtuse civility of the age, must have been overpowering.

To alleviate the strain, many couples separated during the day; the bride was often left indoors alone, to wait for hours whilst her husband went off exploring by himself. [9] In many ways this was a foreshadowing of everyday married life: the woman confined to domestic duties, the man at work, out in the wider world. Everything about Caroline's character, though, suggests that she would have refused to miss out on Archibald's explorations, however pedestrian; after all, she had already given ample warning that she would not embrace the traditional stay-at-home wifely role.

As well as learning about each other's personality traits, there were more intimate discoveries to be made. It was assumed that a man, particularly one in his thirties like Archibald, would be experienced in lovemaking; Caroline, however, fully ensconced in the prim middle class, was not only expected to be virginal but also totally innocent of any sexual awareness. This paradox, of course, was a direct reflection of nineteenth-century hypocrisy, as well as widespread discrimination against women based on their social status and the country of their birth. Whilst middle- and upper-class maidens were treated like fragile flowers that would wilt if presented with lustful realities, it was tacitly accepted that working-class women, prostitutes and foreign females (such as

Archibald would have encountered in India) could be exploited for the benefit of a man's sexual education. In a curious caricature of the female advice books, there were numerous publications, directed at males, detailing where to find women for sex. They reveal the extraordinarily brutal attitudes of some men towards women. One such publication reported, for example, that at Madame Matileau's establishments for young ladies in Soho and Brompton Old Road,

> this Abbess ... of the French flesh market does not keep her meat too long ... Nothing is allowed to get stale here; you may have your meat dressed to your own liking ... Her flock is in prime condition, and always ready for sticking; when any of them are fried [diseased], they are turned out to grass ... Consequently the rot, bots, glanders, and other diseases incidental to cattle are not generally known here.[10]

The book, costing a shilling to purchase, was first printed in about 1830 and was updated and reprinted numerous times, suggesting a keen and constant demand for the information.

Whether Archibald had any sexual experiences before wedding Caroline is not known. What is certain though is that his attitude to women was unusual for his time, as would be evidenced by his total support of Caroline's endeavours with vulnerable girls and young women on two continents. Whilst Caroline was the inspiration and driving force behind the couple's later work, Archibald's constant and dedicated assistance could only have been possible if he had genuine respect not only for his wife but also for the females she helped. It is not surprising that she looked for a consort to complement her ambitions; what is remarkable is that she found one so ready to acquiesce to her view of the world.

Still, there was a lot for Caroline to learn about the mysteries of marriage. The chief purpose of a nineteenth-century honeymoon, of course, was to decorously initiate the bride into her role in the matrimonial tryst. Another contemporary conduct author explained why it was expedient for a couple to go away together: "As the bride is the object of the utmost interest; it is desirable that she should be removed from the observation of her circle. Such a course is particularly acceptable to female modesty and adds fresh charms to the delights of connubial bliss."[11] This helps explain why honeymoons became so popular among the conservative middle class in the 1800s.

Even though Caroline was twenty-two years old she probably knew absolutely nothing about sex, nor was she likely to have received any clear advice at the time of her wedding. Married middle-class women who could have passed on valuable information did not discuss such matters.[12] Conduct books were so euphemistically couched as to be virtually useless: "The duty of a wife is what no woman ever yet was able to render without affection," was the confusing and inadequate description of marital sex written by author Sarah Stickney Ellis.[13] As for the medical profession, if anything, it was even worse. A well-publicised text by Dr William Acton, written for men, boldly stated that "the majority of women (happily for them) are not very much troubled by sexual feelings of any kind", and went on to explain that if a woman was inclined to enjoy sex she would be identified as either a whore or possibly a nymphomaniac who belonged in a lunatic asylum.[14]

Caroline fell pregnant almost immediately, within the first week or two of marriage. Whilst there is no evidence as to Caroline's sexual appreciation (apart from her giving birth to eight children), it is very possible that the ease with which she became pregnant may have helped define her views on sex, women and what she perceived as a need for single females to learn to protect themselves against predatory males.

Vulnerable women who engaged in premarital sex not only became social outcasts but also risked further ostracism and deprivation if they had illegitimate children. With little ability to claim any support from the father, these women faced the choice of struggling to bring up the child on their own (often after being thrown out of their family home), turning to prostitution to survive, or attempting an abortion, which in the early nineteenth century was something akin to a death sentence. Birth control methods such as coitus interruptus, condoms devised from sheep's intestines and cervical caps made from hollowed out lemon halves were only used by a few members of the upper classes and some prostitutes and their clients.[15] Problematic at best, contraception in any case was outlawed by most religions, making it unavailable to the vast majority. Always attentive to moral and pious concerns, Caroline would later seek to offer susceptible females an alternate pathway. What is most interesting is her attitude to the "fallen" women she dealt with. Her patience, empathy and lack of condemnation suggest that she understood not just their practical but also their carnal needs, and that she lay the blame for their plight squarely upon rapacious men who had used and then abandoned them. Such an approach argues that Caroline acknowledged female sensuality, whilst refusing to accept that working-class women were little more than shameless whores.

From Brighton, the couple may have travelled directly back to Northampton, but more likely they enjoyed a longer sojourn in Scotland. Either then or sometime in the following few months, Caroline was introduced to Archibald's relatives. Both his parents were dead, but he still had two brothers and a bevy of cousins and in-laws in the North. Meeting them was no doubt a daunting prospect for Caroline, for not only had she emerged from an inferior social class but she had also been brought up in a very different religion. Caroline was an outsider among the staunchly Roman Catholic Chisholm clan. Three hundred years of tumult, suspicion and prejudice separated their understandings of God, in an age when religion was one of the cornerstones of identity. The Chisholm tribe would have been shocked initially by Archibald's choice of wife; the infiltration of a southern heretic of inferior birth would not have matched their idea of what was due to them. There is no sign, however, that Caroline was intimidated by Archibald's relatives; indeed, there is evidence of ongoing friendship and correspondence — even as late as 1869 there were visits to Archibald's family in Scotland.[16]

Caroline's introduction to Archibald's clan may well have been the occasion when she most clearly displayed the flexibility and liberalism she had inherited from her father — like him she welcomed change with exceptional ebullience — for around this time she became a Catholic. There is no firm evidence as to why she decided to convert, although it is reasonable to suppose that she did so simply because Archibald was a Catholic. Caroline, however, was not a weak-willed creature who could be moulded to her husband's convictions. Her decision would have been taken rationally and after considerable thought. The precise date and place of her conversion is unknown, but from the beginning she embraced her new creed wholeheartedly and seems to have swiftly adopted the more mystical beliefs and elaborate rituals of the Catholic Church while maintaining her clear and practical understanding of human nature. By converting, Caroline also took another step away from her siblings, yet this does not seem to have brought any recrimination from them. How remarkable that William Jones's diverse brood would end up straddling three different mainstream religions — Church of England, Wesleyan and Catholic — while maintaining a harmonious family network.[17]

Like her understanding of a woman's sexual needs and vulnerabilities, Caroline's pragmatic tolerance of all religious backgrounds, developed in childhood, continued to grow following her marriage and ultimately became one of her defining characteristics. Later on, in India and in New South Wales, despite the fears and preconceptions of various senior clergy and laity, Caroline rejected dogma and prejudice while seeking to provide assistance to women of any creed, even those of non-Christian backgrounds, such as often-ostracised Jewish girls.[18]

Caroline's own decision to convert to Catholicism acknowledged her husband's status as the ostensible governing force of their union, the arbiter of their values. Archibald certainly would have expected his children to be baptised within his faith, making it not just an emotional but an expedient imperative for Caroline to enter the Catholic fold. In doing so, she was conforming to prevailing beliefs regarding the importance of religion in a happy marriage, as echoed in contemporary conduct tomes: "It is desirable that the husband and wife belong to the same Christian denomination; and that the family they constitute may worship in one church," recommended one such work.[19]

Despite Caroline's enthusiasm for her new religion, the welcome from Archibald's family and the understanding from her own, her conversion set her at odds with the predominantly Protestant society in which she lived. The last of the Catholic Emancipation Acts had only been passed within the previous eighteen months, finally allowing Catholics the right to sit in parliament at Westminster, and join the judiciary and upper echelons of the civil service. Caroline would have known that the bill had been strenuously opposed in Northampton by the anti-Catholic Brunswick Club[20] and by senior Church of England clergy who even petitioned parliament.[21] Like most of the country, Northampton was furiously divided on religious grounds. Yet this was her home, the place where she had grown up a Protestant — with little thought of being anything else until she met and married Archibald — and this was the place she returned to with her husband to learn to be a Catholic. There is no evidence that she was self-conscious about her changed circumstances, either material or religious; her emotional resilience was unwavering, giving her the strength to ignore or deflect the prejudices of others. It was a strength that would stand her in good stead some years later in Sydney, when her religion would make many in the colonial establishment suspicious of her motives.

The newlyweds chose a home in Leicester Terrace, an ideal compromise, being an affluent area but only a few minutes' walk north of the older, working-class Mayorhold and close to where most of Caroline's family lived and to the property left to her by her father. Just as importantly, it was an even shorter stroll south from the newly built Catholic Chapel, and around the corner was the home of the presiding Catholic priest.[22] The location was a testament as much to Caroline's improved social position as to her new religion.

By mid-1831, Archibald had already extended his two-year furlough from the East India Company by a year. Now he sought and was given a further six months' leave. Obviously keen to be in England for the arrival of his first child, due in early October, he would have been equally concerned about his wife surviving the harrowing experience of childbirth. For Caroline it would be her most terrifying ordeal yet.

CHAPTER 3

Life and Death

1831–33

Leicester Terrace, Northampton, early October 1831

Hours dragged by, the pain grew steadily. The others chattered from time to time or ate the meals sent up to them. Now and then, they took turns walking outside or dozing in a chair, but there was no such luxury for Caroline. She lost all track of time; with windows bolted and curtains drawn, there was no way of telling that the night had turned into day and now the day was fading back into night. The intensity of the spasms worsened with every passing minute; it was all she could do to stop from screaming out in terror as the exquisite pain came in waves. She had never questioned her strength of mind, but now she was unable to control the confusion of her aching body, and incapable of concentrating on the priceless reward that awaited her at the end of it all.

She was trapped in a breathless, dark world. The room, lit only by dull gas lamps and a blazing fire, was stifling, suffocating. Caroline felt she was entombed in a nightmare, eerie with flickering lights. She called out for wine and was given weak tea to drink. The doctor was saying that if the baby didn't come soon, he would bleed her — he held up a bottle of leeches, the black parasites sliming over each other. She vaguely remembered him saying something about bloodletting reducing fever, but it didn't seem important to her now, no more than the sight of him scratching the cat with the end of the forceps. The pain had dulled her mind; nothing seemed to make sense to her.

By now Caroline was all but hysterical. Sweat trickled over her face; her heavy clothes, wet with perspiration, clung to her body. As another shuddering contraction engulfed her, she screamed again, clenched her fists and sobbed. Her strength was almost gone. The agony eased for a moment and she lay back on the damp pillows, closing her eyes during a short but blessed reprieve.

Finally, the midwife announced that she could see the baby's head. The doctor poured a measure of laudanum into a glass and told Caroline's maid to make her mistress drink it as soon as the baby was out. Clutching the metal forceps, he positioned himself at the end of the bed without once looking at Caroline. Then, feeling under the sheet covering the lower part of her body, he located the baby's skull, positioned the blades on either side of the child's head, and pulled.

Caroline could never later even describe the searing pain. She heard screams, but they were so divorced from her own body that she did not realise that she was the one shrieking. She dimly heard the order to push. With one final blood-curdling howl, she felt the baby move out of her body. Exhausted, barely conscious of the activity around her, Caroline had no idea what had happened. She could not even focus on the child. Then she heard a faint mewing and knew it was her baby's first voice. Instinctively, she held out her hand. "My baby, let me hold my baby," she gasped.

Ignoring Caroline's outstretched arm, the midwife snatched the child away to clean it up. Desperate, Caroline called again for her baby. In response, the midwife came back and tipped the dose of laudanum down her throat. Caroline slipped into unconsciousness, not even aware that her infant was a baby girl.[1]

Nothing could have prepared Caroline for labour. Being the youngest child in her family, She was unlikely to have been present at any births, and, as with sex, little information on childbirth was available to women. The scarcity of detail cannot only be attributed to self-censorship by squeamish authors, although without doubt that did play a part. Curiously, in a world where mathematicians had devised calculus, scientists the telescope and engineers the steam engine, doctors and midwives were still guided as much by folklore and pseudoscience as by genuine medical knowledge. The first reliable surveys were not conducted until 1850, but it's estimated that close to six per cent of women died in childbirth in Britain at that time; it's therefore reasonable to suppose that twenty years earlier the risks were even higher.[2] Caroline was one of the lucky ones.

The greatest killer was puerperal fever, an infection transmitted from one birthing woman to another by the midwife or attending physician. It would be another fifteen years before a Hungarian doctor, Ignaz Semmelweis, realised that infection could be prevented if the medical staff simply washed their hands after each procedure. Incredibly, his findings were initially considered so dangerously radical that they were ridiculed and rejected by doctors, who, moreover, resented the suggestion that they were to blame for many deaths through their poor hygiene.[3] Similar ignorance extended to other female concerns, such as menstruation. Caroline would have been totally unaware that her failure to bleed for nine months was related to her pregnancy because it was only in that same year (1831) that a French doctor linked menstruation and ovulation. Until then, it was widely believed (amongst a raft of other bizarre superstitions) that women bled monthly because, being intensely sensitive creatures, they needed to dispose of superfluous blood to cool their overheated emotions.[4]

Over the next twenty years, Caroline would endure eight pregnancies and give birth on three continents and even at sea, often in primitive, sometimes harrowing conditions, without any apparent lasting damage to her own health. This first birth, though, ended in tragedy — a tragedy that would shape her future. The infant, named Caroline after her mother, died just three weeks later and was buried on Wednesday, 26 October, near her grandfather, William Jones, in the graveyard of the Anglican Church of the Holy Sepulchre in Northampton.[5]

Previous biographers have either ignored this daughter or glibly passed over her demise. Certainly, children dying was not unusual in the nineteenth century — some sixteen per cent of infants perished in their first two years of life in Britain in the 1840s and 1850s.[6] Confronted with such overwhelming data, it's tempting to shrug a metaphorical shoulder, but that is to neglect the likely emotional impact on Caroline. The baby was not just another statistic. A young woman devoted to her god, in love with her husband and passionate about her humanity could not lose her first child without the consequences lodging deep within her psyche. She had carried the baby for nine months, had nursed her for just three weeks and within that time had invested her own hopes and dreams in the infant she had planned to take with her as she ventured across the seas. The heartbreak of burying a tiny daughter, one who, moreover, carried Caroline's own name — a sure sign of not just tradition but also strong maternal devotion — would profoundly affect her. Seventeen years and the births of four sons would pass before Caroline had another daughter. In the intervening period, she would be drawn, almost

An early portrait of Caroline Chisholm *(courtesy of Don Chisholm)*

subconsciously, to protecting helpless and broken young women. She seemed determined to defend other women's daughters, as if to make up for not saving her own. When she had told Archibald that she intended to lead a life of charitable work, she was still unaware of what direction that would take. The death of her baby most likely helped define her path.

It's hard to know how long Caroline grieved for her child, but little more than two months later she was left alone with her heartache. Archibald was on the high seas, bound for India. They had been married for just over a year, and it would be more than eighteen months before they were reunited.

A number of reasons could explain why Caroline did not initially accompany Archibald to Madras (modern-day Chennai). After such an extended furlough, it was obviously imperative that Archibald rejoin his regiment as soon as possible; he sailed from Gravesend on the *Elphinstone*, departing on 6 January 1832.[7] It is unlikely that Archibald and Caroline had ever envisaged travelling together. If the child had lived, they would no doubt have wanted her to be older and stronger before undertaking an arduous four- to five-month sea voyage with only limited medical assistance on board. Then, too, Caroline may have needed extra time to recover, both physically and emotionally, from the birth — middle- and upper-class women of the era were advised to stay in bed for at least seven days after a confinement and not to undertake anything more strenuous than a slow, short stroll until at least a month later.[8] Caroline would have been counselled against undertaking, within two months of the birth, the rigorous preparations for departure, let alone the 130-kilometre coach journey from Northampton to Gravesend followed by months at sea in an East Indiaman sloop. Finally, there may have been practical concerns of a different kind. Sometime just before or after her marriage to Archibald, Caroline's property in Bearward Street seems to have been sold to her tenant and brother William Jones.[9]

The sale of the property could have funded Caroline's passage to India in March 1833; it probably also paid for, amongst other things, a curious little side trip that she took by herself before leaving England. Humans are complex creatures and Caroline was no different. At this point it seems that her own inner strength and fervent belief in herself and God may have faltered a little. Perhaps it's understandable. At almost twenty-five and despite an absent husband, her married state gave her more autonomy than she had ever enjoyed previously; but still her circumstances were challenging. She was living in Leicester Terrace, apart from her siblings and without her husband's support, grieving for her first child and now facing the enormous challenge of sailing some eleven thousand nautical miles from Gravesend to Madras, on a boat full of strangers, to then be disgorged into an alien world. The prospect, however exciting, was also daunting.

Probably seeking reassurance, Caroline turned to a prevailing fad, the hocus-pocus pseudomedical technique called phrenology. On 30 January 1833, about two months before she left England for Madras, she visited one of its most famous practitioners, James De Ville, to seek what she would have hoped to be a true reading of her character and her abilities.

Exponents of phrenology claimed to deduce personality and aptitude by examining the shape and size of bumps on a patient's skull. In twenty-first-century terms, James De Ville could have been described as a "phrenologist to the stars": amongst his clients were the Duke of Wellington, Prince Albert and the poet William Blake. With such patrons, his services would not have been inexpensive. Although he was based in London, Caroline saw him in Brighton.

De Ville's four-page report on Caroline was not written up until July of that year, by which time Caroline was on her way to India. It was presumably posted to her there, although no doubt De Ville would have divulged part of his findings to her at the time of the consultation. The report reveals that he believed Caroline had an extraordinary memory, a very high sense of justice and religion, would be equally proficient at mathematics or poetry, was cheerful in society, had few but very strong friendships, and was kind and benevolent as far as her means allowed her to be. Most notably, though, in the overwritten and repetitive report, De Ville continually identified Caroline's organisational ability as her key attribute, describing it as "amazingly powerful, more destined by nature for a Male than a Female head".[10] Obviously the highest of praises.

The rage for phrenology lasted until the early 1840s, by which time attacks from both the scientific community and religious groups had diminished its prestige.[11] Despite that, Caroline evidently gave credence to the report, enough anyway for her to stipulate on the final page of the document that when she died it should be given to Henry, her oldest surviving child.

If her self-confidence had been dented by the agony of her first child's death and the eighteen-month separation from Archibald, De Ville's account of Caroline's abilities no doubt went some way to repairing the damage. Heading out alone to India, she would need every ounce of her poise and temerity to reconnect with her husband and establish herself in an exotic new environment.

CHAPTER 4

India

1833–38

Madras, 4 August 1833

Clutching the ship's rail, Caroline strained to glimpse her new home. She was as nervous and excited as a young girl attending her first ball. Little of her anxiety at the moment, though, had to do with arriving in India; what was driving the blood through her body in rapid, spasmodic bursts was the thought of seeing Archie again.

It had been a long separation, their time apart more than they had spent together as a married couple, and she worried about what might have changed between them. Her heart and her mind were in fearful dispute. Once you are together, said her mind, it will be just like when you were first married: you will both be happy, in love. Her heart wasn't so certain. When Archie had left England, she had still been recovering from their baby's death, in mourning, a cold and distant wife. She had seen the hurt in his eyes as she had rejected him, but had been unable to give herself to him then. What would happen now? What would he be thinking? Had he been pleased to get away from a morose, weeping wife? Would he still love her? Would he think she had changed? How would he seem to her? She was twenty-five, but he was thirty-five. Would he have aged, begun to look dull and worn? What if I do not love him anymore, she asked herself? What if … ? Her heart harped on, but her mind refused to give in. Now you are sounding hysterical, it argued back.

The sloop edged closer to shore. Caroline felt the heavy weight of the sun sear through her brocaded cotton dress. Turning her face towards the slight breeze off the sea, she noted other East Indiamen anchored close by. It was still only early morning, but on land the buildings were shimmering and glowing in the first rays of the sun, conjuring a fairy-tale town. Behind rose the imposing walls of the East India Company's Fort St George.

Madras had no harbour. The vessel dropped anchor in deep water off a long, white, sandy beach and was immediately surrounded by a flotilla of masoolahs — traditional Indian surf-boats — bobbing on the tide. Each small craft was crewed by dark-skinned natives, naked apart from a few yards of cloth wound about their nether parts, who were ready to convey passengers and luggage ashore. Caroline, like the other women on board, tried not to notice the bare bodies glistening in the hot sun, but the allure was almost too much. It seemed the more she tried to avoid watching the boatmen, the more her eyes were drawn to them.

Then she was being ushered over the side of the boat and, clasping tight to the rope ladder, descending fearfully, slowly, a difficult matter in inadequate shoes and long skirts. Arms reaching up received her as she stepped down onto the lurching boards of the boat, then seated her next to other passengers. Twelve men at the oars rowed the boat through the rolling surf towards the shore.

As the small craft pitched onto the sand, an army of natives hauled it up the beach. When Caroline rose unsteadily from the wooden bench, callused hands were thrust in front of her. Gingerly, she took hold of one and, carefully lifting the hem of her dress, just a little, climbed out of the masoolah.

Finally, she was on dry land. Unsteady after months on the ship, she stumbled, almost tumbling to the ground as her shoes sank into the soft

*sand. A hand steadied her. "Why Mrs Chisholm, anyone would think
that you were a drunken sailor for all your time at sea," a soft Scottish
voice whispered into her ear. She looked up into the glaring sun to find
her Archie silhouetted against a brilliant cerulean sky. He was holding
tightly to her elbow and smiling down at her. She turned and slid into his
arms, all her fears and worries melting away. His arms closed around her
and he held her tightly against him for a few seconds before releasing her
to give her a chaste salute on her cheek. He drew her arm through his and
his eyes lit up with a boyish grin. "Come along, Caroline, I have much
to show you."[1]*

A rchibald was stationed more than one hundred kilometres
west of Madras, at Vellore, but one assumes that he would
have been there on the beach the day Caroline arrived. He must
have felt that fortune was now firmly on his side: only a few
months earlier he had been promoted to captain in the 30th
Native Infantry, giving him not only greater responsibility but
also an improved income of about £420 per year; and now his
wife had finally joined him.[2]

Caroline was now living the life that she had dreamt of since,
as a little girl, she had played her colonisation game, with its boats
crossing the oceans to carry her dolls from one foreign country to
another. Madras must have been staggering for a young woman
who had spent most of her twenty-five years in rural obscurity.
The light in England had been soft, the weather damp and cold;
the summer smelt of roses and honeysuckle, the food was mainly
roasted meats and heavy puddings. Here the light was luxurious,
even dazzling, the atmosphere was hot and breathless, and the
perfumes of tropical flowers filled the air, along with the aromas

of pungent spices, rich curries and fragrant rice. Nor was it just the vision of scantily clad locals that would have unnerved her: there were so many curiosities constantly assaulting her senses. According to Julia Maitland, the wife of a British judge then living and working in India, the snake charmers were amongst the most extraordinary sights: "One day we had eight cobras and three other snakes all dancing round us at once, and the snake-men singing and playing to them on a kind of bagpipes. The venomous snakes they call good snakes: one, the Braminee cobra, they said was so good his bite would kill a man in three hours."[3]

The most challenging aspect for Caroline, though, would have been personal. Apart from the emotional aspect of resuming married life with Archibald, Caroline found that she had been transported not just into a different culture but into an entirely different social world, which in many ways was at odds with her nature. British ladies resident in India, known locally as memsahibs, were generally a languid, phlegmatic bunch, who were taught that exertion was dangerous because their European constitutions were too delicate for the Indian climate. In reality, there was little need to expend much energy on anything. Nineteenth-century middle-class women in England, apart from the extremely wealthy, rarely engaged more than two or, at most, three servants. In a world of large families, before the mechanisation of many domestic chores, there was still much for women to do at home. In India, it was vastly different. When Julia Maitland first arrived there in 1836, she noted not just the ridiculous number of servants but that each had separate responsibilities: "one to sweep my room, and another to bring water. There is one man to lay the cloth and another to bring in dinner, another to light the candles, and others to wait at table."[4] It was not unusual for couples to have upwards of fifteen to twenty servants. Even the animals

Fort St George and the town of Madras, India, around the time Caroline arrived
(Alamy)

had attendants: "Every horse has a man and a maid to himself —
the maid cuts grass for him; and every dog has a boy. I inquired
whether the cat had any servants, but found that she was allowed
to wait upon herself; and, as she seemed the only person in the
establishment capable of so doing, I respected her accordingly."[5]
Caroline would not have fitted easily into the lethargic role of an
Anglo-Indian memsahib.

After Vellore, it appears that she and Archibald returned to
Madras to take up quarters in Fort St George, or White Town
as it was known. It was there that she found an antidote to her
inactivity and the endless inanities of social visits and gossip that
prevailed amongst the majority of the wives of the East India
Company officers. Caroline saw that many of the daughters of
the ordinary soldiers were left with few or no formal activities,
thereby becoming prey to idleness and sloth as well as moral
dangers. "In budding womanhood the playthings of passion, in

their youth loathsome and abandoned, and in their prime the tenants of a premature tomb,"[6] was how one of Caroline's earliest biographers, Eneas Mackenzie, rather dramatically described their predicament. By contrast, as soon as their brothers were old enough they were taken into the army and given purpose, a career and an income.

The sight of these girls, many little more than children, may well have reminded Caroline of the daughter that she had lost not so long ago. She noticed the girls hanging around the market place almost as though they were on show for any passing soldier. More observant and more caring than other officers' wives, she became aware of how exposed these youngsters were to pregnancy and disease. Her personal experiences, without doubt, would have made her especially determined to help them. That decision would become her first venture into large-scale philanthropy. She opened a boarding school for girls.

Despite the general indolence of most of the memsahibs, there were a number who, along with various missionaries and other senior civil servants, had already established schools throughout India, including Julia Maitland. Maitland's school, though, like most of the others, was just for local boys; there was significant resistance in India to educating females.[7] The children of British officers and gentlemen were already provided for and in any case most of those children were shipped off to boarding school back home by the time they were seven or eight years old.[8] Caroline's Madras school would be unusual on two counts: not only was it just for girls, but those girls were also the daughters of the common European soldiers, the sort of "riff-raff" usually ignored by the ruling class.

Establishing the school provided Caroline with excellent experience in negotiating with powerful men and bringing them round to her point of view. Although Archibald was a well-respected captain, an approach by his wife for aid to found her school would certainly have raised eyebrows amongst the elite. Other women who interested themselves in such activities either assisted their husbands in the endeavour or worked with the ladies' committees of missionary and church institutions.[9] In either case, very few of the women actually made it their business to facilitate or run the schools. Undaunted by either her sex or her background, Caroline sought out Henry Chamier of the Madras Secretariat and, through him, the Governor of Madras, Lieutenant-General Sir Frederick Adam.[10]

Caroline would have known of Sir Frederick well before she arrived in India. Some twenty-five years earlier, he had commanded the 3rd British Brigade at the Battle of Waterloo, twice leading his men into decisive attacks against Napoleon's Imperial Guard. Though he lost close to a quarter of his soldiers, he was nonetheless hailed as one of the heroes of a battle that is still remembered more than two centuries later. Caroline probably had dual motives in appealing to Sir Frederick. She would certainly have needed some funds to start the project, but, just as importantly, where he led others were sure to follow; his backing would no doubt guarantee enough money for the school's ongoing support. Caroline was obviously taking the advice of that unnamed friend back in Northampton who had advised that she needed influential backers and financial help to make the most of her philanthropic work.

Was she intimidated by appealing to such a man? Maybe. Once again, though, her enthusiasm and confidence would win the day. Possibly the very boldness of Caroline's approach would have struck a chord of recognition in an old soldier who knew the value of courage. As a Scotsman, too, he may have been more willing to support the wife of one of his Highland captains. Whatever the reason Sir Frederick "subscribed £20, and in five days 2,000 rupees were raised by a few officers and gentlemen".[11]

So Caroline had her boarding school, which she rather grandiosely named The Female School of Industry for the Daughters of European Soldiers. Although the actual date the school was opened is not known, it was probably sometime during the first few years that she was in India, when Archibald was either stationed in or near Madras. At first, she set it up within Fort St George, but she soon realised that there the girls were too close to the soldiers. So she moved not just the school but her own household too. Leaving the exclusive lodgings within Fort St George, Caroline relocated to Black Town, which was not far from the fort's protective walls and inhabited by the families of the ordinary soldiers and other poor European settlers. Here, close to the beach, she re-established the school and stipulated that no male visitor was permitted without the sanction of one of the managers. Caroline's conduct in moving to Black Town would have been considered by the other officers' wives as radical, and it may be that they thought her eccentric, particularly as there were often reports of disease and immoral behaviour in Black Town. Whilst Caroline would still no doubt have been welcomed by the ladies back in the fort, it is unlikely that any of them would have sought to return the visit. There is no evidence, but it must have been somewhat difficult for Archibald to have had his wife display such a singular disregard for expatriate norms of behaviour. Yet Caroline had warned him how it would be if he married her. In this first venture into philanthropy she showed that she was willing to forgo her comfort if it meant she could connect directly with the people she sought to help. It was an approach that she was to replicate again in Sydney and London.

Apart from banning men, Caroline wrote up other rules, including provisions for the girls to enjoy daily recreation on the beach, as well as prayers and religious teaching, although she didn't insist that they follow any particular religion. It may have been that to garner financial support, particularly from Sir Frederick and other officers, she had to agree to instruction from the Church of England. But, as she was to prove again later in Sydney, Caroline, whilst being deeply committed to Catholicism herself, was no proselytiser. Her overarching code was moral rather than religious.

A matron and a mistress were hired to supervise the everyday running of the school. The matron, in charge of teaching the girls domestic skills, was described as "an excellent housewife ... more suitable for not being able to read or write" (thus the responsibility for compiling reports and calculating budgets fell on the young girls who were also being taught to read and write).[12] The mistress would have been accountable for the rest of the girls' education and the overall running of the school, particularly when Caroline was absent from Madras, accompanying Archibald on his tours of duty. Even when absent, Caroline was determined to maintain her influence, so she penned an address to the students, which the mistress read to them regularly. Within that address was a plea to the girls to maintain a loving relationship with their parents, particularly their mothers as they grew old. Maybe Caroline was thinking of her own lost daughter when she wrote, "You cannot, my children, think how dearly a mother loves, and the comfort she would feel in having a daughter for a nurse."[13]

Whilst most of the other schools in India taught English, some arithmetic and the Bible, Caroline's school was primarily a vocational institution. In other words, she knew that learning to read and write and studying rudimentary mathematics and religion would not necessarily equip young women to support themselves. Her aim was, in modern terms, to "future-safe" the girls by providing them with the skills to earn a living.[14] Caroline's school therefore also offered practical lessons in such activities as needlework, home economics and caring for the sick. Children as young as eight were required to shop, cook and manage both finances and rations.

One problem, of course, was that in India, where servants were so plentiful and cheap, there were few openings for British maids and there was no guarantee that these girls would be repatriated back to Britain, where they were more likely to find appropriate work. So, Caroline also made sure that the girls were trained to be competent mothers, housekeepers and wives, to make them more suitable candidates for a respectable marriage. Either way, Caroline was determined to help stop them falling into prostitution or ending up cohabiting with men who had no legal or financial imperative to take care of them.

Modern feminists have vehemently criticised Caroline's limited ambitions for her charges. In this respect, there is some substance to their condemnation, but only from a twenty-first-century viewpoint. Across the globe in the early nineteenth century, female education was woeful, as were the chances of women gaining and maintaining autonomy. What Caroline did for the forgotten European girls of Madras was to provide them not just with an elementary education but also with a range of basic skills, which would at least afford them some options in life.

With the school securely underway, Caroline's life was about to take another turn. By August 1835 she was pregnant again. Was she hoping for another daughter or was she afraid that she might lose this child too? Her second child, a healthy son, named Archibald after his father, was born in Madras on

4 May 1836. An army doctor may not have been present at the birth, as it was still considered immodest by many expats in India to have a man attend such an event, but there would certainly have been a European midwife there.[15] Whatever the case, a doctor would have visited Caroline shortly afterwards and in succeeding days to ascertain her health, though more through conversation than examination. Medical science had not really progressed much in the five years since Caroline's first pregnancy, and some bizarre methods were still being employed. One well-respected army doctor who published a book on raising children for European women in India devoted at least two chapters to breastfeeding. He suggested that if a woman suffered from lumps in her breast whilst feeding her infant then the nurse should suck the breast dry with "her own mouth" before rubbing it with oil and brandy, after which up to two dozen leeches should be applied to the lump. Then to make certain that the treatment was successful the lump should be "fomented with hot water, so as to encourage the bleeding".[16] No wonder doctors in India recommended that white women should not leave their beds or receive visitors for at least two to three weeks after delivering their baby.

In fact, except in the very first few days, European women were usually told not to suckle their infants themselves because of the oppressive climate. Instead, doctors advised that they should use local wet-nurses or amahs.[17] "No infant thrives so well in India as those fed by these women," said one authority. It was not unusual for doctors to offer to examine Indian women and their children before they were employed as amahs, to ensure that they were clean and healthy. It was, nevertheless, often the sort of close bodily scrutiny that the doctors would have thought indecent to give a British woman.

However commonplace it was for European women to employ amahs as wet-nurses, it must have been difficult for Caroline to watch another woman breastfeed her baby. Very possibly she resented the close physical bond developing between the amah and her newborn son. It may have meant that she failed to bond as she might have done with her child, and possibly a vital connection between them was lost; she may also have been unaware that the lack of intimacy was retarding her love for the little boy. Certainly, in future years she would send her sons away so that she could concentrate on helping the women of New South Wales, and she would also withdraw them from school so that she would have enough funds for her immigration work. In each case, she was troubled about her actions, but went ahead with them. Caroline seems to have managed to avoid the classic twenty-first-century woman's anxiety about the conflict between work and family.

There would have been little time for soul searching in India, however. Within two months of the birth, and no doubt despite medical advice that she should rest, the family was on the move again. Archibald had been posted about 630 kilometres to the northwest of Madras, to Secunderabad, and then later further north again to Bowenpally. On the journey, Archibald would have ridden with his men, but Caroline and the baby and amah would most likely have travelled in a palanquin, a type of wheelless litter strung between two poles and carried by at least four men. At walking pace, it must have been a remarkably tedious journey, despite the exotic scenery.

A little over six months after Archibald Jnr was born, Caroline was pregnant again. This second child was born in Bowenpally on 6 September 1837.[18] Another son, he was named William after both Archibald's brother, who had been killed in India almost twenty years earlier, and, of course, Caroline's father, the indomitable William Jones.

The end of 1837 found the family still in Bowenpally. Caroline was now a twenty-nine-year-old mother of two boys under two years of age. Her early narrow world view had expanded, as had her understanding of dealings in a curious foreign land that she may not even have imagined as a child in Northampton. Moreover, she had successfully engaged in her first philanthropic endeavour, through which she managed not just to influence the lives of vulnerable girls, but also to gain vital experience of how to manipulate authority and harvest the respect she needed to achieve her goals. Along the way she had proved herself both diligent and extremely well organised.

Judging from Caroline's own writings and those of her contemporary biographers, her school appears to have been a success. However, little is known about what happened to it after Caroline left India. In the *Madras Almanac and Compendium of Intelligence for 1839,* published a year after she departed from the subcontinent, there is mention of the "Ladies Institution for the Education of the Daughters of Europeans and their Descendants in the Presidency of Madras". The school was based "in the Vicinity of Black Town" and took both day girls and boarders, although it did charge some fees, which were not mentioned in documents pertaining to Caroline's school.[19] An unusual trait in Caroline was that she always seemed too busy looking forward to notice what happened behind her. Once she left India she appeared to forget all about the school. It was almost a counterintuitive feature of her character, that having worked so hard for an outcome, she could then just walk away from it with barely a glance backwards. She was to do the same in Sydney and in London.

In February 1838, the clock was ticking, and there was still half a world to navigate. Archibald, on the threshold of his fortieth year, was unwell. He applied to visit Madras preparatory to requesting leave to travel to New South Wales.[20] It's unclear what was behind Caroline and Archibald's decision not to return home. Possibly they thought that the milder climate in Sydney would benefit Archibald, or maybe they headed to the New World in a spirit of sheer adventure. Whatever the reason, that choice was to have an immeasurable impact on the burgeoning colony.

CHAPTER 5

The Bounty Girls

1838–40

Sydney, 1840

The girl raised the bottle she was holding and swirled the light brown liquid around inside it before taking a long draft from its neck. Caroline reckoned her to be little more than fifteen years old. Propped against a stone wall, with her dirty brown hair falling loosely about her freckled face, the girl looked at Caroline for a moment, with green eyes listless and indifferent. Her dress bespoke her calling: a red bodice only partly laced over a grubby blouse hardly troubled by breasts that had not yet fully developed; a stained white chemise slipping off one thin shoulder; and an oversized skirt, a hand-me-down of some sort, kept in place by a gaudy red ribbon, beginning to fray.

Only a short time earlier, passing the Military Hospital in George Street and the elegant abode of the trader Robert Campbell, one of Sydney's richest men, Caroline had plunged into a twisted coil of footpaths that led her into the rancid heart of the Rocks. Located at the fag end of the Sydney Cove settlement, the Rocks was surrounded by water on three sides and fused into the hills above west Circular Quay. Along the waterfront and around the cool rim of the promontory rose the lavish homes of the wealthy traders, but crammed within its febrile belly were the dilapidated dwellings that seemed to spread like a virulent rash from the edge of town. Bordering a maze of narrow passageways, they were home to the colony's poorest families, who fought for survival amidst the crime, booze and carnal pleasures of their neighbours. Dotted among the hovels were a smattering of honest businesses, but also grog shops, pubs and brothels frequented by convicts, the vilest of the emancipists and rough seafarers — the sort of lowlife to be found in the underbelly of most ports.

Caroline was unused to such squalor; it seemed that all the ugliness of London's slums had been transported to this insignificant corner of the Empire. She was out of place here and she knew it, but that very fact kept her safe. A couple of scraggy boys had run after her, only to be called back by their mothers. "We don't want no trouble," the women had shouted at the boys.

On almost every street, Caroline saw young women already beyond her help. They hung around in doorways, the dregs of their youth destroyed by the life they led. Something about the green-eyed girl had stopped her and forced her to speak. She tried again, asking how long the girl had been in the colony and, finally, offering to help.

The girl laughed at her, but with little humour; it was more the sound of tired resignation, past hope of any salvation. She turned from Caroline, swirling her skirt, and headed towards a loutish looking sailor, at least three times her age, making his way up the hill, calling out to catch his attention. Caroline watched as the man put his arm around the girl's waist and drew her to him. That child was someone's daughter; a woman had brought her into the world, fed her, guided her first steps, taught her to speak, laughed with her. All to what end? The tragedy of that one girl felt to Caroline like a physical ache. She had to get to these girls, before desperation led to ruin.[1]

By 1838, the British colony of New South Wales was past the foetal stage but still in its infancy. It would be another five years before even a limited vote for the Legislative Council was extended to wealthy landowners and more than sixty years before the creation of the Commonwealth of Australia brought about an albeit imperfect nationhood. When Caroline arrived in Sydney, she found numerous and disparate strands of humanity cohabiting in an uneasy, often fractious arrangement.

Scratch the surface and it was riven by conflict. Apart from the obvious struggle between the convicts and the soldiers, there were so many other bubbling hostilities, such as the dispute between wealthy free settlers, the Exclusives, and the emancipists; the prejudice shown between the English and Irish, and, similarly, amongst the Anglicans and Roman Catholics; and the restless push for democracy, led by William Charles Wentworth and others, against the governor's rule. Whilst animosity fermented between the white settlers, they turned almost as one to subjugate the Indigenous people, the original owners of the land. Sydney was a plaything of Janus: it had beauty, opportunity and wealth, yet it was also promiscuous, angry and greedy. "Money, money, money. Nothing is considered disgraceful here but the want of money. It covers an immense multitude of sins," wrote one commentator.[2] New South Wales needed direction and morality if it was ever to throw off its brutal past.[3]

It is unlikely that Caroline and Archibald had any idea of the turmoil seething within the colony when they first arrived. What they saw on that early spring day in September when the 501-ton *Emerald Isle* sailed through Sydney Heads was enough to gladden their hearts. As one contemporary writer described it,

"The entrance to Port Jackson is grand in the extreme ... The countless bays and inlets of this noble estuary render it extremely beautiful."[4] Sailing into that almost virgin harbour with Caroline and Archibald were their two young sons and three Indian maids; it was the end of a journey that, including extended stopovers in Mauritius, Adelaide and Hobart, had taken six months.

Leaving the boat and the Indian maids (who were returned to Madras), the family initially put up at an inn, probably in Jamison Street, not far from the still incomplete Circular Quay. The thoroughfare was named after their neighbour, the somewhat irregular, first titled free settler, Sir John Jamison. In many ways he typified the paradox that was colonial society. Born to middle-class Anglican parents in Ireland, he went to sea as a naval physician and was knighted during the Napoleonic Wars. After inheriting vast tracts of land in New South Wales, he moved there in 1814 at the age of thirty-eight. By the time Caroline reached Sydney, Sir John was well established, incredibly wealthy, a member of the governor-appointed Legislative Council, and co-founder of what would become Sydney University, the Bank of New South Wales (later Westpac) and the horse-racing industry. This paragon of the new elite also supported liberalising the political and legal institutions and, maybe most shockingly, had numerous illegitimate children from various working-class and convict mistresses, most of whom he recognised and who carried his name. One bastard daughter of a convict servant even married into the colonial establishment, with the governor attending her wedding.

Despite some serious attempts to vanquish it, the fluidity of the social order in New South Wales, where the child of a felon could rise to lawmaker, was one of the most obvious differences between this New World and the old one, where social mobility

EMIGRANTS AT DINNER.

Emigrants eating dinner below decks en route to Australia *(National Library of Australia, nla.obj-135889370)*

was much more limited. Many settlers from the upper ranks, though accustomed to clear class barriers, had already started to rethink and accept the unstoppable waves of change, and many more would follow suit as the century unfolded.[5] This was a community that Caroline could understand. One can almost see the spectre of her father, William Jones, with a satisfied smile on his lips, cheering her on. In this small but strangely altered reproduction of Britain, there was scope for Caroline to carry out charitable works whilst entering the highest echelons of society, moving beyond the traditional confines of her own class and, indeed, her sex also.

So, Caroline met with a fractious, confused society, still taking shape, much like the physical town itself. After the teeming populace of India, New South Wales must have seemed strangely empty. Its allure or otherwise was in the eye of the beholder, and opinions varied. Much of the bone work of the town, including buildings such as Sydney Hospital and Hyde Park Barracks, all representing the growing sophistication of British rule, had been built some twenty-five years earlier, in Governor Lachlan Macquarie's day; by Caroline's time, the town was described by a Scottish businessman as being "elegant and perfect in its design ... and is not surpassed by that of any modern town in either hemisphere".[6] The quality of the shops was disputed, though. One long-term resident, an Anglican minister, was scathing about their pretentions: "Look at our splendid shops — some of them fully equal to those of second-rate in London."[7] Another, a woman with an eye to fashion, was more complimentary, describing Sydney as "a large busy town ... full of good shops exhibiting every variety of merchandise".[8] One of those shops, opened just a few months before Caroline arrived, was situated on the corner of George and Barrack streets; the proprietor, a Welsh immigrant named David Jones, offered the finest goods "bought in the best English Markets".[9] Other observers, however, had no hesitation in poking fun at Sydney's attempt to emulate London: "George Street seems to be ... the Pall-Mall ... of Sydney, and up and down its hot, dusty, glaring, weary length go the fair wives and daughters of the 'citizens', enjoying their daily airing."[10] At the same time, parts of Pitt Street were praised for their rural tranquillity, being "remarkable for [their] neatness and cheerful appearance ... most of the cottages with ... small garden plots before them [and] shaded verandahs ... recall the rustic beauties of Old England."[11]

On the edge of Hyde Park, the one place that Caroline would definitely have visited shortly after her arrival was St Mary's Church. Built in 1821 with the blessing of Governor Macquarie, it was a simple cruciform stone structure in the Gothic style.[12] Despite most governors being tolerant of religious diversity, it wasn't until 1835, and after much negotiation between London and Rome, that John Bede Polding, an Englishman, was appointed by Papal Briefs to be the first Bishop of Sydney (and in 1842 became the first Archbishop of Sydney). The 1841 census showed that just over a quarter of the colony's 130,000 souls were Roman Catholics, the vast majority of those being Irish convicts and poor working-class immigrants.[13] Yet there were also by then a number of eminent Catholics, particularly in the judiciary, including the Attorney General, John Hubert Plunkett, and lawyer and future judge and politician Roger Therry. It is likely that Caroline made their acquaintance, possibly through the church, when she first arrived in Sydney. Certainly, there is evidence that Caroline maintained a close friendship for some years with Therry's wife, Ann.[14] Later Roger Therry was to devote a section of his 1863 book, *Reminiscences of Thirty Years' Residence in New South Wales and Victoria,* to Caroline and her work with immigrants.

Caroline's first impression of the colony was no doubt coloured by the views of those early friendships. Or maybe, as so often happens, she was drawn to people whose opinions corresponded with her own. Whatever the case, in Therry and Plunkett she certainly found important men with surprisingly liberal views for the era, notably on the rights of Australia's Indigenous people. Despite public opinion being strongly against them, both men were instrumental in prosecuting the white men responsible for one of the most heinous attacks on Aboriginal people documented since the advent of European settlement. It happened at Myall Creek Station, about 360 kilometres northwest of Sydney, on the Liverpool Plains, on 10 June 1838. (Caroline was still on the boat on her way to Australia when the massacre took place.)

On the evidence of one brave convict station-hand, a local magistrate, Edward Denny Day, and the station owner, eleven men (a mix of convicts and emancipists) were charged with murdering thirty Aboriginal people, mostly women, old men and children. It was a premeditated slaughter. With the young men of the tribe away, the rest had been inveigled to seek protection on the property. Then they were butchered with swords and their bodies burnt.

In the first trial in the middle of November 1838, in Sydney, all eleven men were acquitted. Their defence at this trial and the subsequent one was paid for by an association of landowners and stockmen who, like most of the white community, supported the defendants. Later *The Sydney Gazette* reported the words of one of the jurors from the first trial, who claimed that he knew that the men were guilty but admitted, "I look on blacks as a set of monkeys and I think the earlier they are exterminated from the face of the earth the better ... I for one, would never consent to see a white man suffer for shooting a black one."[15] Almost immediately Plunkett and Therry found evidence to recharge seven of the men and go to a new trial. (The other four men, plus one free settler also believed responsible, were released, never to face any legal reprobation.) This time, all seven were found guilty, and they were hung on 17 December 1838. The expectation throughout the colony had been that the new Governor, Sir George Gipps, would intervene with an order for clemency, but none was forthcoming. *The Sydney Gazette* reported that before their executions the men asked to be allowed to embrace: "They kissed and shook each other's hands, and with eyes streaming with tears, bade each other a last adieu ... They mounted the scaffold ... The cries of the men to God for mercy were distinctly audible and they were soon launched into eternity. Throughout the whole of the time they remained in the yard they appeared to pay much attention to their devotions ... although they expressed no contrition for the crime."[16]

The men were the only whites in all of New South Wales to be hung for crimes against the Indigenous people during the colonial years. Sir George Gipps came in for severe criticism from the newspapers. *The Sydney Herald* on 5 July 1838 described as "mawkish sentimentality" his statement that Her Majesty's Government expected an increase in the "just and humane treatment of the aborigines of this country".[17] It seems extraordinary, from a twenty-first-century perspective, that such a statement would even need to be made, but two hundred years ago white society had no perception of equality, be it racial or sexual.

Caroline would have been very aware of the bitter social divisions created by the massacre and subsequent trials. It gave her an initial insight into the broad social opinions of many of the powerful men within the colony, as well as those of lesser individuals. Although she was to become primarily concerned with British immigrants, she exhibited significant sympathy for the plight of the Indigenous people, though true to her main focus, it was Indigenous women who interested her the most, particularly when she discovered that many had been victims of rape and possibly murder at the hands of settlers. An example of her attempting to intervene on behalf of Aboriginal people is a letter that she wrote almost ten years later, when she was able to trade on her status as one of the best-known philanthropists within the colony and exert some influence. Dated February 1847, it was addressed to Earl Grey, Secretary of State for the Colonies in London; she suggested to him that the "frightful disparity" of the sexes in New South Wales was responsible for subjecting the Indigenous population to misery and crimes and pointed out that "this ... may be traced in a great degree the gradual but certain extermination of those unfortunate tribes ... the original holders of the soil".[18]

Strife of a different kind was also invading New South Wales by the late 1830s: the colony was on the verge of depression. There were three major causes for the crippling economic slump.

The first and possibly chief reason was the type of boom and bust that is not unknown in twenty-first-century Australia. Back in colonial days it was the result of land and stock speculation. From 1831 Crown land had been sold at auction from five shillings an acre, but in 1838, at a time when there were more free immigrants wanting to invest in the New World, that price rose sharply to twelve shillings an acre. With no taxation in the colony, land sales provided much-needed revenue to the government, and the profits from the sales were deposited with Sydney banks. In a dangerous circular effect that left both sides vulnerable, the banks then lent the money out immediately on interest to other eager settlers, often people with little collateral, only a burning desire to buy land that, in many cases, they had not even seen. Many also borrowed to invest in livestock, especially sheep. The Reverend David Mackenzie, writing about the colony after living there for a decade, suggested that speculators needed rather a "cargo of strait-jackets, and a place in a lunatic asylum".[19] He went on to tell of several young men he knew who had taken out five-year loans at ten per cent interest to buy flocks of sheep at £3 a head, only to find that by the time the loan had matured, the sheep were worth no more than six shillings a head.[20]

The second cause originated on the other side of the world. Just as the colony's boom was reaching its zenith in the late 1830s, Britain's economy sneezed and soon New South Wales caught cold. For mostly domestic reasons, the United Kingdom lurched into depression at the end of the 1830s, resulting in the colony's trade with the homeland being slashed. During the seven years from 1833, New South Wales's exports to Britain had increased on average each year by close to thirty per cent. In 1841 they fell by nine per cent; loans from back home were also called in, further draining colonial funds.[21]

The third cause was beyond anyone's control: drought. Lasting for some six years from 1837, it destroyed crops and livestock and sent the price of food soaring. Soon "wheat was at an enormous price in Sydney ... *twenty-seven shillings* per bushel".[22] On Wednesday, 10 October 1838, *The Sydney Monitor and Commercial Advertiser* wrote on its front page: "The dust is flying in clouds under the impetus of a parching wind ... We are old hands, but we never heard of the owners deliberately killing the lambs because there was nothing to eat for the mothers ... Mr Peters ... out of 900 lambs has lost 600."

The combined fallout from these three devastating events was significant. Upwards of one thousand of the colony's largest stockholders and merchants went bankrupt, along with at least two of Sydney's banks. Thousands of sheep, the economic lifeblood of New South Wales, were "boiled down for tallow and fat on the outskirts of town".[23] With the colony teetering on the brink of financial disaster, the effects of the depression on the colony's inhabitants were exacerbated by an influx of poor bounty immigrants, both men and women.

In 1838, when Caroline took up residence, the drought was certainly causing some concern, but it was still only in its early days and the other ills were not yet apparent. One of the main reasons was the dilatory nature of communications: boats sailing between Sydney and Britain could take up to four months each way, so that by the time an official communiqué had been sent, a response decided upon and an answer given, the better part of a year could have elapsed, leaving both governments on either side of the world playing catch-up with the changing conditions.

With the boom in the mid- to late 1830s, and knowing that London was planning to stop the transportation of convicts and, hence, the free supply of labour, squatters and farmers were crying out for workers. Sir George Gipps responded by applying for more free bounty immigrants to meet these needs, and, to counter the imbalance of the sexes, there was also an active decision by the Colonial Government to increase the numbers of women.[24] For every fit and healthy female of good character they delivered to the colony of New South Wales, ships' captains were paid a bounty of about £15 (worth $18,900 today). Some character references were real; others were forged by bounty agents.

The trouble was that by the time the majority of free but poor and often unskilled bounty immigrants reached Sydney, the economy had turned; depression, unemployment and harsh conditions became the welcome mat laid out for their arrival. The increase of immigrants was staggering. Just over 6500 landed in 1840; by the next year, that number had risen to more than twenty thousand, in effect a surge of fifteen per cent of the total population of New South Wales. As Margaret Kiddle has pointed out, "Even without the depression, such a number would have been too great ... to absorb quickly."[25]

In the spring of 1838, when Caroline arrived, there was barely an inkling of the impending trouble. Certainly Caroline saw disparity between rich and poor, but that would have seemed inevitable in such a society. Sometime in those first few weeks, for example, she and Archibald came across a group of Scottish Highland men, free immigrants who had been unable to find work. Their money was virtually gone, they were incapable of supporting themselves or their families, and their plight was exacerbated by their lack of English. Archibald spoke to them in Scottish Gaelic and, though it's unclear whether it was his idea or Caroline's, gave them some coinage. It was probably only a few shillings, but it wasn't just a handout, it came with a business plan, a suggestion to the men to use part of the money to "purchase tools and wheelbarrows, whereby they might cut and sell fire-wood to the inhabitants".[26] This sounds very like Caroline. It was typical of the problem-solving in which she excelled and which was based on a commercial understanding rare among her sex at that time. Whilst concerned for the Highlanders' immediate predicament, she was well aware that the only way to safeguard against lifelong poverty and destitution was to acquire marketable skills. It was the same strategy she had adopted in teaching household skills to her girls in India, and it was becoming her modus operandi.

After a short stay in Sydney, Caroline and Archibald decided to settle in the country, choosing Windsor, some fifty-six kilometres to the northwest, along a dry and dusty tract of highway via Parramatta. This tollway was considered so dangerous that some coach drivers refused to travel by it.[27] Bushrangers were also a very real threat, including one of the colony's most notorious highwaymen, Jack Donohoe, otherwise known as the Wild Colonial Boy. To avoid these risks, the Chisholm family may well have taken the scenic route: a boat up the coast from Sydney to Pittwater then along the Hawkesbury River to Windsor. Steamers had become something of a familiar sight on that particular stretch of waterway, and provided the locals with everything from "sugar to shoes and from farm implements to haberdashery"; they were, indeed, the lifeblood of Windsor.[28]

There's no obvious explanation why Caroline and Archibald decided to live at Windsor. Perhaps, after the rigours of India, they both craved the peace and tranquillity of country life, and the matter of travelling a few miles along a major watercourse would have seemed of no great import. Moreover, the town would have been described to them as a well-established community with good homes, churches, schools, a police force and a courthouse. Windsor was probably the most successful of the five towns founded in the area by Governor Lachlan Macquarie about 1810 and developed as the colony's breadbasket; in the 1830s fruit and vegetables replaced wheat as the main crops. By then there was also blood on the ground: the original inhabitants, the Darug people, had been mostly killed or pushed out and the area occupied by some eleven hundred white settlers.

The family's first Australian Christmas came and went. Children of India, the boys had not known a cold English yuletide, and would have found nothing strange in the heavy, hot, oppressive days or the relentless buzzing of cicadas and other insects. Maybe they listened without understanding as the grown-ups lamented icy windswept landscapes and freezing nights around warm, smoky fires or even the harsher winter climate of Archibald's Highlands, with its snowdrifts, frozen rivers and long hours of darkness followed only by the weakest daylight.

As 1839 waxed, little seemed to infiltrate the respite that Caroline and Archibald were enjoying from a troubled world. Having engaged a nanny for the boys, a Miss Galvin, they settled down to enjoy a halcyon period of family life. The only time reality intruded was on their trips into Sydney. Whenever rural serenity palled a little for the innately adventurous couple, Caroline and Archibald left the children and travelled to the town to socialise with their new friends. Once there, they became aware of the slow emptying out of the colony's prosperity; and it was during these visits that Caroline witnessed firsthand the dreadful plight of growing numbers of young bounty girls, wandering the streets with few prospects.

Although the girls were meant to travel to Australia under the aegis of a married woman, many of them had little real protection on board the boats, either during the journey or when the vessel docked. Once they arrived in Sydney, they were allowed to remain on their boat for ten days with full rations, but as well as legitimate employers, brothel owners and single men looking for short-term "housekeepers" were permitted to board the boats to engage either willing or unwary girls. Moreover, once the ten days were up, the girls were forced to go ashore. Unable to find lodgings, many walked the streets looking for honest work.

As Caroline became increasingly disturbed by the predicament of these females, she started to bring a few back to Windsor, housing them until she found them local employment. At one point she had up to nine girls staying with the family.[29]

In July 1839, an Australian child, a third son, Henry, was born to Caroline and Archibald in Windsor. Thereafter, the harmony of their recent reprieve was to be short-lived, and never really reoccur. At the end of the year, Archibald received orders to return to the subcontinent. He was needed there to help replace East India Company officers who were being sent to China, where Britain was engaged in a dispute that would go down in the history books as the Opium Wars. Britain had developed an unquenchable thirst for all things Chinese, particularly tea, and the Chinese had been more than happy to sell it to them, but only in exchange for silver. That had created a difficulty for the British traders because of the increased cost. Then the British had discovered and fuelled a ravenous desire among the Chinese for the Indian-grown opium drug, leading to the balance of trade swinging significantly back in favour of the British. Now the Chinese were attempting to make opium illegal and stop its sale altogether. So the East India Company troops were sent to China, in a tactical display described as "gunship diplomacy", to prevent the Chinese from destroying the British opium trade. Several skirmishes ensued, ending in the Treaty of Nanking of 1842, which, among other conditions, ceded Hong Kong to Britain.

It was not just a clash of two cultures, but a war for mercantile supremacy.

Shortly after the Chisholms' second Christmas in New South Wales, Archibald set sail for India. It was January 1840; Caroline stayed behind with their three sons: Archibald Jnr, soon to be four years old; William, almost two and a half; and the baby, Henry, just six months old. It would be close on five years before Archibald returned; by then he would carry the rank of major, but his health would have suffered. Caroline, on the other hand, would be in her prime.

One wonders why Caroline remained in Australia when Archibald departed. Maybe she was unwilling to subject herself and the children to the stringency of living in India again or, more likely, in New South Wales she had found a society that not only needed her but in which she could flourish. She had lived in this would-be replica of the Old World for sixteen months, long enough to appreciate both the dissemblance and the possibilities behind its rugged, ruthless exterior. Before he left, Archibald, witnessing her growing empathy towards the bounty immigrants, had suggested that they would be "fit objects for her charitable zeal and energy".[30] India had given Caroline experience; now Australia would make her famous.

CHAPTER 6

Flora's Story

1840–41

Sydney, 1840

Skirting behind Petty's Hotel, she became aware of a young woman, just a few yards ahead, scuttling away, avoiding her. Caroline stared and her heart jumped; there was something familiar about that girl: the way she walked, the turn of her head, bowed now as she hurried forward.

Determined to overtake her, Caroline ran a little, and, catching up, laid a hand on her arm. The girl stopped. For a few seconds she stood, head bent, chest heaving, and then she raised her face. There before Caroline stood the wreck of her "Highland Beauty", Flora. How different she was now from the lovely girl Caroline had first seen in a tent near the Immigration Barracks. Gone were the modest dress and the shining blonde locks in demure ribbons. The ruddy rose of the Highlands was changed for the tinge of rum; she had been drinking, but she well knew what she was about.

"Tell me where you are going," asked Caroline.

"To hell," scoffed Flora, walking on past.

Caroline kept pace with her. "Let us talk," she tried again.

The girl stopped, sneering, "No, Mrs Chisholm. You can't help me. I'm not one of your good girls." She turned aside but called back over her shoulder, "Get away from me. You're no use to anyone."

She headed for Lavender's Ferry. Caroline was determined not to lose her, and stayed with her. She asked again where Flora was going.

"Over there," she pointed across the bay. "My mistress lives over there."

"Then I will go with you. I want to say a few words to you," said Caroline.

"Do what you want," she shrugged.

Caroline paid the fare for both of them and sat next to Flora as the boat crossed to the other shore. No words were spoken. Disembarking, the girl ambled along by the water. There was a look on Flora's face that Caroline recognised, a desperate agony, beyond words. She looked from the girl to the water, glittering silver-grey in the late afternoon sunlight. There was something about Flora's manner that suddenly made Caroline aware of what she was planning. She felt an icy coldness rising within her.

She tried to distract the girl. She knew what had been happening in Flora's family, so she asked softly, "Did you see your mother die?"

The girl stopped and sank down on the rocky beach as though punctured by a pin prick. "No, she died happy," came the self-mocking answer.

"Are you a mother?" asked Caroline as gently as possible, as she sat down beside her.

Flora gasped, shook her head slowly, eyes intently seeking Caroline's. She took Caroline's hand and held it over her heart. "God is merciful," she whispered. "I am not with child."

"May I see that letter?" Caroline asked, noticing for the first time a piece of paper tucked into Flora's partly exposed bosom. Flora nodded and handed it to Caroline, who spread it open. It was from Frank, Flora's brother, who had been with their mother in Sydney when she died. The letter told of her final hours and taunted Flora for the life she now led:

"You have humiliated our family, we all share a part of your shame. Thank God our mother knew nought of it. I do not know if God or I could or even should forgive you ..."

The words were harsh, but Caroline saw something else in them. "Your brother loves you, even now. Will you let me speak to him?"

"No, no," cried Flora. "He is better off without me. I loved my brother better than anyone, anyone save ... him ... But Frank curses me for my life now."

"Were there any in your family that ever committed suicide?" Caroline asked abruptly.

The girl shuddered. "It's there I mean to drown myself," she whispered, pointing to a distant spot where the rocks were jutting out into the last of the sunshine winking off the water. "It's there we went often and there I mean to die."

"You must not," Caroline responded urgently, taking Flora's hand and cradling it between her own.

"Why should I not? What is there for me in this life? He tricked me. Now I'm a slut, a harlot, a whore. Degraded, my brother says. The only decent thing I've done was to keep it from my mother."

"Your mother knew you for a good girl. There is a way back to virtue." Tentatively, Caroline put out her arms to Flora. The girl dropped her head onto Caroline's shoulder, clinging close like a child. Then Flora recounted her story.

Shadows lengthened and the air chilled as dusk crept across the water and onto the rocks where Caroline sat with her fallen Highland Beauty. Flora told of the past few months since she had gone with the man who had taken her from the Immigration Barracks. She had believed he meant to marry her. He gave her clothes and pretty bits of jewellery, but after a few weeks, having satisfied himself, he grew bored with her. He told her he had a wife, and said he wouldn't marry the likes of her anyway. Then he left her. That's when she started drinking.

"He turned me into a filthy whore, Mrs Chisholm. If you only knew how dirty I feel. I'll never be clean again. No one will ever want me."

"Do you have a mistress over here?" asked Caroline.

"No, I have no mistress, save the drink. I just said that to get rid of you," she answered.

"My poor child," whispered Caroline. Flora finally let go. She sobbed, her young body racked by shudders. When the weeping eased, Caroline spoke gently to her, describing all the love a mother has for a child and a brother for a sister. Then of the future. "I will help you. I can, you know." Caroline said. "But first, you must vow to me that you will not attempt to end your life. You are too precious."

Finally, Flora promised, and agreed to let Caroline approach her brother. They crossed back to the other side in the ferry. Caroline procured cheap but respectable lodgings for Flora, not far from her own inn. In the morning, they would go together to look for Frank.[1]

Caroline was obsessed with Flora. According to her own account, the young "Highland Beauty" was the catalyst that propelled her towards helping the destitute bounty women. In Caroline's eye, Flora was the living, breathing embodiment of the dangers present in Sydney and what Caroline fervently believed to be her personal moral duty to minimise those perils.

It was probably quite early in 1840 when Caroline first became involved with Flora. With Archibald back in India, she was spending less and less time in the relative wilds of Windsor. Although she did involve herself with the local community there, including helping to collect subscriptions for an orphan school and a Catholic girls' boarding school — contacts which were later to be useful to her — it was still obviously not enough to keep her occupied.[2] Maybe the community in Windsor was too limited, or possibly she was lonely or bored. Whatever the case, Caroline gravitated towards Sydney. Her relative freedom of movement suggests that either she left her three young sons in Windsor with Miss Galvin or else brought the nanny and the boys with her to town. Certainly, while delving into the haunts of the bounty women, she was not hampered by her children.

Having already helped a few of the bounty girls, Caroline's concern for their sisterhood was growing. Between 1840 and 1841 it was estimated that some six hundred girls were on the verge of penury in Sydney, being unable to find employment.[3] Caroline visited the immigrants' camp near the old Immigration Barracks, where many of the bounty women and families were living. If they had not found work and accommodation before they were forced ashore, most were offered some shelter in tents set up next to the Immigration Barracks on Bent Street, near the Governor's Domain. Others though, unable or unwilling to chance the encampment, found shelter in the streets or in the nooks and boulders of the public gardens.[4]

It was on her initial inspection of the camp that Caroline first saw Flora. In her own words: "About five in the evening, my attention became fixed on a young and beautiful Highland girl (in tent No. 1): the arm of a gentleman was round her waist. I am a great admirer of beauty, and her style pleased me exceedingly. On my two following visits, I still saw the same gentleman; I observed, too, a little extra *finery* on Flora."[5]

As Caroline soon learnt, Flora was not a lonely, defenceless girl like so many others, but had arrived in Sydney with her mother and brother and at least one male cousin, all of whom may have been expected to protect her — yet they didn't. Although she was unable to discover the gentleman's name, Caroline was suspicious

Caroline meeting immigrants as they arrive in Sydney *(Alamy)*

of his motives, so she attempted to caution Flora's mother: "The poor woman said, there was no fear of Flora for her head had never rested but on her mother's hearth. She was all innocence — the mother all hope."[6]

The very next day in George Street, Caroline saw the same man enter the store where she was shopping. She couldn't fail to notice that an elegant woman "hung on his arm". Caroline quickly found out the man's name and that the woman was his wife. With the pedantic precision that became her hallmark, she then double-checked her facts, going next door to inquire if anyone knew who owned the carriage in which she had seen him arrive. Receiving the same information, Caroline said that she "no longer doubted his intentions".[7]

The next evening, she again noticed the man in the tent with her Highland Beauty. At this stage, though, Caroline had been in the colony less than two years and still felt herself to be a "stranger".[8] She was also obviously nervous of a confrontation with a gentleman, one moreover who was probably her social superior — she was to find out later that he was a friend of Governor Sir George Gipps — and although she suspected he was a libertine, she had no firm claim against him. Making further inquiries, Caroline was told that a Ladies' Committee had already been established to care for the female immigrants but that these ladies failed to help the girls in any meaningful way because they "never visited the institute or in any way interfered"[9] — thus opening the door to men of any condition to prey upon the girls without fear of discovery.

Lacking any influential support, Caroline was "obliged to leave Flora to her *fate*".[10] That sounds strangely unlike the confident, decisive Caroline who had in the past and would again in the future display considerable temerity when faced with moral and practical concerns. Indeed, she later felt extremely guilty that she hadn't managed to prevent Flora's seduction. When the girl vanished from the barracks with her beau, Caroline kept an eye on her family, and learnt a little later of her mother's death. Flora's fate continued to haunt Caroline. The girl was Caroline's first failure. It was a word that did not fit comfortably within her lexicon. Whenever she saw or heard of other girls tricked by lascivious men or deliberately turning to prostitution, she felt she was at fault because she had not done all in her power to prevent it.

Her inactivity did not last long. As though propelled by an irresistible force, Caroline could not help but involve herself in the crisis she saw surrounding her. Later she wrote, "As a female ... I naturally felt diffident ... [but] ... I was impressed with the idea, that God had, in a peculiar manner, fitted me for this work ... On Easter Sunday, I was enabled, at the altar of our Lord, to make an offering of my talents to the God who gave them ... and determined ... never to rest until *decent protection* was afforded them."[11] Caroline clearly wanted to show her devotion to God, but there was obviously also little doubt in her own mind that she was capable of taking on the enormous task ahead of her or that, having resolved to do so, she would be successful. Her confidence now restored, Caroline would no longer let herself be handicapped either by her social position or her sex.

It was whilst grappling with how to shelter the girls that she conceived the idea of a dedicated home to keep them safe whilst she looked for suitable work for them. She knew that each ship disgorging its cargo of single women increased the need for such an institution. Caroline identified the old wooden Immigration Barracks, which was mostly vacant, as an ideal building for her purpose.[12] It had the added advantage of being next to the immigrants' camp. To proceed, she required the governor's permission and the funds to make it work. After hesitating for three weeks whilst she weighed the various possibilities, she threw herself headlong into the project. "I now considered the difficulties, and prepared my plan," she wrote.[13] She was about to revolutionise the social policies of the colony.

From the start Caroline's methods were, yet again, contrary to what was expected of a nineteenth-century woman. She acted on her own volition — there was no husband, or any other "responsible male", to set restrictions or determine her path. Nor did she race into action without a comprehensive understanding of the problem and how to mitigate it. As she had done in India, she took a highly practical, long-term view. Her aim was not just to relieve the present stress but also to ensure ongoing security for the girls. It was an approach that required both imagination, to devise the plan in the first place, and strong organisational and people skills, to instigate it. Caroline was effectively setting up a residence and employment and transport agencies with satellites throughout New South Wales, at a time when gas lamps had only just started lighting the streets of Sydney and train services were still more than a decade away. In the twenty-first century, the skills required for such an enormous undertaking would first be honed on various tertiary courses, ranging from law and business to marketing, accounting and human resources; and the project itself would require the support of trained employees as well as a range of advanced technology. Caroline had none of those benefits. She implemented her plan drawing only on her own raw ability and resolute pragmatism.

Having laid her strategies, Caroline launched a multi-pronged attack. Cognisant of the immediate need to support the steady flow of immigrants, she attempted to meet as many of the boats as possible. Soon she became a familiar figure dockside, boarding vessels to talk to the bounty women and rubbing shoulders with genuine employers, as well as, no doubt, the more nefarious variety. She hoped that by explaining the prevailing conditions in New South Wales and advising naïve girls how to avoid the traps laid for them, she would be able to negate the influence of the bordello madams and the philanderers. By January 1841, she was far enough advanced in her planning to take a major step; she wrote to the governor's wife, Elizabeth, asking for her aid in applying to her husband for permission to use the Immigration Barracks. She also wrote to Sir George Gipps directly, but initially she received only a short letter of acknowledgement.

Intuition is a potent force that reveals secrets with a clarity defying ordinary perception. Caroline's instincts told her that she must publicise her plan if it was to gather any traction. She needed friends in high places and funding. Although she knew that the women of the Ladies' Committee would be useful only for providing her with a certain social propriety and helping raise funds, nonetheless, as autumn turned to winter in 1841, she approached all of the committee members — Lady O'Connell, Lady Dowling, Mrs Richard Jones, Mrs Roger Therry, Mrs W. Mackenzie, Mrs J. Wallace and Miss E. Chambers — and was pleased that "not one refused me — all expressed themselves as *feeling an interest* in the work".[14]

When she broadened her appeal, to friends and acquaintances, both in Sydney and Windsor, Caroline received positive responses and promises of support. This initial success was not to last. She soon came up against one of the sacred cows of colonial society: religious sectarianism. As little as she shunned what society classified as fallen women did Caroline eschew women of other faiths. "I promised to know *neither country or creed,* but to try and serve all *justly* and impartially," she wrote.[15] If she made a mistake in this regard, it was probably in being too open and honest.

In an attempt to engender as much support as possible for her scheme, Caroline had tried to publicise it as widely as possible. The problem was that Sydney was still a small, parochial society that fed intently on gossip and rumour. Churchmen on all sides of the religious divide, and for varying reasons, saw her plan as a threat to their congregations. Caroline's subsequent struggle with religious leaders was to prove one of the most difficult of her career. The Anglican establishment was wary of her, fearing she was organising a "Popish Plot" designed to proselytise for her own church; even harsher criticism came from other Protestant leaders, such as the Presbyterian minister John Dunmore Lang. All that, to some extent, was to be expected. What bewildered and dismayed her most, though, was the antagonism from her own church, from Catholics who feared that her ecumenical approach meant that she wouldn't do enough to promote Rome.

All at once, it seemed that many who had previously backed her had now changed their minds: "Even some of my first promised supporters withdrew their pledges," Caroline wrote. She was daily requested to give up all thought of her "Home". Two gentlemen, one a clergyman, visited her and urged her to renounce her plans, and she received a letter from a friend that she described as being "of so painful a nature that I am astonished how my mind held out". And yet, through all of this she maintained her self-belief: "I had nothing to cheer me but an assurance of success, if there were no failing on my part."[16] The resilience of her childhood reasserted itself. Here she was, in her own words a stranger in a small, hypocritical and censorious society, pitting her judgement and instinct against what seemed to be the rest of the colony. Her husband, the one person she could rely on to stand by her, was almost half a world away. How isolated she must have felt, and yet she still intrinsically believed not only that she was right but that she had the wherewithal to stare down her detractors and accomplish her mission.

Yet, even as she strove to counter the condemnation, there was worse to come. A priest, Father Michael Brennan, whom she had counted as a friend, published a highly critical letter in the Catholic biweekly newspaper, *The Australasian Chronicle*, on 18 September 1841. Whilst acknowledging the need to assist the bounty women, Father Brennan rejected any suggestion that the public should subscribe funds, categorically asserting that the problem was best left for the government to address. On a more personal note, he described Caroline's scheme as a waste of energies and as "Utopian ... only excusable as the effect of an amiable delusion".[17] It's possible that Caroline was as offended as much by this attack on her understanding as she was by the criticism of her plan. She labelled the letter a "missile" and it certainly found its mark. "I felt a dreariness of spirit creep over me," she wrote. That same day, she decided to take a break and accept an invitation to visit friends in Parramatta for a few days, even though she had been invited to a gathering in Sydney in the evening.[18]

Setting out to walk to the wharf, she was overtaken by a friend in King Street who offered her a lift, saying that he too was running late and they were both in danger of missing the steamer to Parramatta. She refused the offer, saying she wanted some time alone to think, and arrived after the boat had already pulled away from the pier. Despite feeling dispirited, she was not one to give in to maudlin humours, so she resolved to attend the party in Sydney. She set off on one of her favourite walks, towards Flagstaff Hill (now Observatory Hill), and began to gather her thoughts. Whether she joined friends in Parramatta or Sydney was almost immaterial; she knew that her scheme would be discussed by everyone. In either case, she was determined not to let anyone know that "during that day my feelings had been used as a door-mat".[19] She wanted to seem cheerful, in good spirits, positive.

Caroline made no attempt to hide her sombre reflections later, but at the time she understood that confidence breeds success and that she therefore had to at least *appear* assured and optimistic. In modern terms, she had to put the best spin on events. In any case, she was a genuinely outgoing character who thrived in company, and, even though a number of friends and acquaintances, including clergy, had withdrawn their backing, there were still many who she knew would continue to uphold her scheme or, at the very least, remain on good terms with her until events unfolded. Preserving her social connections was critical for Caroline's wellbeing and future success.

It was whilst she was walking towards Flagstaff Hill after missing the ferry that Caroline spied Flora and persuaded her to accept her help. Though the encounter with her Highland Beauty left her drained, this small victory restored her resolve and swept away her despondency: "I was able to join the promised party. My spirits returned; I felt God's blessing was on my work. From this time ... I increased my exertions ... From the hour I was on the beach with Flora, fear left me."[20]

For Caroline, the successful outcome of the meeting with Flora was a sure sign that she had been correct to pursue her aims: to do all in her power to help the bounty girls and to establish an immigrants' home. What she'd thought had been her first failure had actually set her on course for a remarkably successful career.

CHAPTER 7

The Immigrants' Home

1841

Sydney, autumn 1841

Caroline set out in good time for the meeting. She was excited but unable to fully rid herself of the strictures uttered by the two friends she had initially asked to accompany her. Both had refused, saying that their husbands would be shocked by such effrontery. As though, she thought, I am seeking notoriety by courting the notice of the press. It was an uncomfortable characterisation.

Still, she had taken even more care than usual with the way she looked today: she wore her best walking dress of sky blue and tan checks, with its elegant drop shoulders and deep pointed bodice embellished with cream lace, and her stylish blue and tan poke bonnet framing her soft round face. Knowing she was fashionably dressed gave her an assurance that already felt like success.

Following her failure to secure an interview with Governor Gipps, Caroline had decided to request a meeting with the publishers of The Sydney Herald. *Her letter to Messrs Kemp and Fairfax had received a warm reply and an invitation to visit their offices.*

The May morning was still warm as she trod up the steps of the two-storey building on George Street, south of Circular Quay. She gave her name to the pimply-faced young man behind the counter just inside the door and followed him down a long dark corridor, up a flight of steps and then along another passageway to the end of the building. From somewhere in the distance came the clanging and rumbling of machinery at work, and the tepid air was laden with a heavy chemical odour she recognised as ink and warm metal. As they halted outside a shut door, she was annoyed to find that she was perspiring slightly. The spotty-faced youth asked her to wait while he inquired within, giving her time to dab her upper lip with a linen handkerchief and to settle her racing heart.

The door then opened wide and there before her were the new owners of one of the colony's most important newspapers, The Sydney Herald. "Hello Mrs Chisholm, I'm John Fairfax," said the taller of the two, bowing formally. Caroline curtsied slightly, putting out her hand as she would have done if they had been introduced at any social gathering. She guessed that he was not much older than she was, but he was a big man with a long face and an already receding hairline. Maybe in compensation, he wore a fulsome beard below a pair of thin lips, but it was his eyes more than anything that took her attention — not their colour, but their directness. She felt that he was a man who made up his mind and acted upon his decisions quickly and efficiently.

His partner, Charles Kemp, was very different: a younger, slighter man, almost elfin yet exuding barely restrained vitality. Caroline remembered that Fairfax had been described as the sober publisher and administrator, while Kemp was said to be the literary power behind the paper. Kemp had been born in London, come to the colony as a child and started his working life as a carpenter. She knew he was a man intent on making a name for himself and realised that could be to her advantage.

Introductions completed, Caroline was invited to sit down and explain why she had requested the meeting. She began by thanking them for seeing her and then set out her case for turning the Immigration Barracks into a home for the bounty girls. "I am certain that you must understand, gentlemen," she finished.

"But what do you expect us to do?" asked Mr Fairfax.

Caroline took a small pile of papers out of her purse, neatly held together with blue ribbon. "If you could see your way clear to support me in your newspaper, then I am confident that, with public opinion behind me, Governor Gipps would listen also." She unfolded one of the pieces of paper. "If you will permit me, gentlemen." And she began to read: "'My name is Mary Cooper. I am a growed woman of twenty-two and was a laundress back in Bath. The Bounty Agent said there'd be lots of good paying work for me. But now I'm near starving and I don't know what will become of me.'" She took out another letter. "'We are three sisters who came on the Isabella in October last and we be desperate and scared. I'm nineteen, Lizzie is twenty-one and Maggie is fifteen. We was taken in by one woman who we thought was kindly. But she took us to a house in the Rocks and we all ran away. Our mother, God bless her, would die if she knew the temptations that had been put to us.'" Caroline stopped and looked up to see the effect on her audience.

Mr Fairfax spoke. "What do you want from us?" he asked again.

She lifted the pile of letters. "If you could print some of these letters, the good people of the colony would surely support me in wanting to establish a home for the girls."

This time Mr Kemp was the first to answer: "Mrs Chisholm you are to be commended for such an endeavour. Before we consider what we could do, please can you tell us how exactly you would choose the girls for your home?"

"Mr Kemp, it is not a matter of 'picking the girls'. Any and every one that is in need will be welcome" — she hesitated for a moment before continuing — "be they English or Irish or Scottish or be they Church of England, or Catholic or Wesleyan. It's the girls I care for, not how they worship God."

He was quick to respond. "I am sorry to have distressed you with such a question, ma'am. We have heard so much already from both sides of the church fence, as it were, that I wanted to satisfy myself of your impartiality." A smile creased the line of his wide mouth. "I feel we should back your extremely worthy cause, but I also firmly believe that we should wait for Governor Gipps to lead the way. Only then can we commit to throwing our full support behind your project."

"And the letters?" she asked.

Mr Fairfax had been leafing through the correspondence. "They are indeed valuable evidence of the dire need of which you speak," he said. "But, for myself, I would hesitate to publish an array of material that will portray the colony in such a bad light at home. No, I think all things considered we should not print these." But then he looked to Mr Kemp and, after an infinitesimal nod of understanding between them, continued: "I speak for both of us, however, in promising that once the governor agrees, we will start a campaign in The Sydney Herald *to fully support your Immigrants' Home and help you raise funds for it. In fact," and now he was smiling, "we will be amongst the first to contribute with a donation of £2, which you may collect on the very day that Governor Gipps gives his consent."*[1]

Unusually for a woman of her time, Caroline showed a keen appreciation of the influence of newspapers on public opinion, and the importance, therefore, of cultivating contacts in the press. *The Sydney Herald* (soon to be renamed *The Sydney Morning Herald*) would join most of the other newspapers in the colony, such as *The Australasian Chronicle, The Sydney Monitor and Commercial Advertiser,* and *The Empire,* to become strong supporters of her philanthropy, both in word and financially, and in subsequent years Caroline would use the print media to advertise and promote her causes and, more broadly, seek to influence public opinion. This not only yielded a potent force of supporters but also ensured her own fame. Later, in London, she would even turn journalist herself, writing about Australia and the benefits of emigration, and during a series of lectures in Sydney between 1859 and 1861, she would constantly promote the value of newspapers to her audience, telling them that "the press was the quickest, the best, and most effectual means of representing and procuring redress of their grievances".[2] At each lecture, indeed, she encouraged her audience to "take" the papers, and went on to mention *The Sydney Morning Herald*, *The Empire* and *The Freeman's Journal* numerous times by name. She was, in effect, engaging in her own marketing exercise.

In 1841, however, it was a series of reports in mid-September that had nothing to do with Caroline that finally pushed Governor Gipps into agreeing to the establishment of the Sydney Female Immigrants' Home. Though the reports concerned just one female immigrant, they highlighted the depth of the despair among the bounty girls.

Mary Teague was a twenty-year-old Irishwoman who had arrived in Sydney, apparently under the protection of a family man but in reality alone, on the ship *Forth* at the end of August 1841. Unable to find work initially, she was "thrust ashore, without a roof ... or the means of obtaining food" and became so desperate that she was contemplating suicide when she was found dishevelled and disorientated in George Street a few days later.[3] Taken for drunk by a constable despite her denials, she was brought before a magistrate, who ordered her to be placed in the stocks in lieu of the fine she could not pay. Released from the punishment, she was discovered the following day "lying in a ditch, in a paddock near the South Head Road, almost dead ... She was unable to stand or walk."[4] A Good Samaritan took her to the General Hospital, where she recovered, but the press, led by *The Australasian Chronicle* and *The Sydney Monitor and Commercial Advertiser*, were extremely vigorous in their outrage and condemnation of the authorities for their callous disregard.

By that time, following assistance from Lady Gipps, Caroline had met with Governor Gipps and received his polite refusal to endorse her project. Now, however, with the press agitating for action, he was finally prepared to acquiesce to her plans for the old Immigration Barracks. Before he gave his final approval, Caroline was required to sign a promise that the Colonial Government would not be responsible for any costs involved in either the establishment or the running of the home.

So, after months of battling, Caroline prevailed. To publicise her campaign and to raise funds, she of course went to the press, who obliged with a number of articles about the founding of the home. On 24 September 1841, *The Sydney Herald* ran a story under the heading "Sworn to no Master, of no Sect am I". It described how the home would be organised and concluded, "Such a 'Home' is much wanted, and should it be commenced, and go on without party influence and sectarian bias, it shall have our cordial support."[5] About a month later, *The Australasian Chronicle* also championed the home: "We are glad to perceive that this institution is about to be put in operation ... and under the prudent and experienced direction of Mrs Chisholm, it will be productive of incalculable good."[6]

With a little help from Mary Teague and the Sydney press, Caroline had effectively cut through official apathy and the sectarian divide — no mean feat in a small, distrustful society, where wealthy settlers jealously protected their privileges. That game she had made up as a child, some twenty-five years previously, imagining a diverse group of religious ministers travelling the world together to create an inclusive new society, was taking seed. In what was a radically eclectic system for the era, Caroline invited clergy from different faiths to attend the home to give guidance and support to girls of their own creed. There was to be no proselytising or favouritism towards any particular sect; all were to be treated equally. The plan did much to bring the clergy and the extended community on side. It also emphasised Caroline's axiom that whilst a belief in God was important, the style of worship was a personal decision.

There were still a few detractors of course, but not many. With the governor's consent and backing from the Ladies' Committee and the press, Caroline's supporters were re-energised. She even received financial aid from senior members of the Church of England, although there was some cloak-and-dagger work involved. The Anglican Bishop, W.G. Broughton, maintained his concern that the Catholic clergy would attempt to use Caroline for their own benefits. Even so, he felt that she was candid about helping the women without partiality. "There is an air of openness and honesty in this lady's declaration," he wrote in a letter to his chaplain, the Reverend Henry Stiles, "which leads me to believe that she has no views other than she professes ... I will therefore beg to place £5 at your disposal, to give from time to time ... I have not the slightest objection to its passing through Mrs Chisholm's hands, or being distributed according to her recommendations: she however not knowing whence it comes." Bishop Broughton also asked local Anglican ministers to preach charity sermons dedicated to immigrant relief in their churches on a Sunday.[7]

With very few exceptions, the Catholic clergy also fell into line, three notable Fathers — Murphy, Therry and Rigney — all donating £10 each to the home's coffers.[8] Many other contributions followed, including from Lady Gipps and members of the Ladies' Committee. Caroline was now widely known and talked about, and her supporters included a veritable who's who of colonial society, spanning religious and national divides. More importantly, she had reminded those in power that diversity, whilst challenging, could contribute to a healthy society, as long as it was attended by equality. It was a theme she was to put into writing on 24 August 1842, in a letter to Lord Stanley, the English Colonial Secretary: "I have no wish to see any power whether English or Irish — Catholic or Protestant — have *too much* in their own hands ... for one might try to oppress the other."[9]

Caroline took possession of the Immigration Barracks, but found that she was not the only one with a claim to the old storeroom that she had planned would be her bedroom and office. This time, fine words would not help so much as grit and imagination. The first night that she slept there she blew out the lights only to hear scufflings and scrapings, as though some living creatures were creeping, crawling and swarming across the chamber. Terrified, she lit her candle — and saw rats everywhere. They were on the floor, the ceiling, the furniture. Her first thought was to throw on her cloak and run out the door. But, realising that deserting her post would "cause much amusement and ruin my plan", she became more pragmatic. She lit a second candle and curled up on the bed "until three rats, descending from the roof, alighted on my shoulders". Even then, she was not about to give in to feminine frailties and be out-generalled by a pack of vermin.

She took two loaves of bread and some butter that was left from her supper and put them in the middle of the room along

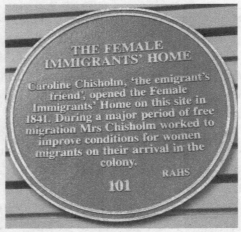

This plaque at the corner of Bent and Phillip streets in Sydney marks the original location of Caroline's Female Immigrants' Home *(Sarah Goldman)*

with a dish of water, then sat reading and watching far into the early hours. Through the long night she counted as many as thirteen rats and never fewer than seven around the food. The following evening, she put out a similar treat — with the addition of arsenic. Within four nights the rodents were gone and she had the room to herself.[10]

The old Immigration Barracks no longer stands, but it seems to have been a roughly made wooden structure divided into several rooms. The bedroom/office that Caroline won from the rats was just over four square metres. After gaining full control of it, the frustration she had endured bubbled to the surface: "My first feelings were those of indignation that such a *trifle* should have been so long *withheld*; but better feelings followed".[11] It was an honest appraisal.

Within days of opening the home in the late spring of 1841, Caroline had invited upwards of ninety destitute girls to take shelter with her. She was responsible for housing, feeding and finding them employment, all on a shoestring budget. Caroline determined that, apart from the donations, the not-for-profit home would be funded by a subscription scheme. Her aim was to place as many girls as possible in jobs outside Sydney, where she believed they would be safe from the immoral traps waiting for them in town. As she had told Governor Gipps at their first meeting, she had written to a wide range of farmers and business owners in country towns, and she now knew what type of servants were needed in which areas and at what cost. She also understood that farmers, squatters and country townspeople could not always travel to town to engage suitable servants.

For a yearly fee of £1, a subscriber to her scheme could request any number of servants of different categories be chosen and sent to them. The employer paid the travel costs. Non-subscribers could hire a worker for £1 a time, again covering all travel costs. To ensure that proper wages and conditions, such as rations, the length of the working week, and travel allowances, were adhered to, Caroline wrote a contract for each person she placed in a job, whether they were single females or, later, single men or married couples with children. Not only that, but the contracts were written in triplicate: one copy was for the employer, one went to the employee and one was kept on file at the home in case of any dispute. Some two thousand of Caroline's contracts were issued between 1841 and 1842, and many more after that date. She wrote them herself, despite the fact she had absolutely no legal training (although it appears that she did seek some advice from lawyer friends in Sydney) and their validity was never questioned before the courts.[12] The following is an example of one of Caroline's later contracts, written in Sydney in 1844:

No. 460/423. Sydney,   20th June 1844
Memorandum of Agreement made this Day between Messrs.
D. and F. M'Connel of Moreton Bay of the one Part, and
Noah Toall, a free Immigrant per Ship "John of London,"
1824, of the other Part.

The Conditions are, that the said Noah Toall engages to
serve the said Messrs. D. and F. M'Connel as a Stockman,
and otherwise make himself generally useful, for the Term
of Twelve Calendar Months; and also to obey all his or
his Overseers or authorized Agents lawful and reasonable
Commands during that Period; in consideration of which
Services the said Messrs. D. and F. M'Connel doth hereby
agree to pay the said Noah Toall Wages at the Rate of
Twenty Pounds (20L.) per Annum, and to provide him
with the following Rations weekly. Wages to commence on
Arrival at the Station. One Half of the Passage Money to be
paid by the said Noah Toall.

Ten Pounds Beef or Mutton.
Ten Pounds Flour.
One Pound and a Half Sugar.
Three Ounces Tea.

In witness whereof they have mutually affixed their
Signatures to this Document.
D. and F. M'Connel,
Per Robert Graham the Agent.
Noah Toall X his Mark.
Witness, Caroline Chisholm.[13]

Caroline did not draw a wage herself, but she did employ a clerk
to help write up and copy the contracts, and also a matron to
supervise cooking, cleaning and washing for the girls within the

home and to ensure its smooth running whenever she was away. Well aware of the cost of the huge amount of correspondence received and sent by Caroline, Governor Gipps made a further contribution to the cause by allowing her to frank her own mail — "the privilege of sending and receiving letters free of postage".[14] At this point, most of the postage and printing costs were for the pamphlets Caroline was sending around New South Wales to let prospective employers know that she was finally open for business.

It was an extraordinary achievement for a thirty-three-year-old woman in the first half of the nineteenth century to effectively set up a retail employment agency. There were and had been other successful businesswomen in New South Wales at that time, such as former convict Mary Reibey, who had been transported in 1790 for horse stealing at the age of thirteen and just four years later had married a successful trader, Thomas Reibey. When he died in 1811, Mary was thirty-four years old, and she was left with seven children and entire control of her husband's business, which under her management was worth some £20,000 by 1820 (well in excess of $36 million today). However, while Mary Reibey clearly needed skills to run her business, she had inherited it as an already highly profitable ongoing concern. Caroline, on the other hand, had, alone, taken her business from the merest spark of an idea and turned it into a flame of triumph.

She admitted to only one personal regret at this time, and that was the fact she couldn't have her three sons living close to her. She had initially brought the boys, now aged five, four and two, to the home, hoping to keep them with her. It didn't take long though before she "found the elder one a source of so much anxiety" that she decided to send the two older boys back to Miss Galvin in Windsor, where she knew they would be "well fed and kindly treated".[15] That "source of anxiety" was, one suspects, trying to keep the boys out of mischief and danger: after all, Caroline had never been required to look after them all by herself. She did keep Henry, the two-year-old, with her when she sent the older boys away, but not for long. Aware that other youngsters had died, victims of disease and unsanitary conditions, she thought the risk too great, so Henry was, within a few weeks, also dispatched to Windsor.

In twenty-first-century terms Caroline was negotiating the work–life balance. Instead of long day care, she was taking the nineteenth-century option of effectively outsourcing her children to a nanny, twenty-four hours a day, seven days a week. It left her entirely free to pursue her vision of empowering other women to establish themselves in a largely chauvinistic culture not used to concerning itself with working-class females. The loss of her children features in Caroline's writings of this time, but rarely again; nor is there regret that Archibald is absent, unable to share either the workload or the success. She may have missed him, but she was busy, she was engaged and she had friends — all panaceas to loneliness. She was a fashionable, attractive woman, eloquent and persuasive, with the ear of some of the most important people in the colony. No wonder she was courted and admired, and not just by the fairer sex.

CHAPTER 8

Going Bush

1841–42

Hunter Valley, New South Wales, mid-1842

Gunshot fractured the evensong of a hundred birds. Silence pervaded the small bush camp, but only momentarily, before it was shattered by hysterical screams and panic, fear radiating like dust spreading out across a dry river bed. Caroline stood up, shaken and bewildered, much like the other women. She threw out her arms, as though to protect all within her sight: the terrified girls, the slow-witted bullock drivers, even the cumbersome beasts themselves.

"Come, don't be alarmed," she said in a soft, calm voice. "It is probably just someone hunting dinner."

But it wasn't.

In the leaching daylight, men on horseback rustled though the dry undergrowth, the embers of the dying sun behind outlining their silhouettes. There were at least six of them, riding with rifles cocked.

Caroline looked at their unyielding faces and tense bodies, relaxing slightly as they took in the sight of some twenty unprotected girls standing mute before them. Even the plainest female can look inviting in youth and amongst this group there were at least two young pearls: Aileen, an ethereal, dark-haired creature destined to be governess to a squatter's children; and Kitty, her inverse, a buxom blonde, all character and dimples, wanted as a dairymaid.

A log fell on the fire; sparks spluttered, wood flared. The men, alert for trouble, edged closer. Caroline watched one in profile as he smirked, licked his lips and raised his gun. Taking a deep breath, she stepped forward, maintaining her poise as best she could. "I am Mrs Chisholm," she said, displaying a confidence more apparent than real.

This, she knew, was a danger unlike any she had ever encountered before, even in India. These girls had placed their faith in her. She had to protect them, whatever it took.

There had been almost forty of them when they had started their journey a little under a week earlier, taking the night steamer up the coast from Sydney to Newcastle. By dawn the boat had turned westwards into the Hunter River as the sun glimmered just above the ocean at their backs. Another few hours had brought them ashore in Morpeth. Stretching after nine hours on board, the girls, travel tired and hungry, looked askance at the small wooden town clustered behind the wharf. Two girls were left there with local women wanting servants to help with chores and children, the rest had walked the three miles to Maitland.

They had stayed three days there at the Mill Street depot, set up by Captain Edward Day, the local magistrate: two rooms, stone walls with a dunny out the back; it was cosy inside with the fire lit. From here a few girls left to work on local farms, a few more stayed with good prospects of finding jobs. Caroline wouldn't let any go where there was no mistress. Then the rest took to the road again, at daybreak, travelling in empty bullock drays, northwest along the wool track towards Scone and beyond. Some girls rode, others walked; then they swapped so everyone could have a rest, even Caroline. All but the bullock drivers. They stayed in their seats. Big-bellied men with hands the size of tree roots, suitable company for their beasts.

They were travelling in mid-winter but the weather was good, the days cool but smiling bright. The sun glanced off eucalypt leaves, red spider flowers danced amongst the green-grey of the foliage, and red and blue parrots turned upside down to suck nectar from yellow bottlebrush, their raucous chatter cutting through the songs of less showy birds. "Larks, if this be winter," Kitty had marvelled, "what will happen in spring?"

Come evening, the bullock drivers would seek a safe site just off the track, large enough for both drays to pull into and with room enough for the bullocks to rest and for Caroline and the girls to find shelter away from any wind or storm that might arise in the dark hours. Most nights a fire was lit, tea made and bread and cheese passed about; then, under Caroline's careful watch, the girls curled up in groups under blankets, weary enough from the long hours of walking and riding to sleep unhindered.

This night would be different.

As though on a signal, the men dismounted, their guns still levelled menacingly. Caroline's mouth went dry. How do I negotiate with bushrangers? she wondered. Where do I begin? As her brain scrambled, one of the bullock drivers suddenly stepped forward. He swallowed, his Adam's apple protruding from his fleshy, stubbled neck.

"We don't have no blunt, nor nuthin' you'd want," he mumbled.

The leader, a whippet-like creature, leapt forward: small, not even Caroline's height, with dark hair, a prominent nose, a scar above his left cheek, and green eyes alight with mischief.

"Are you really Mrs Chisholm?" he asked. "Better for you not to know my name, but if you are Mrs Chisholm, then I'm honoured to meet you, ma'am," he said with a flamboyant bow.

"Yes sir," Caroline replied, thinking it best to humour a dangerous man. "Indeed, I am." Then hoping to garner a little sympathy she added, "I am taking these girls to find work, we're heading for the New England country."

His eyes ran appreciatively over the young women standing behind Caroline, grinning and winking at them before bringing his gaze back to Caroline. "A fine brood. Very fine. But none, I think, as winsome as their leader." Turning to his men, still standing with guns at the ready, he asked: "What say you boys?" They grunted agreement. There was a whistle.

As changeable as he was curious, he was off now on another tack. "It is growing late," he said. "You will be wanting your rest. You still have many miles to Armidale." Then calling one of his men over he whispered an order. The man shrugged and disappeared from view. Whilst he waited, the bushranger asked Caroline about her work. Unsure where it was all leading, she told him about her home and her hopes for settling girls like these safely out of harm's way. She remained on alert, though, wondering what devilry he was planning.

The other man returned carrying a large canvas bag. Rummaging inside, the bushranger pulled out £25. "We've had a good few days," he said, holding the money out to Caroline. "Plucked a few rich birds, we did. You take this, call it a donation." He laughed. "After all, we have plenty more. Eh, chaps?"

Startled, Caroline stood undecided. Then, as he became agitated and insistent, she took the money. "Good girl," he said. With one final bow, he was gone, his men dissolving into the gathering darkness behind him.

The girls, the bullock drivers and Caroline stood bemused. It had been real: she was holding the £25 to prove it.

"Larks, if they be bushrangers," Kitty's voice sang out, "what will honest men be like?"[1]

———————

Caroline had originally planned to send groups of girls into the countryside on their own. However, the first time she attempted it, having assembled two bullock drays to carry them, the girls had refused point blank to go. It appeared they were afraid of the unknown, be it bushrangers, strange animals or dangerous insects. With the flexibility and pragmatism that defined her, Caroline sent the bullock drivers away and organised more for the following day, when she made herself available to accompanied them.[2]

It was the first of many journeys she made travelling with the girls on the wagons or, later, riding her own horse, Captain. Her expeditions went "as far as 300 miles into the far interior, sometimes sleeping at the stations of wealthy settlers, sometimes in the huts of poor emigrants or prisoners; sometimes camping out in the bush, teaching the timid awkward peasantry of England, Scotland and Ireland, Protestants and Roman Catholics, Orangemen and Repealers, how to 'bush it'."[3] Where possible, Caroline and her charges travelled by the steamers that hugged the coast as far north as Brisbane; most of the costs she outlaid for these journeys were refunded to her by the employers. When travelling overland, she usually sought free rides in bullock drays returning home after taking wool or produce to Sydney to sell. Both small farmers and the wealthy squattocracy supported Caroline — after all she was bringing them the workers they needed to run their properties and their homes.

Travelling inland with her girls meant negotiating the dirt tracks that crisscrossed New South Wales. Caroline's cavalcades from Sydney ventured out as far as Armidale in the central northwest and along the road to Gundagai on the Murrumbidgee River in the southwest. Today Gundagai is 375 kilometres from Sydney by road — less than five hours drive; in 1842, however, Caroline and her convoy would have spent weeks travelling to get there. It was a rugged, inhospitable land, vastly different to the Old Country. Like the light, the odours were sharp and pungent.

Instead of the lush, velvet-green, cultivated and settled land of home, with its farmhouses and villages, the drays wound through a seemingly vacant landscape covered by scrub and forests of native trees. There were animals aplenty, including the strange kangaroos that travelled in mobs and the lugubrious wombats that stole out at night, but there was little sign of humanity, European or Indigenous.

When they reached habitation, it was cause for celebration, even if it was only an overnight stay near an isolated, roughly made farmhouse or a country inn. Few of the bush people charged Caroline for accommodation or food. Longer stops were allowed at the various depots that Caroline had arranged for local police magistrates to set up, like the sandstone cottage at Maitland that Caroline's home rented. It still exists, at 3 Mill Street, East Maitland.[4] The depots were dotted in small towns along the routes. (Caroline was to reprise the idea of the depots some thirteen years later, in Victoria.) Either with Caroline or at her behest, thousands of immigrants were moved throughout New South Wales to employment. With the combination of her talent for organisation and the respect that she received, she was able to achieve this huge migration extremely frugally. During the seven years of her work in New South Wales her personal expenses at inns amounted to only £1 18s 6d (about $1700 today), although she did admit to other financial outlays for which she received no remittance, such as clerical fees.[5]

The nomadic life suited Caroline. From Britain to India and Sydney and then out along the sheep and cattle tracks of Australia, she seems to have been almost constantly on the move. As more and more girls were placed in jobs, along with, later, some hundreds of single men and families, Caroline became something of a celebrity in the towns and byways throughout the bush. There were numerous descriptions of her travels, like this one from her friend, colonial judge and elected parliamentarian Roger Therry (later Sir Roger):

> I remember ... meeting her on the Goulburn road, as early as 5 o'clock in the morning, when the first burst of an Australian spring loads the air with the perfume of the acacias, and the glades of the open forest are clothed in a mantle of bright green ... Mrs Chisholm herself, wrapped in a loose cloak, was seated on the top of a dray, laden with casks and bales of goods ... Besides her and around her were seated twelve or fourteen young girls. Alongside of the dray walked about thirty others.[6]

One of the shelters used regularly by Caroline, at 3 Mill Street, East Maitland, NSW
(photo by Athel d'Ombrain, courtesy of the University of Newcastle)

Sir Roger creates a romantic picture, but Caroline was essentially a realist rather than an idealist. Her interest in immigration had certainly been fomented by the bounty girls, but as she delved further into the source of their difficulties she also began to identify the systemic problems that prevented the sort of social cohesion that New South Wales desperately required. She realised that she needed to investigate this further and gather convincing evidence if there was to be any chance of her helping the settlers. So she made the most of her travels through the bush, speaking to everyone, the wealthy squatters, the small farmers and their workers, collecting the stories and thoughts of ordinary men and women, not just regarding their current conditions but also, more saliently, their aspirations for the future.

Back in Sydney, there was still plenty of work to do. Caroline started another employment registry to help single men and families. Each placement contract was still copied in triplicate and fair wages and conditions, such as rations and days off, had to be agreed to by all parties. In each case, Caroline tried to match the immigrant and the employer as carefully as possible. Although she had branched out, the girls still remained Caroline's main focus. As boats came in, most of the unattached girls were sent to her home. She grew bolder in her fight to save as many as possible. When told that one young and very pretty girl had not come to the home but had instead been taken to the North Shore by a ship's officer, Caroline hired a boatman to row her over there. Accosting the couple, she threatened the man with exposure to his captain and the press unless he relinquished the girl. He did so. Returning to the Sydney shore with the girl, Caroline offered the boatman his hire. He refused, saying, "You do not know me, ma'am, but I know you; and may my arm wither from the socket if ever I touch money of yours."

Surprised, Caroline asked the man who he was. "Flora's cousin," he replied.[7]

Caroline was, moreover, finally able to take some revenge on the man who had seduced Flora. Whilst his unsuspecting wife was in Caroline's office questioning a prospective maid, Caroline found the husband wandering around inside the home inspecting the girls. He indicated one pretty female, suggesting to Caroline that she would suit the position. Caroline was firm. "No," she told him, adding that the girl was too young, too pretty and too inexperienced to be in his house. "His face showed symptoms of apoplexy," and he asked Caroline what she knew of him. Her reply left him in little doubt: "All that Flora has told me."[8] After that he complained of the heat and left his wife to complete the business. This last of the Flora stories shows just how assured Caroline had become within herself and in her role in Sydney society. A year earlier she had not been brave enough to stand up for what she knew to be right. Now, she not only was able to belittle the perpetrator of Flora's troubles but, although she did not use any names, also felt secure enough to highlight her story in her first public booklet called *Female Immigration Considered, In a Brief Account of the Sydney Immigrants' Home*. She knew that doing so would mean that one man, at least, would henceforth be wary of his actions.

Published in 1842, the pamphlet carried numerous accounts of the girls that Caroline helped, and others that she was unable to protect. In detailing their histories, she turned them from faceless figures into living, breathing creatures. There was the naïve fifteen-year-old orphan who was brought to Caroline by a woman who found her walking the streets. The girl's rate of pay should have been about three shillings per week, but the mistress who had engaged her off the boat had told her that she didn't have to work, just walk between two particular streets, where, she was told, a "gentleman is to give me £2". A ship's captain asked Caroline to rescue another girl who had been engaged from his boat by a man well known to approach single girls when they first arrived in Sydney; however, in this case Caroline was unable to remove the girl from his home.[9]

Not everything to do with the home was desperate or immoral; there were lighter moments too, reflecting Caroline's love of the ridiculous. Unlike many overtly religious people, Caroline also admired personal beauty and acknowledged its attractions. However, she also believed there was a place for everyone, even those less favoured, such as the young girl named "Little Scrub". She had been given that ignominious sobriquet by her shipmates on the voyage to Sydney, who noted "her hair not combed, her face not washed, and her clothes [looking] as if she had jumped into them". Little Scrub arrived with some sixty other girls just as Caroline was having difficulty satisfying a somewhat fastidious client. The woman, who had a husband and grown sons, had already sent back three girls, saying they were not suitable as servants. Caroline had just realised the reason for the woman's dissatisfaction: she was worried that her husband or her sons might take too keen an interest in any new, attractive maid. So, with some delight, Caroline presented Little Scrub for inspection:

The lady looked at the poor girl with a keen and scrutinising eye; her countenance betokened satisfaction. Addressing me, she said, "I will take the girl; I dare say she will turn out a good servant. You will make the agreement for six months. Ah, 'tis safe to have something a little *repulsive*." I opened the door, desired the clerk to enter the agreement, and returned to my own room, [where] … I indulged in an irresistible fit of laughter.[10]

Another well-to-do woman from the bush came to Caroline looking for a governess for her younger children. On spying a qualified but very attractive young woman, she immediately chose her. Explaining to Caroline that she had an older son at home who was somewhat wild and she feared that he would make a "foolish match", she went on: "Tho' he can neither read or write, he's uncommonly cute. Now I think, she'll tempt him to stay at home; and then, when I see ... his heart is touched ... the clergyman shall settle everything, and it will be a good thing for us all, ma'am." The governess was engaged for one year on a good salary of £16 per annum plus board and keep.[11]

For many men in the bush, their future was blighted by their lack of female companionship. Unashamedly, Caroline promoted the idea of marriage between her bounty women and rural men. With only a sprinkling of subtlety, probably more related to morality than coyness, she attempted to place suitable females within sight of eligible men, many of whom had asked for her help in providing them with a spouse. In 1845 she wrote: "To supply flockmasters with shepherds is a good work; to supply those shepherds with wives a better. To give the shepherd a good wife is to make a gloomy, miserable hut a cheerful, contented home; to introduce married families into the interior is to make squatters' stations fit abodes for Christian men."[12] She hammered the point a little harder three years later in London, when writing an open letter to Earl Grey, then Secretary of State for the Colonies: "If Her Majesty's Government be really desirous of seeing a well-conducted community spring up in these Colonies, the social wants of the people must be considered ... For all the clergy you can dispatch, all the schoolmasters you can appoint, all the churches you can build, and all the books you can export, will never do much good, without ... 'God's Police' — wives and little children — good and virtuous women."[13]

Caroline's advocacy of marriage, and her justification for it, were major objects of criticism from twentieth-century feminists. In her notable book, *Damned Whores and God's Police*, Anne Summers took issue with the suggestion that "good and virtuous women were the much needed civilizing agents in a rough and ready colonial society". She described as sexist the notion that such qualities belong only to females, and asked: "Why not encourage their nurturance in men, just as we have fostered in women the belief that no ambition is now beyond them?"[14]

In fact, Caroline did believe that men, even those who had suffered brutality under the transportation system and in the hell-holes of Norfolk Island and Port Arthur, could also be inherently decent and moral without recourse to feminine influence. In her 1847 open letter to Earl Grey, she wrote about former male convicts: "While there is hope of heaven, there is hope on earth ... vast numbers ... have gained through the force of an innate virtue ... a respectable position in the ranks of social life." She continued: "Wandering for hundreds of miles in ... New South Wales ... I have shared in the hospitality of all classes ... I have had opportunities of gaining an intimate knowledge of the peculiarities and feelings of the people, and these justify ... my recording here my humble testimony to the sterling worth and exemplary conduct ... of the emancipists of New South Wales."[15] Caroline was in no doubt that "goodness and virtue" were intrinsic *human* qualities, and not confined to the female sex.

She did, however, consider that "goodness and virtue" were the necessary traits of the women needed to redress the imbalance of the sexes; in fact she believed that to import "immoral" women would be cruel because they would not be wanted for regular employment or as wives. Caroline was lobbying for the type of female that she thought essential for creating a fruitful and, even more significant, happy community. She believed that any hardworking, well-behaved females would not only address the frustration and loneliness of the bushmen but also help develop the colony. She wrote, "Those who, at home, have been accustomed to work, and are willing to do so in this country: these ... stout, *strong* girls that can milk cows, wash, boil a potato, scour the floor, and are willing to try to do whatever their mistress bids them: for these, the demand is very great, both as servants and wives."[16] She was, in effect, cherry-picking the type of immigrant she thought would be most beneficial to the community; in that she was doing no less or no more than governments of all complexions have done since Australia was first invaded by the British. Unlike many of those governments though, she was listening to the people and addressing their needs, and she was seeking to alleviate a social ill.

Her other motive was to offer the female flotsam and jetsam washing up on Australian shores an opportunity to build substantially better lives than the ones that they had left behind. Certainly, she was often sending them into situations where they would meet marriageable men, but they were not being forced towards the altar. Caroline was no white slaver prostituting girls on exclusive long-term agreements. Marriage was not being offered as the lesser of two evils but as a means to an end. Caroline was arranging for the girls to work, but with the safeguard of a contract that stipulated a reasonable rate of pay and fair conditions at a time when only the most incipient rumblings of workers' rights were being raised in Australia, and those purely for men. Effectively, she was giving the girls far more autonomy than they had ever experienced, and certainly more than they would have had access to in Britain. Putting it into context, it would be close to another 130 years (1973) before the Australian Conciliation and Arbitration Commission finally accepted the concept of equal pay for females.[17] While Caroline did not advocate equal pay, she did ensure that the girls' remuneration and conditions were adequate: for example, a governess she contracted on £16 a year plus board and keep, as well as defined workdays and hours, enjoyed an arrangement that compares favourably with that of a shepherd (not a beneficiary of one of Caroline's contracts) who two years later was receiving between £16 and £20 per annum plus board and keep but without any definite days off or limits on hours per week.[18] Some thirteen years later in 1855, writing a letter to the editor of the Melbourne *Argus*, she said, "We ought not to forget that if this country is to become a great nation, we must endeavour to uphold in the females who come here principles of self-reliance and independence."[19] There is little doubt that Caroline believed women were entitled to be both self-sufficient and free to make their own choices.

To criticise Caroline for promoting agricultural and domestic work for women along with marriage is to ignore the metaphysical fog of the era and to undervalue Caroline's attitude to female ability. During an emigration lecture in her home town of Northampton in 1853, she stated, "I never can imagine that Almighty God sent females into the world to be cooks and housemaids all their days."[20] New South Wales in the 1840s was mostly subject to British laws, and although there was a young woman on the throne of the United Kingdom she was caged in by male advisors and her husband. It would be another seven years before women were allowed entry to tertiary education in Britain and, even then, it was only to a secluded London house well away from the traditional bastions of learning, the exclusively male-inhabited universities. In Australia, where the first university was not established until 1850, it would take until 1883 for the first woman to graduate. Universal female suffrage in the United Kingdom would not happen for almost ninety years (1928), although it would be introduced considerably earlier in Australia (1902). Meanwhile, the woman described by the *London Post* as the "Queen of nineteenth-century science", Mary Somerville, was prohibited only by her sex from being made a fellow of the Royal Society, the pre-eminent British association for mathematicians and scientists.[21] (The first women were not elected fellows until 1945.)

So, to condemn Caroline as a promoter of female subservience is to totally misunderstand and misrepresent her achievements. Nineteenth-century society did not value women, except as mothers or sex objects, and that variance depended on their social status. The most vulnerable were those of the lower classes, especially those with little or no education or financial independence. Caroline was a fierce advocate for these women, giving many of them a degree of autonomy well in advance of the precepts of the era and, in turn, instilling a level of self-respect that abetted the move from serfage to suffrage. In later years, Caroline would even start conversations about women politicians, and men doing their share of domestic duties.

*

Throughout her early work with the immigrants, Caroline received many requests from countrymen looking for wives. To Caroline the bushmen working the land, who were often alienated, depressed and in need of succour and love, were not just statistics, they were real people with real needs. One of the many letters she received was from a farmer who was well known "as a person of integrity". As a one-man-band he could not leave his holding to spend time in Sydney looking for a wife, but he obviously carried heartache in his solitude. This is what he wrote to Caroline:

Reverend madam,
I heard you are the best to send to for a servant, and I heard
our police magistrate say, it was best to leave all to you;
and so I'll just do the same, as his honour says it's the best. I
had a wife once, and so she was too good for me by the far,
and it was God's will, ma'am; but I has a child, ma'am, that
I wouldn't see a straw touch for the world; the boy's only
four yeare old: and I has a snug fifty-acre farm and a town
'lotment, and I has no debts in the world, and one teem
and four bullocks; and I'se ten head oh cattle, and a share
on eight hundred sheep, so I as a rite to a desent servant,
that can wash and cook and make the place decant; and I
don't mind what religion she bey, if she is sober and good,
only I'se a Protestant myself; and the boy I have, I promised
the mother on her death bed, should be a Catholic, and I
wont, anyhow, have any interferance in this here matter …
I wouldn't, mam, on any account in the world, be bound to
marry; but I don't wish it altogether to be left out. I'll get
her fourteen wages, and if she don't like me, and I don't like
her, I'll pay her back to Sydney. I want nothing in the world
but what is honest, so make the agrement as you like, and
I'll bide by it. I sends you all the papers, and you'l now I'm
a man wot's to be trusted. I sends you five pounds; she may
get wages first, for I know some of the gals, and the best on
um, to, are not heavy we boxes; and supposing anything
should happen, I would not like it to be said she come here

in rags. I wants, also, a man and his wife; he must be willing to learn to plough, if he don't now how, and do a good fair day's work at any thing: his wife must be a milker, and ah dustrious woman; I'll give them as much as they can eat and drink of tea and milk, and, whatever wages you set my name down for, I'll be bound to pay it. With all the honer in the world I'se bound to remain your servant till death.[22]

Apart from the pathos of this letter, what is notable here is that it shows a man wanting a companion, not just a sex partner. He was cognisant, moreover, that the female as well as the male had rights within a relationship: "and if she don't like me, and I don't like her, I'll pay her back to Sydney. I want nothing in the world but what is honest." Such an attitude would have appealed to Caroline. And it did. She wrote: "There was something in the character of this honest bushman to admire; he had gained his freedom, sent home money to his parents, and, during a long and tedious illness of twenty months, he had tended his sick wife with patient care. Who would not get up an hour earlier to serve such a man?"

Caroline took time to look around for the right girl and eventually discovered one at the home who she thought would be ideal. The girl was "at the wash-tub; she was at work with spirit; she was rather good looking, very neat and tidy". Investigating further, Caroline found that she was related to a married couple, so she sent the three of them to her petitioner. Even so, she made sure the girl still had a choice, by giving her letters of introduction to three ladies living nearby. One engaged her within a few days of her arriving in the district, but she does not seem to have remained there long, as Caroline learnt: "About a fortnight after, the bushman wrote to thank me, for sending him the married couple; and concluded by saying, 'With regard to that other matter, upon my word, you have suited me exactly; and, as soon as our month is up, we is to be married.'"[23] (The "month" referred to the banns, or notice of intended marriage, which had to be issued three times in a parish church before a wedding could take place.) Caroline acknowledged that she received more than forty requests for wives, but insisted that this young woman was "the only one she sent into the country with a *direct* matrimonial intention".[24]

CHAPTER 9

The Trouble with Men

1842–44

Sydney, 22 February 1842

It was mid-morning in late February, one of those heavy, stifling days: the air hanging wet, a dirty haze rising over a fetid road, the sun a furnace, the sky cobalt. Caroline pulled the bell at the entrance to her friend Ann Therry's house and heard its urgent clanging behind the cedar doors. Like an excited child, she wanted to share her news with someone and, in the absence of Archie, Ann was the natural choice.

The door was opened by a maid, who curtsied and said that Mrs Therry was entertaining in the front drawing room. "Please follow me ma'am," she requested. Caroline stopped for a moment inside the door. It was deliciously cool there, the thick sandstone walls a fortress against the heat.

When Caroline entered the drawing room, Ann flew out of her chair to grab her by the hand. "My dear! The very person I was hoping would visit," she exclaimed. The irrepressible Ann was about to continue, but Caroline swiftly interjected.

"No, Ann, you must listen to me first. I have such wonderful news, astonishing you will say." Excited and ebullient, Caroline clutched her

friend's hand. "The governor has agreed to the prosecution. I've just come from his office. Ann, your own Mr Therry will be in charge." Caroline was glowing. "He will win, I know he will. What's more, Sir George says that I will be called to testify. I depend on you to advise me."

"Caroline! How simply wonderful. And yes, I am certain that my Roger will win, he is so clever. But how on earth can I help?" Ann was brimming with delight at being asked. "Of course, I will do anything for you my dear, but you speak so well. I don't think I can add much."

"I know very well what to say," said Caroline. "But you must advise me how to dress for court. There is no one better."

"Indeed, I don't think I could improve on the way you look at this very moment," replied Ann, turning to her visitor, a young man, who was standing on the other side of the room staring appreciatively at Caroline. Ann repressed a gurgle of laughter and inquired impishly, "What is your advice, Mr Callaghan? A man has such a different eye to a woman." And then, "Oh, where are my manners, Caroline. This is Mr Thomas Callaghan, of whom you have heard me talk, and this, you must know Mr Callaghan, is my very dear friend, Mrs Chisholm. Now I command you to like each other."

"Oh, I do," breathed Mr Callaghan, bowing then coming across the room to take Caroline's outstretched hand. "Simply perfection, ma'am. I would not change a thing," he twinkled at her. "All the lawyers will think themselves most fortunate men to be in the same room with you, as do I."

Caroline responded immediately to Thomas's lightning smile. He was tall and slender, with a long face set amongst carefully brushed brown locks; his fulsome side-whiskers gave him a distinguished appearance. What Caroline found surprising were his eyes: they were a soft, honey brown and had an almost soulful expression. He was maybe a little younger than she was but had so much natural confidence that the age difference seemed insignificant. He was fashionably dressed too, even elegant, and she found herself wondering if he was a sportsman — he had the physique of one.

She was confused by his admiration. At thirty-three and the mother of three children, Caroline thought of herself as a staid matron, certainly not a female trying to attract attention. What she hadn't allowed for was the bloom in her cheeks from the walk to Ann's, tinged with the exhilaration of her news. She looked for all the world like a china doll in her dusky green, taffeta dress with its low, white lace-trimmed neckline and the bodice tapering down to an impossibly small waist. Apart from her wedding ring, her single adornment was a black ribbon tied around her throat, which emphasised the smooth alabaster of her skin. If Archie had given her such a look, she would have been thrilled, but she was unprepared and somewhat nonplussed by such attention from a stranger.

At Ann's behest Caroline sat down and told Thomas about the case of Margaret Ann Bolton, a young woman who had been brutalised by the captain and surgeon of the Carthaginian, *and how finally, after she, Caroline, had petitioned the governor, he had agreed to prosecute the two men. "If he had not, I would have done so myself," said Caroline, unaware of the effect of her passion on Thomas Callaghan.*

She would have continued, but just then the maid entered with tea and cakes. They began a light-hearted discussion about the correct attire for a woman to wear to court, and Thomas Callaghan made the ladies giggle time and again with outrageous suggestions and stories. Ann, delighted to see her friends so amiable, turned to Caroline with a knowing look and said, "My dear, if you flirt with the judge the way you are doing with Mr Callaghan, I'm certain that you will win without my Roger's help."

Caroline's cheeks turned fiery red. She looked up at the mantelpiece clock and rose, saying that it was time she left. Straightaway, Mr Callaghan offered to escort her wherever she was heading.

"Thank you but no, Mr Callaghan. It is very kind of you, but I have work to do and it is only a short walk back to the home," she said, drawing on her gloves.

"I insist, Mrs Chisholm. It is the least I can do after leading you astray with my foolish stories." His voice was sober, though his eyes still held that twinkle.

Caroline finally acquiesced and they left the house together. On the street, Thomas offered his arm. She hesitated for a heartbeat, before tucking her hand into the crook of his elbow.

"So, which way are we headed?" he asked.

She smiled slightly, managing to avoid his eyes. "To the Immigrants' Home on Bent Street. I would prefer to be going back to Jamison Street, though. That's where the captain and I first stayed when we arrived here in '38. He's back in India, you know, and I do miss him." As soon as the words were out, she wondered why she had said them and wished she had not. Would he think her a good, devoted wife or imagine that she was lonely and offering him some sort of invitation?

Looking grave, he said something about how difficult it must be for an army wife, then turned the conversation back to the coming court case. "The law moves slowly," he warned. "It may not come to court for some months. Therry is a good man, though. I wonder if he would accept my help?"

"Would such a case interest you?" she asked, resisting the temptation to look at him.

"Mrs Chisholm, anything that interests you interests me." That did bring her eyes up to his, but there was a sudden frown across her brow.

"No, really," he assured her, "I am, mostly, a sober individual, a man of the law, you know, and it greatly concerns me that a young woman could be treated in that way."

"Then, indeed, I do hope that you can assist."

"And may I visit you at the home?" he asked. "I would like to bring you a donation."

There was a long pause before she answered. Making a pretence of smoothing out her gloves, she nodded her agreement. "Yes," she spoke softly, "in that case, Mr Callaghan, I would welcome your visit."[1]

Caroline was determined that the men responsible for the heinous violations on board the immigrant boat the *Carthaginian* should be brought to justice. The fact that they were the very people who should have protected the immigrant women only made it more imperative to her that the law should intercede.

Margaret Ann Bolton, a slender, twenty-six-year-old seamstress from Ireland via Liverpool, had arrived at Caroline's home at the end of January 1842. She was near physical and emotional collapse. Described by a Catholic priest on the *Carthaginian* as a "modest well-behaved woman", she had disapproved of the lewd and loose behaviour of others on board and not been afraid to express her opinions with an acerbic tongue.[2] Most of her fellow travellers disliked her and she was nicknamed "The Old Maid", becoming the butt of derision from both passengers and crew. Late one night during the last few weeks of the voyage, there was some sort of ruckus in the steerage cabins, with several women playing "ghosts" and screaming. Margaret Ann Bolton was not one of them. Nevertheless, she was dragged out on deck wearing nothing but a thin nightgown, handcuffed by the captain, and made to stand whilst the surgeon hurled buckets of cold water over her thin frame, after which she was left shivering and alone in the dark for at least two hours before being released. Even then, she was unable to change out of her drenched nightdress until the morning because, with no lights allowed in the cabin, she was unable to find her key to unlock her bag.

Caroline's doctor diagnosed a severe pulmonary infection.[3] Horrified by the tale Margaret Ann Bolton told, Caroline interviewed both the ship's captain and the surgeon. Realising that they had indeed ill-treated the woman, she petitioned the governor to charge both men. When Sir George hesitated, she was insistent: "I am ready to prosecute: I have the necessary evidence; and if it be a risk whether I or these men shall go to prison, I am ready to stand the risk." If Caroline had prosecuted and lost the case, it is likely she would have been fined or even possibly faced a jail term.[4]

The trial, in mid-April 1842, with Roger Therry leading the prosecution, held the colony in thrall. Other immigrants had suffered bullying and brutish behaviour on the high seas, but few thought they had any redress against someone as powerful as a ship's captain, let alone that the law would hold him to account for his ill deeds. This case was to prove that both were possible. The captain and the surgeon were each sentenced to six months' jail and fined £50. Reporting the verdict, *The Australasian Chronicle* noted that "the result of this trial will give masters of ships to know that they have no power to punish passengers at their caprice".[5] The case would also bolster Caroline's subsequent appeals for substantial changes in conditions on boats transporting immigrants around the world. It was a cause she took up first in her 1842 pamphlet *Female Immigration Considered,* where she suggested that "the rate of remuneration to the surgeon-superintendent ought to be increased so as to secure the services of properly educated and responsible individuals". Some ten years later she would give similar evidence to government committees in London and help redesign the interiors of immigrant ships during her work with the Family Colonization Loan Society.

In 1842, however, although the conviction of the ship's captain and surgeon brought a certain peace of mind to Margaret Ann Bolton, it was not to significantly alter the story of her sad life. In Roger Therry's words:

Poor Margaret Ann Bolton lingered for a few months in the Colony ... she found relief in sitting, for a few hours each day, in the verandah of my house, which was in a cheerful situation, and where a gentle breeze breathed from the sea in the hottest days of an Australian summer ... Missing her accustomed visits, I made inquiry about her; and found that some days before she had surrendered her subdued and bruised spirit, and had been consigned to an humble grave.[6]

Nor did punishment persuade the *Carthaginian*'s surgeon, Richard William Nelson, to change his ways. Not long after finishing his prison sentence, he set up a successful medical practice in Sydney. He married a wealthy local lady and "sported a carriage, the usual indication of professional prosperity". At the height of his success, though, news reached him that the wife he thought was still safely in England was, in fact, expected to arrive in Sydney within days. "With wonderful rapidity of action, he sold his carriage, horses, furniture, etc. and stole away from the Colony in a ship sailing at night, bound for California."[7] His fate thereafter remains unknown.

Roger Therry was indeed assisted in the *Carthaginian* case by Thomas Callaghan, then a twenty-seven-year-old, somewhat impecunious lawyer who had arrived in Sydney from Dublin in 1839, a year after Caroline. Seven years younger than Caroline, Callaghan was immediately captivated by her when he met her at Ann and Roger Therry's home for the first time on Tuesday, 22 February 1842, writing in his diary, "Only that she is a little too old *and* married I should not be unlikely to transfer to her my home affections ... I think that she has a kind heart and I consider her decidedly good looking."[8] A series of meetings and an exchange of notes between the two followed immediately, mostly initiated by him, but not always. There is no suggestion of an affair between them, but in the way of sudden and mutual attraction between two people, they managed to communicate on six of the next seven days. Callaghan was clearly besotted with Caroline.

There is no evidence as to how he affected her, although Thomas Callaghan believed that she was "very friendly" towards him. Caroline may have been responding in a normal cordial manner and anything warmer may have been just wishful thinking on his behalf. Then again, she may have been lonely and genuinely charmed by the attentions of a good-looking younger man about town. Caroline was an elegant, fashionable woman, an extrovert who, despite her work, still managed to collect friends and enjoy society. Her children were tucked away at Windsor with Miss Galvin and her husband had been absent for more than two years. There would certainly have been ongoing communication between Caroline and Archibald but, given that

Portrait of Thomas Callaghan, by W. Baker, 1847 *(National Library of Australia, nla.obj-148456420)*

mail was still transported by sailing ships, it would have taken months for letters to reach their destination. Caroline must have felt herself to be very much alone, but also free to live the life she wished.

With time on his hands and being a socially insouciant character, Thomas Callaghan decided to pursue his new acquaintance. The very day after meeting Caroline, he visited her home to give legal advice on the contracts that she was drawing up for the immigrants. In his diary he painted firsthand the scene he encountered: "She was sitting there writing hard amidst a bevy of women assembled round her in a small and crowded room. She looked very well and happy: but this must be terrible work for a lady, and it is apparently done for charity's sake." And then, "Our interview was short and satisfactory to me."[9] His description reflects the belief then prevalent among middle- and upper-class men that women were too frail to work.

Two days later he was successfully chasing donations for Caroline's home from leading criminal lawyer George Turner. Then, furthering his claim for her attention, he sent Caroline a contribution of one guinea of his own money. In present-day terms, that one guinea was worth about $180 — not an insignificant amount from a man whose diary constantly alluded to his financial difficulties. The next entry expressed his delight when Caroline sent back a note "kindly written". Like a love-struck schoolboy, he exclaims to his diary, "Her name is Caroline!"[10]

The following Sunday, returning from church, he met her again and she gave him a "very friendly salute", which inspired him to return home and to write her a long letter. He received her reply later that evening and although he doesn't describe it in detail in the diary, it sounds as though Caroline, aware of his growing interest in her, was trying now to hold him at arm's length. He says her letter was "kindly and anxiously written."[11] Given the frequency and the rapidity of the messages between them, their notes must have been hand-delivered by a servant.

The budding friendship then fell into an enforced hiatus. Thomas Callaghan was sent to Maitland and Windsor for more than a month to attend the local Quarter Sessions Court. There is a considerable gap of about two months in his diary entries, aside from references to other lawyers and the various cases with which he was concerned. It is likely that Caroline was out of Sydney for some of this time, travelling with her immigrant girls. On Monday, 2 May, he recommenced writing, endeavouring to fill in some of the lost days, before going on to comment on the *Carthaginian* case. He described Caroline being questioned by the senior defence lawyer, Edward Broadhurst, a close friend of his, to whom Callaghan had admitted his infatuation: "Mrs Chisholm was a witness in the case and was politely cross-examined by Broadhurst who was quizzing me in court about her. She gave her evidence with a great deal of nervousness ... I like being on intimate terms with women of station and character." Yet while Thomas Callaghan's words suggest he was still fond of Caroline, his next statement makes it clear that he now felt it would be foolish to pursue a married woman: "I am very fond of female friendship and I have pleasure in thinking that there are such women ... who take an interest in my fortunes. But there is no-one in this country who can be more than a friend to me."[12]

There is very little about Caroline in Thomas Callaghan's diary during the next eight months, apart from a note saying he was not impressed by her 1842 pamphlet, *Female Immigration Considered*. There were, however, large gaps between entries, as he acknowledged in January 1843: "I have been more than usually dilatory in making up this history of my fortunes."[13] When he does mention her again, in late January 1843, it seems that his interest in Caroline has cooled further. Although unwell from colic, he is once more dining at the Therrys' home. Caroline is there and seems to have been teasing him about his matrimonial prospects. His reaction is unequivocal, "I don't think as much of Mrs Chisholm as I once did."[14] There are few references to her thereafter.

With one exception, all other biographies of Caroline fail to mention Thomas Callaghan.[15] His cameo in Caroline's life was short, but to ignore him is to discard a fascinating insight into Caroline both as a woman and as a prominent member of colonial society. His diary accentuates two aspects of Caroline rarely highlighted: her sex appeal and her social mien. Few biographers have paid any attention to Caroline's physical appearance, and where she is described or depicted she is almost always portrayed as stout and sexually unappealing. The only early biographer to describe her was Eneas Mackenzie. It appears unlikely, considering a few of the inaccuracies in his manuscript, that he knew Caroline well, although he would probably have seen her in Sydney in the early 1840s.[16] Showing Victorian "delicacy against gratifying a mere morbid taste by rudely peering behind the veil of domestic life",[17] he gave very little detail about Caroline the person or her family, although he was unable to resist a short description of her near the end of his book: "Mrs Chisholm is tall, embonpoint, and ... her eyes are grey, penetrating in their glance; and her countenance beaming with kindness ... Her voice is musical, without the slightest provincialism, she speaks with fluency and appropriateness of phraseology, and, as occasion calls forth, can be affecting, sarcastic, or witty."[18] Mackenzie published this account in 1852, some ten years after Thomas Callaghan found her so attractive. Caroline was admittedly only forty-four years old, but she had, by then, taken eight pregnancies to full term. No wonder she was "embonpoint", as he puts it, meaning "stout". Few women who had given birth eight times would have retained a slender figure, and the prescribed female fashion of the day, with its crinoline cage, would likely have exacerbated the impression.

Down the ages, Caroline has been portrayed as rotund and frumpy, but that wasn't the case in her early years, and in fact she was probably never dowdy. Evidence from two disinterested men, Sir George Gipps, who described her as "a handsome stately young woman",[19] and Thomas Callaghan, who was very obviously smitten, indicates that she probably exuded as much sexual allure as was possible for a conventionally dressed Victorian woman. Then, too, her husband, Archibald, was another man clearly attracted to her.

Caroline noticed when other women, such as Flora, were beautiful, and she understood well the attraction between the sexes. There is no doubt that Caroline was a committed Roman Catholic and felt morally driven to use her abilities to help less fortunate people, but to suggest that therefore she must have been a sexless, drab creature with no interest in her own appearance or appeal to the opposite sex is not just a mistake, it also serves to deny her real character. In later years, she was, according to Mackenzie and various illustrations, overweight, and yet she still maintained her enjoyment of fashion and style. A story that has come down through the family recounts how, when she was in her late sixties and very unwell, she was being driven in a carriage from one part of London to another. All at once she asked her driver to stop, so that she could do a little window-shopping and study the latest modes in women's fashions — hardly the act of someone not interested in appearances.[20]

Similarly, it would be ignoring the truth to suggest that her character was universally admired. Even Eneas Mackenzie described her as "sarcastic", while Thomas Callaghan goes further at times in his diary, saying that she "wants judgement" and "is a very unreasonable and indiscreet woman".[21] He even quotes Ann Therry as agreeing with his summation. In Thomas Callaghan's case, it is likely that he had been irritated by her teasing him about his possible love interests in Sydney; however, Caroline apparently admitted to being imprudent and lacking judgement, according to another of her early biographers, Samuel Sidney. In his 1850 book, *Sidney's Emigrant Journal,* which includes a chapter on Caroline, he described how she asked him not to mention the name of the pamphlet she had written about immigration eight years earlier, *Female Immigration Considered.* Apparently "in spite of [using] dashes and asterisks" instead of names, she had caused "dismay among … many of the wooing husbands and Don Juanic bachelors of Sydney". Wrote Sidney, "We respect the scruples of the writer; and … we will circulate no scandal."[22] Caroline's pamphlet no doubt caused something of a stir within the colony and she obviously thought better of revisiting troubled waters, even if it would have given her pleasure to allude to the real men who were the hidden lechers of the city, so that they could be shamed. She may have made that decision to minimise any distress caused to the wives and families of the men involved.

There is no doubt that Caroline was a remarkably gifted woman who contributed to the betterment of thousands of immigrants. But to ignore her anchorage in our temporal world, with all the fluctuations of temper and character that involves, as though she were some sort of superior deity, is to diminish her capabilities and achievements and suggest perhaps that divine interference, rather than skill and courage, was responsible.

As for Thomas Callaghan, he had a successful albeit short career in Australia, becoming a Crown prosecutor before being appointed in 1858 as one of the first three judges in the Court of Quarter Sessions. A few years after first meeting Caroline, he married Eliza Milford, the daughter of a Supreme Court judge; they had two sons and a daughter. Unfortunately, he was only forty-eight when he was killed in an accident involving a horse at Braidwood, in the New South Wales Southern Tablelands.[23]

*

Success is not measured by the length of a project, so much as by its efficiency. Caroline's home operated for just seven months, yet within that time she placed some two thousand immigrants in work, 1400 of them women, mostly outside Sydney. The home closed in mid-1842, when there was no longer any demand for its services, as the backlog of unemployed had been cleared. Soon after, Caroline documented the story in *Female Immigration Considered*. When publishing the pamphlet in late 1842 she claimed to be "the first lady in Australia who has ventured in the character of an author, to appear before the public".[24] She was wrong. A year earlier, in October 1841, a children's story had appeared in the Sydney *Gazette*, titled *A Mother's Offering to Her Children,* and dedicated to Master Reginald Gipps, son of the governor. The writer ascribed herself only as "The Author", although she is now believed to have been Charlotte Barton, an immigrant governess who also made legal history by winning guardianship of her four children from an insane, alcoholic and violent second husband.[25]

Despite Caroline's success with the Immigrants' Home, as 1843 ventured onto the horizon the economic outlook seemed little improved, with the colony still beset by depression and drought. It would be another two years before there was any recovery. Although she had closed the home, Caroline kept the registry open to help new immigrants find work; that also gave her an excuse not to return to the rural tedium of Windsor. Leaving her home office in Sydney, she moved first to Glebe and then took a lease on a cottage with a large garden at Albert Park, about eleven kilometres from town on the Liverpool Road.[26] At the same time she retrieved her sons from Miss Galvin in Windsor. They were growing up: Archibald Jnr was seven, William six and Henry four years old. Little information exists about their private lives at this time, but it is likely that at least Archibald Jnr, and possibly also William, received formal tuition, either privately or in a day school. Miss Galvin was no longer with them, but undoubtedly Caroline would have hired other nannies and servants. Her husband was still in India, and Caroline was not about to become a homebody.

There was change, too, in how New South Wales was to be governed. Like a first-term foetus still snuggled in the womb, wholly dependent on its mother, the colony was preparing for its birth as a fledgling democracy. The Legislative Council had existed since 1824, but its ten to fifteen members were appointed by the man they advised, the governor. Now, in 1843, the council was extended to thirty-six men, twenty-four of them elected by a restricted franchise of adult, white males who met strict financial criteria. Put another way, the "property-owning electorate had produced a property-owning Council … [it was] overwhelmingly Protestant, prosperous and conservative".[27] Nonetheless, it was a beginning and it at least held some sort of limited potential. Moreover, there were exceptions to the rule; it wasn't a totally homogenous entity. Amongst the elected members were pro-democracy agitator William Charles Wentworth; Caroline's friend Roger Therry, a Catholic who had been acting Attorney General for the previous two years; and also the Presbyterian minister, immigration campaigner and abrasive firebrand John Dunmore Lang.

Within three months of the election, Caroline was invited to give evidence to one of the first committees established by the new Legislative Council, on the existing conditions for labourers and skilled workmen.[28] If any further indication was needed to confirm her extraordinary position in the colony, this was it. The committee consisted of seven men; they interviewed fifteen expert male witnesses, plus Caroline. In a society where only a small percentage of men were even allowed to vote, and where women's suffrage wasn't discussed, the invitation to contribute was a clear acknowledgement of the value of Caroline's work.

In what was probably the start of her publicising her more radical views, Caroline upset many of her erstwhile supporters in the landed establishment when she made a proposal to the committee for a new scheme for settling immigrants on private acreage outside Sydney. Most of the members of the Legislative Council disliked the idea. Landowners were reluctant to offer their unimproved property on non-financial leases; more significantly, they were concerned that turning poor immigrants into landowners would adversely affect the supply of labour.

Caroline, however, was not dependent on them, for she had already persuaded an extremely wealthy landowner to donate four thousand acres of unimproved land on the Shellharbour hinterland, eighty-five kilometres south of Sydney, as well as rations for the new settlers for the first five months — something of a coup. Captain Robert Towns could afford it. He either owned outright or had a share in more than nine thousand square kilometres of real estate in Queensland alone. Townsville was later named after him; however, he was considered by contemporaries a far from charitable person. He was a prime instigator in bringing Islanders to work in the north, and although he was described as "bluff and peppery, with simple habits ... respected by all for his honesty, reliability and never ending speculative spirit", to his "employees he was known as a cheese-parer, full of furious criticism for failure but few words of praise for success".[29] An unlikely philanthropist indeed.

The land was made available for six years rent-free in exchange for the settlers clearing and improving it. The idea was that each family would establish a small farm and at the end of the rent-free period they could either start to pay rent or purchase the land. Caroline initially gathered some fifty interested families, though in the end, only twenty-three families took up the opportunity and boarded the Wollongong steamer to Shellharbour to start the trial settlement. Caroline engaged a schoolmaster and employed three bushmen to show the new arrivals how to clear and crop the land. The work was slow and physically demanding, the area being heavily timbered, with cabbage-palms dotting the thick scrub.[30] Caroline expected a type of barter system to prevail amongst the settlers; for example, the schoolmaster would not be paid with coinage, but with labour and produce from the parents of his students.

Caroline proved that, for the most part, immigrant families could work together to subsist in the Australian bush whilst establishing moneymaking farms. Later, though, she admitted to some failures and she did not seek to replicate the scheme. Few people, least of all Caroline, seemed concerned that she was, in fact, experimenting with people's lives. In this case it appears that it was beneficial. Later, in December 1849, *The Sydney Morning Herald* ran a story from a correspondent in Jamberoo which stated that the settlers were all doing well, and went on: "As one said to me — 'They can all get a living. Mrs Chisholm, I am told, brought down many of these persons, and she thus did good.'"[31]

In 1844, Caroline was again called to give evidence before another committee, on jobless labourers.[32] This time she was given top billing, having been asked to compile numbers and details of the unemployed and their dependents in Sydney. Her efforts proved that, whilst still not strong, the economy was certainly showing signs of recovery, with almost two thousand fewer people in distress compared with the previous year — quite a significant proportion of Sydneysiders, given that the whole population of the town was only about thirty thousand. Another noteworthy statistic from Caroline's data revealed that the number of children under eight years of age was almost equal to the number of adults — evidence, if it was needed, that the white population of Australia was increasing rapidly.[33]

Loathe to let the jobless and distressed become just mere statistics, and obviously feeling that her work was not complete, Caroline took to the road again with a group of immigrants in October that year, to find jobs for them in the bush. This time she had some financial support from the government and also from private donors, such as William Bradley, the Australian-born son of a sergeant in the New South Wales Corps, and one of the wealthiest men in the colony, who owned vast tracts of land on the Goulburn Plains and further south on the Monaro. It must have seemed an unwieldy convoy: some one hundred people, mostly in family groups, walking and riding in drays. They had, however, a very adept marshal in charge. The cavalcade took about a week to reach Goulburn from Sydney, by which time Caroline had placed most of the immigrants in work at farms and townships along the way. In less than two weeks she was back at her office in Sydney.[34] Just a few weeks later, in early December, she was off again, with twice as many people. This time she took them as far as Yass and Gundagai, eventually placing everyone in a job — another sure sign that the economy was improving.

Caroline returned to Sydney to be with her sons just before or possibly just after Christmas 1844. At thirty-six years of age, she was at the height of her powers, one of the most recognised and influential people in the colony — and she had only resided there for five and a half years. The next year, 1845, would bring new endeavours, fresh challenges — and significant change.

CHAPTER 10

On the Move

1845–46

Sydney, 11 March 1845

"Poor bugger," muttered the servant under his breath, a rheumy eye taking in the swell standing before him. *"This one must 'a been bush'd, otherwise he'd not be here asking for Mrs Chisholm."*

In a rare moment of compassion he opened the door a little wider; speaking out loud, though, he offered little sympathy. *"She ain't 'ere. Closed registry afore Christmas."* As he smirked he revealed a few yellowed teeth in a foul, cavernous mouth.

"Do you have any idea where she may be?" asked the man at the door.

"Could be 'ome, could be away or could be 'bout town. Always on the move, that's our Mrs Chisholm." The servant shrugged and shut the door.

The man was left staring at the roughly hewn wood, wondering where to go next.

It was a strange homecoming. If home it was, and that wasn't settled either. Somewhere within this colony, this shifting conglomerate of humanity, lived his family: his wife and his children. After so many years away, would it be the same, or just different quarters in another part of the Empire?

He'd landed only that morning. Leaving his bags on the boat, he had stretched his legs walking up from the dock to the old Immigration Barracks. It had been good to feel dry land beneath his feet again. Three months at sea was a long time. He'd noticed changes too. The town was growing. The first surprise had been that massive Gothic castle up on the headland as the boat had drawn in towards Circular Quay. The new Government House, he'd been told. His austere Scottish soul disapproved of the folly as much for its excess as for its incongruity, a palace lording it over a population of felons and charlatans like Gulliver in the Country of the Lilliput. The recently built Customs House down in front of the quay had pleased him, though, a respectable building that one. Then he'd spied a pair of camels wandering about the grounds of the old Government House. He'd laughed out loud — as though this country didn't have enough of its own strange creatures without importing them.

Outside the Immigration Barracks now, he turned on a whim, down towards George Street. Finding himself outside the Bull's Head Inn, which he had frequented some years previously, he decided that he could do with something to eat. It was early in the day, so the inn was not too busy. Ordering a pint and a dish of mutton stew, he settled into a small cubicle by the door where hints of sunshine filtered through the window. He took up an old copy of The Australian newspaper left lying on the table, and squinting in the gloom, began to read about the happenings of the colony.

An item on page two seized his attention. Under the heading "Mrs Chisholm's Expedition", he read: "This eminently benevolent and enterprising lady has returned, from her expedition into the interior to find service for the unemployed and distressed operatives who accompanied her and who ..."[1]

"'Scuse me, sir. You be wantin' anythin' else?" asked the barmaid. She was looking over his shoulder as she picked up his empty tankard and plate. "That Mrs Chisholm, she be a wondrous lady. It's she what got me this job. Saved me life." She nodded across the room to a couple of men talking near the bar. "See Bert there? 'E's the one with the ginger 'air. She found 'im work too."

"But this must be unusual, such a long article about Mrs Chisholm?" he asked.

"You must 'a just arrived. It almost seems as though there's always somethin' 'bout Mrs Chisholm in the papers, sir. She's found work for so many people an' she's been talkin' at those committee things an' all. Then if she sees somethin' not right she's a'writin' letters in the paper too. An' people take note of 'er. Why, sir, I would say she's as well known as the governor 'iself. An' for me, well, I reckon she's a damn sight better 'an him. If you'll be 'scusin' me language."

Later he decided to try Ann and Roger Therry's home. They could well know whether she was in Sydney, at home or elsewhere. By now it was mid-afternoon. On the way he stopped at Mr Jones's George Street shop to buy a necktie; it still felt strange to be out of uniform. It was there that he overheard the name of Mrs Chisholm being mentioned again, this time by a couple of gentlemen discussing her plan for settling immigrants on small blocks of land. It caused an odd sensation in his breast to hear her spoken about by complete strangers, men too, so casually and in such a public place. He had not been prepared for such notoriety.

The maid opening the front door explained that Mrs Therry was entertaining guests for afternoon tea, but, when she heard his name, insisted that Mrs Therry would gladly welcome him. He followed the girl across the hall to the drawing room, where she announced him. The babble of confused, mostly feminine chatter froze on the instant as though suspended in air. From somewhere to the left of the room came a single word: "Archie."

Caroline stood, a little unsteadily, shock robbing her momentarily of her usual sang-froid. He watched her advance towards him with her hands held out, the colour rising in her soft round face, her large green eyes *sparkling, her lips parted. Had he forgotten how lovely she was or how desirable?*

The silence shattered. "Captain Chisholm, what a surprise. How wonderful!" Ann Therry was bubbling. What a coup this afternoon tea party would be for her; it would be discussed for weeks.

Relinquishing Caroline's hands, Archie turned to Ann Therry, bowed, shook her hand and apologised for arriving uninvited at her party. The next thirty minutes passed in a daze as by habit he responded to the necessary social requirements before he could suggest that he and his wife leave.

When they were finally alone, strolling back down to Circular Quay, there was an uncomfortable silence. Looking down at her, he wondered what she was thinking. Did she resent his presence, had she managed better without him, was she shocked at the sight of him?

Slowly he began to talk. He told her how much he had missed her, how happy he was to be with her again. She held his arm tightly, smiled up at him, said that she had missed him also. "I don't understand," she said. "Why didn't you take the coach home, to Albert Park?"

"I didn't want to frighten the bairns. It's been so long since they saw me I thought they might not know me. I needed to see you first. You have done so much: everyone knows you, talks about you. I wasn't sure if you would be pleased to see me."

They had reached the shady side of the new Customs House building. She stopped, turning towards him, standing close. He bent his head to kiss her.

From somewhere behind them came a gasp: "Mrs Chisholm! Well, I never!"[2]

When Archibald returned to Sydney on the *Coringa Packet* after his final five years' service in India, it was the early autumn of 1845.[3] It's not known whether Caroline was waiting for him or he did indeed need to search her out, but undoubtedly he would have been bemused to discover the extent of Caroline's celebrity. She was certainly starring in a lesser firmament than India or Britain but, still, as a member of the middle class and a woman she was inhabiting an extraordinary position in colonial society — and thriving on the exposure it gave her.

Having retired from the East India Company, Archibald did not seek to replicate his command in civilian life, nor to dominate domestically. Instead, he seems to have been satisfied to be the helpmate, the follower rather than the dynamic innovator — he left that to his wife. It was not a role reversal; he was no house husband. Instead, their relationship displayed the sort of equality accepted as normal in the twenty-first century, but which was almost inconceivable in the nineteenth century.

There are various possible explanations for Archibald's decision to retire whilst still in the prime of life. The most likely reason was his desire to support Caroline in her work. Very possibly also, after more than two decades with the company, mostly on the Indian subcontinent, he may well have just wanted a change. At forty-seven — ten years older than his wife — Archibald was not an old man by mid-nineteenth-century standards, and as Caroline's consort he could still expect to have a fulfilling and busy life, although very different to the one that he had left behind. Other biographers have intimated that after so many years in the Indian climate his health was broken; but this seems an unlikely reason for his retirement, given that within a short time of arriving in Sydney he set off to rove for months with Caroline along the rough bush roads of New South Wales. Moreover he would spend the next thirty years travelling backwards and forwards between Britain and Australia engaging in numerous activities, none of which were sedentary, and die only just short of eighty years of age, considerably older than the average life expectancy of the time.

What is clear, though, judging from his commitment to Caroline and her various undertakings on behalf of Australian immigrants and settlers, is that Archibald never once shied away from the promise he gave her, all those years ago, when he asked her to marry him. He continued to support her unconditionally, both privately and publicly, and, as far as possible, financially. Theirs was not just a marriage built on love and admiration, but a true partnership.

At the end of his twenty-three years of combined service, Archibald, although a captain, qualified to retire on a major's pay of £292 per annum. That was about £100 more than a captain's pay and no doubt justified Archibald spending the last five years in India, albeit as a member of the Invalid Establishment with the 2nd Native Veteran Battalion. When he reached retirement age in late 1854, Archibald would receive a major's pension along with the honorary title of major, despite never commanding at that level.[4]

There was another and considerable cash-in-hand monetary inducement for Archibald to quit soldiering too. Promotion in the East India Company was based on seniority alone; it was accepted therefore, that junior officers would band together to offer pecuniary encouragement for an older man to stand down. "The average for a majority was about £2500 to £3000", a staggering sum for someone on Archibald's yearly pension.[5] Although the Chisholms were seldom well-off and money concerns would be an ongoing anxiety for them both — one colonial newspaper, almost ten years later, would describe their circumstances as "with an income barely equal to English notions of a decent competence"[6] — this windfall would have allowed them to enjoy some financial stability for a short time at least. They had nowhere near the means of the colony's affluent squattocracy, but they would have easily fitted financially as well as socially into the middle strata, high above the working class. As a comparison, a married shepherd or a farm labourer with four children would have received wages, rations and rent totalling just over £57 per annum — substantially less than the Chisholms' income.[7]

A lack of money was the reason that Caroline had deferred travelling through the bush seeking information from ordinary settlers and emancipists about their circumstances and progress. It was evidence she was keen to collect to substantiate her proposals to the home government that Britain's excess population of working poor could successfully relocate to Australia, so long as more women were sent out and divided families reunited. When appearing before the New South Wales Legislative Committee in 1843, she had asked for funds to defray her costs whilst collecting statements, but despite backing from both William Charles Wentworth and, perhaps more surprisingly, John Dunmore Lang, a motion supporting her request was defeated by seven votes to six.[8] In later years Caroline would maintain that she did not accept government funding because it would compromise her independence. The fact that in this instance she asked for funding is something that she seems to have conveniently forgotten.

Needing to find the money herself, Caroline was obviously wary, at this stage at least, of spending a considerable amount without discussing it first with Archibald, saying, "I could not incur the responsibility of its expense, without the sanction and approval of my husband."[9] As soon as he arrived in Sydney, Archibald of course gave his consent and engaged fully to accompany her. Together they traversed New South Wales, north to Armidale, south to Gundagai and Yass and west over the Blue Mountains to Bathurst, meeting and talking with as many people as possible and recording hundreds of statements.

Apart from documenting the sort of details found in government surveys such as names, dates, holdings, incomes and relationships, Caroline also focused on the minutiae that are often the true measure of human happiness. More than half a century later Caroline's daughter described her as "having some knowledge of many sciences" and, certainly, her manner of investigation had a scientific rigour about it.[10] She had no use for hearsay, supposition or fantasy; she dealt only in facts. As she had done before the establishment of the Sydney Immigrants' Home only a few years before, she compiled a set of standard questions, so that she could easily compare the answers. Her methods would bear scrutiny today, and were akin to modern market research. She was scrupulous, for example, in making certain that she had a wide representation of respondents and took their answers down verbatim. "They were written down in all manner of dwellings, but chiefly among the humbler; in cottages and bark huts; on the roadside; ... in the field, on a plough; in the forest, on the first log of a frugal bush servant's first freehold. There were nearly eight hundred of these statements from natives of almost every county of the United Kingdom, from emigrants, from 'old hands', and from ticket-of-leave men."[11] The statements proved that men and women who had arrived either as convicts or very poor free settlers were, within a relatively short period of time, able to make a good living and become financially secure on their own land, with many of them subsequently becoming employers themselves.

Collated and compiled, the statements formed the basis of Caroline's second written work, part of which was published in

The exterior of a settler's hut in the Australian bush, 1849 *(Alamy)*

Sydney and India under the somewhat daunting title of *Prospectus of a Work to be Entitled "Voluntary Information from the People of New South Wales" Respecting the Social Conditions of the Middle and Working Classes in that Colony.*[12] It in turn provided the material for her testimonies on immigration before the New South Wales Legislative Council in September 1845, and the Committee of the House of Lords in London two years later. Making the most of the material, she would later refer to it in an open letter that she published in London in 1847, entitled *Emigration and Transportation Relatively Considered* and dedicated to then Colonial Secretary Earl Grey.

On a personal level, writing *Voluntary Information* showed just how far Caroline had advance from her father's world of the itinerant day worker. Not only was she confident enough to address directly the acme of colonial authority in London, but she wrote of the working class with a condescension that suggested that her family had never been part of its commonality — like any rising star she was too busy moving forwards to look backwards. She wrote, "Their language may be rude, but their hearts are kind and true. To improve the condition of these people is my object."[13] *Voluntary Information* also further established Caroline's credentials as an authority on immigration to New South Wales and was praised as presenting "a more perfect, truthful and valuable picture of bush life painted by servants and settlers, than had ever been drawn in travellers' tales or parliamentary blue books".[14] Bridging the gap between the highest and the lowest of the white classes in the colony, Caroline gave voice to the concerns, needs, wishes and achievements of the ordinary men and women who were populating the land.

The statements highlighted healthy attitudes to hard work, a fulsome optimism, and a predominant belief that Australia was a land with greater equality of opportunity. They also captured, however, the loneliness, heartache, and guilt of leaving loved ones behind in the Old Country, be they children, parents or siblings:

Statement No. 12: William K. from Kildare
I arrived here by the ship Sir Charles Napier; was single; engaged as labourer to Mr William Lawson, Prospect; wages £18 per annum, with a weekly ration of nine pound of flour, nine pound of meat, two pound of sugar, and three ounces of tea; remained in service two years and six months ... taken a farm from Mr James M'Arthur, of Camden; expect to get on very well ... Got married to a native of King's County. Have four bullocks; employ one labourer, give him 7s per week, and his food. What do I think of this country? Why I think very well of it; I think I'll get on better here; a man that is willing to work will get on here; ... I have one sister, if she were here I should be proud. Wife says, "I think well of the country; better off here." October 1845

Statement No. 5: Ellen W. from London
I arrived in 1833; I am married to George W.; We are
doing well; I wish to have my sister out … Her name is
Emma; she is about twenty-two years of age; will give her a
comfortable home … neither of us has wanted for anything
in this country … We pay eight shillings a week rent, but
it is well we get on. Oh, what a difference there is between
this country and home for poor folks. I know I would not go
back again, I know what England is. Old England is a fine
place for the rich, but the Lord help the poor. 11th March,
1846

Statement No. 11: Patt D. from Kildare
It is six years since we arrived in the ship; we brought two
children with us and left one at home, named P.D.; he is
about ten years of age. Oh! How we was pushed to get out
when the money was to be paid … We are, thank God, well
to do now. We have seventeen cows … We leaves our child
wi' a poor widow woman, one Betty Hurley; she did live in
Barrack-Street, thirty-two miles from Dublin. Don't rest till
you find him, and may God reward you if you send my poor
child to me. 29th January 1846[15]

The reasons why families split up varied. Convicts of course had
no say in the matter. The cost and risk of immigration meant
that many free settlers would strike out alone or with maybe only
one or two family members whilst their aged parents or younger
siblings remained back in the old country. Possibly the most
heartrending cases were parents who had been encouraged by
bounty agents to leave their small children at home because they
were too young to work and therefore considered an unnecessary

burden. Once in Australia, even when they prospered, communication with families in Britain was extremely difficult. Apart from the tardiness of the mail services, many of the lower classes were partially or totally illiterate, and although some did send money home, often it vanished before reaching the intended recipients. In nearly every case that Caroline documented, there were requests for close relatives to be found and sent out to the colony, to reunite families and to lessen the isolation and hardship of those trying to put down foundations in a new land.

When the British Government had ordered the invasion of Australia to start its prison colony it may have been founding a strategic foothold in the Antipodes, but more certainly it was also creating a dumping ground for its teeming, dispossessed riffraff and meeting the need to exorcise from its overpopulated cities both the desperate and the petty criminals that inhabited its underbelly. Human rights did not yet even exist as a concept, let alone as a consideration in policy debates. Very few of the powerful cared about the lower orders; there was no need, as the working class and the majority of the middle class had no vote or say in the running of the country. In 1788, when Captain Arthur Philip established Sydney, only one in seven males over the age of twenty-one had the right to vote for Britain's lower house of Parliament; there was no election for the upper house, the House of Lords, where holders of hereditary titles sat to determine legislation; and, emphasising the elite's callous disregard of humanity, slavery was still legal. Even almost sixty years later, in 1846, when Caroline was collecting her statements, although slavery had been abolished throughout the Empire, the proportion of men enfranchised in Britain had only risen to one in five and was based on financial standing. It is doubtful whether Archibald would have been amongst them had he been living in the United Kingdom. So, whilst Britain was prepared to divest itself of its excess poor, and to use them to improve its own economy at home with increased trade to and from the colonies, there was no imperative to address the misery caused by such a massive human displacement — until Caroline discovered the need and sought to redress it.

Based on the research she had gathered, Caroline identified three main issues that she believed the British Government should address: the shortage of females in New South Wales, the need for a family reunion policy for former convicts and settlers, and the beneficial effect on Britain's population congestion of sending its poor to a country that would provide them with a full and healthy lifestyle and some equality of opportunity.

These three points Caroline put forward with some force in Sydney, when she was requested to give her opinion to a third committee, on immigration, established by the Legislative Council in September 1845 and chaired by the Reverend John Dunmore Lang. To support her arguments, Caroline read from some of the statements that she and Archibald had collected. She also put forward the idea that single women should only travel on ships with married families and never with single men. The committee was interested and respectful, but unwilling to pursue her ideas.

Since she had first commenced her work with immigrants, Caroline had settled some "11,000 souls".[16] But to achieve more she needed the British Government on side. It was time for her to return home.

*

Almost eight years earlier, Caroline had slipped into Sydney unknown and unnoticed. Now at the age of thirty-eight, her departure would make news throughout the colony. The

Chisholms gave up their lease on the property in Albert Park and took rooms at the Queens' Head Inn on the corner of York and King streets.[17] They planned to sail on the *Dublin* in March 1846; however, the captain of the boat postponed leaving Sydney until mid-April, thus allowing Caroline time to proceed, almost regally, on a farewell tour.

Amongst the visits she made was one to Camden Park, some seventy kilometres southwest of Sydney, a Regency-style mansion that was home to the Macarthur family. Although eighty-year-old Elizabeth Macarthur, the matriarch of the Australian wool industry, was in residence, Caroline was not there at her behest but that of her daughter-in-law, the much less well known Emily Macarthur (née Stone). There were just two years between Caroline and Emily, both were well educated and both had lived on the Indian subcontinent, but that was where the similarities ended. Born in Bengal, the daughter of a successful banker, Emily had returned to England at five years of age. She was described as a plain-featured spinster in her thirties when she married James Macarthur within months of meeting him in 1838. Unkindly, biographers have suggested the marriage was more of a business deal than a love match: "The most spectacular feat of [James Macarthur's] visit to England was his unromantic but most useful marriage to Emily Stone, daughter of a Lombard Street banker."[18] Emily, however, had more to her than just a well-connected and wealthy father; she was a remarkably good artist. Amongst her paintings were various depictions of her daughter Elizabeth, the eventual heir to the Macarthur fortune. The daughter was only six at the time of Caroline's visit. Later, as Elizabeth Macarthur Onslow, she would head up a major dairy company that would in turn lead to the establishment of the Dairy Farmers' Co-operative Milk Company.[19]

The friendship between Caroline and Emily appears to have been of long standing and quite close. Caroline stayed three days at Camden Park, her visit documented by Emily's young Swiss guest, Herminie Chavanne, yet another contemporary whose firsthand account describes Caroline as beautiful.[20] It is also interesting to note that Caroline's visit was without Archibald. Maybe he had other engagements, or maybe after so many years apart and then so many months travelling around New South Wales together, she enjoyed having a little space to herself again.

Back in Sydney, and almost on the eve of her departure for London, Caroline was once again the centre of controversy. The combination of Caroline's religion and her interest in immigration were lambasted by John Dunmore Lang, one of the most strident anti-Catholics in the colony. Scottish by birth, this Presbyterian minister had a very real, although somewhat narrow, interest in encouraging immigration to Australia, believing there were already too many Roman Catholics in New South Wales. In a fluctuating career, Lang had been both praised and scorned for his work and beliefs. As one of the first elected members of the Legislative Council in 1843, representing Port Phillip, he had served with Caroline on three council committees, at times supporting her against the majority, so there is no doubt that they were well acquainted with each other's views and work. In early 1846 he was, like Caroline, preparing to return to Britain (and Europe) to further his latest plan: to encourage Swiss and German Protestant vine growers to settle in the Port Phillip area. He was convinced that they would make a financial and social success of the enterprise and also hoped they would help offset what he saw as a flood of Catholic economic immigrants that had arrived in the early 1840s, mostly from Ireland.

In early March, the Catholic newspaper *The Morning Chronicle* severely denounced Lang's vine growers plan and his highly biased attitude towards immigration. A furious Lang then launched an energetic diatribe at his detractors. Whilst his letter to the editors of *The Sydney Morning Herald* on 14 March certainly attempted to explain the reasoning behind his scheme, most of its three-thousand-word tirade took vicious aim at the religious affiliation of the *Chronicle*'s editors and what he claimed was the threat that the colony would fall under the "dictatorship of a Romish priesthood". Caroline's work with immigrants and her own Catholicism were swept up in his somewhat confused verbal assault. He attacked Caroline for being an unwitting tool of the priesthood, describing her as a "zealous and devoted Roman Catholic, who ... will, as a matter of course, render her influence and efforts ... to the extension and prevalence of Romanism in this colony and hemisphere", before backtracking to say "I do not say that Mrs C will do so" and even going on to describe her as a "truly benevolent lady" who had rendered valuable service to "many poor immigrants in this Colony for years past". Even so, he warned that Australia could be "transformed into an Irish Roman Catholic Colony" and expressed his desire to "live and die among my own people", suggesting that he would have been in favour of some sort of Protestant theocracy.[21]

Caroline's much shorter reply was also published in *The Sydney Morning Herald*, six days later. Obviously distressed by the vitriol launched partially at her, but more certainly at her faith, she displayed an air of fatigue and despondency that was unusual in her. She may have despaired of ever defeating such entrenched bigotry, or, after managing alone with the physical, emotional and mental exertions of the past few years, she may have just been genuinely tired. Denying that she held any sectarian principles, she maintained that "there is something unkind in all this; I feel conscious that I do not deserve it". Addressing directly Lang's desire to "live and die among his own people", Caroline once again outlined her vision of a multicultural society, albeit in nineteenth-century terms: "My idea of good neighbourhood is not so contracted; I have lived happily amongst pagans and heathens, Mahometans and Hindoos — they never molested me at my devotions, nor did I insult them at theirs; and am I not to enjoy the same privilege in New South Wales? ... Am I not to be allowed to address my Maker after a weary day's work in the way that my conscience dictates."[22] It was an appeal that won her many friends from across the religious divide.

It seemed, however, that despite the respect that Lang insisted he held for Caroline, the colony was too small for both of them. As it would transpire, even Britain would not be large enough to hold them both without further verbal aggression, but that was still in the future.

In April 1846, strangely, given his professed views, John Dunmore Lang was one of the first people to subscribe one guinea (£1 1s,), the maximum amount allowed, to the collection for Caroline's farewell testimonial from the people of New South Wales. The list of contributors to the testimonial read like a who's who of the colony, being headed by Governor Sir George Gipps and including magistrates from across New South Wales, clergymen, merchants and members of the Legislative Council, most of whom also donated one guinea. They were not the only ones desirous of expressing their thanks to Caroline. From across the colony, from Sydney to the furthest outback towns came pledges from the faceless settlers, ticket-of-leave men and women and emancipists that Caroline had aided, people like Betsy McMahon and Patrick Guines, who each gave 2s 6d, or

Ann Clark, who forwarded 1s 6d.[23] The total collection raised a staggering 200 guineas, more than two-thirds of Archibald's yearly pension. Knowing that Caroline would not accept money, the organisers used it to buy her a commemorative plate, and presented it to her just two days before she left Sydney.[24]

The *Dublin* finally sailed on 14 April 1846. For Caroline, it would be the first time that she had set foot back in Britain since she had left to follow her husband to India in 1833. Then she had been twenty-five years old, mourning the loss of her first child and uncertain about the future, a far different creature from the assured and motivated woman who was undertaking this trip as part of her mission to improve the lot of immigrants and settlers. Family ties, although of some importance, would be relegated to second place. For her three sons — ten-year-old Archibald Jnr, nine-year-old William and seven-year-old Henry — going back to Britain would be a revelation: after the wide-open spaces of the scantily populated colony, they would finally become acquainted with what all white Australians still referred to as "home".

As the *Dublin* sailed out through Sydney Heads and pitched into the open ocean, there would have been much excitement amongst the five Chisholms, but there would have been considerable anxiety too. For the delay in leaving would have significant consequences. Caroline was pregnant once again and now she would, in all likelihood, give birth on the high seas.

CHAPTER 11

Back Home

1846–47

Somewhere between Hull and London, August 1846

"Wheesht! There's enough commotion without you laddies adding to it." Archibald, taciturn and forbidding, glared at the three boys rumbling over each other and fighting for the window. Abashed, they sat down in some disorder, but the excitement throbbing through their veins meant that as soon as Papa's head was turned, there were sly pinches and elbows, kicks and punches, until they flared again into full-blown noisy dispute. *"Ach! One more twitch and you'll be outside to continue your brawl. That's yer last warning."* The startling threat had the desired effect.

They were, all of them, locked within the great lumbering belly of a steaming iron coach, hurtling along, according to Papa, at an extraordinary twenty-eight miles an hour. Outside, they saw England passing before them through a steamy white haze: the countryside with its soft, rich fields and little hamlets, and the towns crammed with dirty hovels backing on to monstrous buildings belching black smoke. Inside the coach, the constant clanging was like some sort of mechanical giant hammering into rocks, and every now and then the locomotive spurted forth an eerie, high-pitched whistle. The boys had dreamt of this journey, but had never imagined being captured by such power.

Little Henry decided to venture a grin, eyes alight, seeking out the warm good humour he knew lay beyond Papa's stern exterior. His father's frown lightened and a self-mocking smile twisted his lips. Papa could never be angry for long. Mama was the strict one, but right now she wasn't taking any notice of the three boys. That was all the fault of the new bairn, as Papa called him. Henry looked across the carriage to where his mother sat, eyes closed, half asleep, holding his tiny brother, Sydney, on her lap. Henry thought the baby was more like a rat than a real person, with his squished up face and sour smell.

Henry would never forget the night Sydney had been born. Mama had grown fatter every day on their sea journey and then, just as they were about to arrive in England, she had started having pains. Henry, his brothers and Papa too had all been sent from the cabin. They had heard Mama crying though, even from up on deck. Only the ship's surgeon and a dirty-looking old woman, a Mrs Doherty from steerage, were allowed to stay. Then there had been a terrible storm, with the boat rocking and tossing on huge seas. Finally, hours later, as the light faded into darkness, the surgeon had called them to see the baby. The boys, crowding around the lamplight, had been disappointed — all that trouble for such a scrawny little thing.

After that, the adults had said that Sydney might die. Mrs Doherty might have looked like a mucky, witchy sort of old woman with no teeth and bad breath, but amazingly had come up with a plan to save their little brother. She took milk from the last goat on board and gave it to the baby from a strange-looking bottle, and that seemed to keep him going. Henry and his brothers thought it was hilarious and kept calling Sydney "the kid", but no one else had laughed, least of all Mama. She just lay on her cot, moaning and sleeping. It scared Henry to see Mama like that; she was never sick.

When they'd reached Hull, they had found rooms in a hotel, and Papa had called in a doctor for Mama and the baby, and found a woman who could feed Sydney. They'd stayed there until both were strong enough to travel.

Henry had seen drawings of trains, but now he was actually inside one. Papa had said that it would only take eight, maybe ten hours to reach London, 155 miles away. The boys grew fidgety, restless. The baby whimpered, but slumbered on.

"Ach, but it's a miracle the bairn sleeps through all this racket," Papa said, turning his head to look at Sydney nestled in Mama's lap. Mama was too tired to answer, but a slight smile creased her lips.

"Papa, how much longer?" asked William. "I'm so hungry."

Pulling his watch out, Papa checked the time against a small booklet. "We should be stopping soon," he said.

Henry was also beginning to feel an empty gnawing in his stomach. It seemed such a long time since they had eaten breakfast. He wriggled in his seat trying to concentrate on the rattling train, the fields of bright yellow flowers, even baby Sydney — anything apart from food.

The locomotive emitted a long, shrill blast and a burst of steam engulfed the windows, shutting out the view momentarily as the chugging slowed and the giant machine eased into a station. A guard ran up and down the platform shouting: "Peterborough, Peterborough, one hour, ladies and gentlemen, one hour."

Henry and his older brothers jumped from their seats. Archibald Jnr asked, "May we be excused, please?"

"Of course," replied Mama, the first words she had spoken since they had left Hull at dawn.

Then, as Henry scrambled down the iron steps onto the platform behind his brothers, he heard his Mama say: "I'll stay here with the baby, Archie. You take the boys for something to eat, but please come back in time, so that I have a chance to stretch my legs too."

Racing along the platform, Henry suddenly felt light-hearted again, his fears subsiding. Mama was back in charge. All would be well.[1]

Some thirteen years had elapsed since Caroline had last stepped foot in England. Time had wrought a remarkable alteration in the untested and heartbroken twenty-five-year-old who had undertaken that first lonesome sea journey to India. Now she was returning to a country that had also undergone many changes in those intervening years. Three great forces had been at work in Britain. The ongoing expansion of the Industrial Revolution had created an impoverished, downtrodden, urban population. This, in turn, had spawned its own antidote: a growing demand for workers' rights. At the same time an unprecedented natural disaster was sweeping through Ireland. In what became known as the Great Potato Famine, Ireland was devastated by the twin evils of massive crop failures and the deadly diseases that often accompany famine. Between 1845 and 1849, some one million people died as a result of starvation and such illnesses as dysentery, cholera, smallpox and influenza. Another one million people are thought to have emigrated, mostly to North America.[2]

These factors would help define Caroline's pathway forward, but it is probable that, at first, she did not even recognise the extent of the changes around her. On arrival in Hull, the need to feed and succour her newborn infant would have been paramount. It is unlikely that Caroline had breastfed any of her sons, hence it would have been extremely difficult for her, at the age of thirty-eight and with a gap of seven years since her last baby, to start doing so now.

When Caroline and the baby were finally well enough to leave Hull, the family travelled directly south to London. It is somewhat surprising that, having arrived in northern England, Caroline and Archibald did not take the opportunity to visit family in Scotland or Northampton, particularly as they had been absent for so many years and were now within striking distance of both locations. Their four sons had been born abroad after all, and it would have given them an opportunity to renew family ties and introduce the children to their relations. Sometime in the next few years, Sarah Laws was probably in London, and she was certainly there six years later during the 1851 census (as mentioned previously). Earlier biographers have speculated that Sarah looked after Caroline's younger children in place of a nanny. It appears, however, that in 1846, when Caroline first arrived back in Britain, she was too eager to start on her emigration work to have time for any family reunion of her own.

The Chisholms may have journeyed to London by coastal steamer, although it's more likely they would have taken a steam train. At the time, Britain was gripped by a speculative frenzy known as "Railway Mania". In 1846, the year Caroline returned to Britain, more than 270 Acts of Parliament were passed setting up new railway companies. It was a rage that would have long-lasting social effects, allowing the poor and working class to travel outside their usual orbit. For Caroline, it not only meant that she would more easily be able to journey around Britain spreading her message of the benefits of living in the Antipodes, but also that would-be emigrants could more easily reach her and access her help. It would have been strangely unlike Caroline, and Archibald too, to have ignored the chance to experience the power of the invention that was already revolutionising the world. Besides which, it was both a faster and cheaper way to travel — not to be ignored when you had four sons to transport, one of them a newborn.[3]

Railway companies assisted Caroline by providing tickets free of charge.
(Museums Victoria)

In choosing a home in London, Caroline, heeded the advice of a visiting colonialist and wealthy squatter, Archibald Boyd, by initially renting near Jubilee Place, off Commercial Road in the East End. Boyd had suggested the location because it would mean that Caroline was within reach of the indigent people wishing to emigrate. It was a far from salubrious location amidst the abject poverty and violence of London's most degraded, grimy slums, where according to one of London's leading journalists of the day, "Pigs and cows in back yards, noxious trades like boiling tripe, melting tallow, or preparing cat's meat, and slaughter houses, dustheaps, and 'lakes of putrefying night soil' added to the filth."[4] There were advantages, however: the rent in such an area would have been much cheaper than more modish surroundings, and it was close to the docks and railways.

It's likely that Caroline hit the ground running. Having no lasting ill effects from the birth, she probably organised a wet nurse to look after Sydney, leaving herself free to pursue her own agenda. Archibald took responsibility for the education of the three older boys, sending them to board at Sedgley Park School in Staffordshire, about nineteen kilometres from Birmingham, where the former Catholic Vicar General of Sydney, William Ullathorne, was to become bishop a few years later. Sedgley Park was a renowned Catholic college, established back in 1763. It accepted boys from seven to fourteen years of age, and at the time that the Chisholm boys arrived had about 140 students from both the middle and upper classes.[5] For a family watching its budget, Sedgley Park was not cheap, costing at least twelve guineas a year per pupil, plus a one guinea entrance fee. Amongst the subjects studied were geography and arithmetic, which also combined book-keeping and land-measuring. Assuming Archibald, with his classical education, would have wanted the boys to learn at least Latin, he would have paid an extra half guinea for each of them. Additionally, there were charges for French, drawing and dancing classes, although it is unlikely, given the Chisholms' financial restraints, that the boys would have indulged in those activities.[6]

Given the location of their home, it was probably just as well that the older children were sent off to school, as it kept them from wandering the local streets amid disease and filth. In this and other ways, Caroline's overriding concern for her emigrants at the expense of all else had a significant effect on her children, and would do so again in the future.

With their domestic arrangements sorted out, Caroline and Archibald began working towards her three main aims, the ones she had identified before leaving New South Wales: to procure more single female immigrants; to ensure a free family reunion scheme for both the wives and families of former convicts and the left-behind children of free settlers; and to help Britain by encouraging its hardworking poor to seek new lives in Australia.

Within two and a half months of settling into London life, at the end of October 1846, Caroline was writing back to a friend in Sydney, confident that although she was still finding her feet, progress was being made towards her goals: "I have taken no public steps, thinking it better to work my way quietly."[7] She was, however, making some noise, letting people know where she could be found, gathering people to her cause and becoming well known as the go-to person for would-be emigrants seeking information about the Australian colonies or assistance with the complicated administrative and financial processes of emigration. Many of the people asking for her guidance had family or friends who had gone before them and were now responding to calls for them to follow. "Numerous letters have been sent me requesting interviews from persons in all parts; some giving long lists of relations who are anxious to emigrate," she wrote to her friend in Sydney.[8] Displaying her usual confidence that she was the person best equipped to select the most promising settlers, Caroline usually wrote back to the applicants asking them to meet her in person.

Caroline knew what she was about. She had already set up one business-like venture, the Female Immigrants' Home in Sydney; now she could call on those skills to lobby the British Government to help her establish a not-for-profit emigration network. She knew that government support was essential.

Like anyone establishing a complex new venture, Caroline, trying to pull together the various strands, was time poor. One of her chief objectives was to enhance communications with both her supporters and, even more importantly, with her clients — those wishing to emigrate. This task was so onerous that there was little time for anything else. "The numerous letters we have received have occupied nearly the whole of my time and the best part of

Captain Chisholm's to answer, and I can see that within three months from this, extra aid will be requisite."[9] Whilst running the Immigrants' Home in Sydney, Caroline had employed a clerk to help write contracts, and she did the same now. The clerk helped her answer the almost 3400 applications she received within the first year of her arrival in England.[10] A prime concern again was the expense of postage. Writing to her Australian friend, she bemoaned that "a letter from Sydney today cost me 2s 3d, and Captain C. paid £1 4s 3d for postage, last week. This is a serious tax; stationery is also a heavy item."[11] The financial burden would only increase, particularly as Caroline was determined to be independent of any outside influences. In Sydney, the Female Immigrants' Home had received some sponsorship money to help with its running costs, and had been self-sufficient as a result of employers paying for the hire of staff. And although the Colonial Government had offered no direct funding, Caroline had been allowed to frank her own mail, a big saving. In London, she was acting as a private citizen and therefore was wary of appearing to be beholden to any particular groups, especially religious ones. It meant, in effect, that the whole financial responsibility of helping the emigrants was initially being borne by Archibald.

Whatever the costs, Caroline pushed on with her plans. Undaunted by protocol, she approached the top echelons of government; the Colonial Secretary, Henry Grey, the third Earl Grey, granted her an interview, as did his first cousin, Sir George Grey, who was the Home Secretary. (Although both men were highly respected, important politicians of their day, neither would be remembered as well as Henry's father and George's uncle, Charles Grey, by succeeding generations. He was not only Prime Minister of Britain, but is the earl after whom Earl Grey tea is named.) Caroline's plan that the British Government should, free of charge, reunite the wives and families of convicts and emancipists in Australia, spanned both jurisdictions. Both Secretaries of State and associated civil servants showed respect for her abilities and her opinions, and she was very pleased with the way she was received: "I am happy to say Earl Grey listened with much interest and humanity to all I advanced ... [He] expressed himself obliged by my affording him so much authentic information."[12]

Following those top-level meetings Caroline made an appearance before the Colonial Land and Emigration Commission. Not long afterwards, she paid two more visits to the Colonial Commissioners' Offices, "and I have every reason to be satisfied with the attention that has been paid to my suggestions."[13] Caroline, focused on promoting her causes, appeared totally unaware of the singularity of her success in gaining access to these high-born and powerful men and then bending them to her will. She had, of course, already achieved similar success in India with the Governor of Madras, Sir Frederick Adam, and in Sydney with Sir George Gipps. Even so, in London she was dealing with the pivotal power-brokers of the Empire, the colonial masters responsible for tens of millions of lives around the globe — and she had only been in the city for three months.

In later years, highlighting the David and Goliath battle that she was conducting, Caroline described the physical hardships that she had endured while pursuing her quest:

Many a weary and cold walk, through the sleet and snow,
for it was in winter I commenced my operations, I had to
undertake from Prince's-street, Mile-end, the eastern part of
London, to the Home-office, before I succeeded in obtaining
a passage to Sydney for those poor people. Although I met

with every consideration and attention from the Home Secretary of State, Sir George Grey, forms and inquiries had to be gone though, and I had also to hunt out the wives and families by postal communication.[14]

It was worth the effort. In April of the following year, 1847, a group of wives and children of emancipists who had been left behind when their husbands had been transported, were granted free passage by the British Government aboard the *Asia,* a vessel taking convict women to Hobart (transportation continued to Tasmania until 1853). From there the families would sail to Sydney, their passages paid for with funds entrusted to Caroline by their husbands awaiting them in New South Wales.

When the women and children first gathered in London, Archibald met the families and, at his own expense, paid for a boat to take them to Woolwich to board the *Asia*. Some of the women were so poor that Caroline begged funds from two wealthy Australians then in London to provide them with clothes for the journey. Amongst those embarking was an "aged wife separated twenty-one years that very day, as she told me, from her expatriated husband".[15] Within two months another group of emancipist families were aboard the *Waverley* bound similarly for Hobart and then on to Sydney to be reunited with their husbands. Within just seven months of landing at Hull, Caroline had launched herself at the British establishment and with dedicated single-mindedness, cut through red tape and achieved success. It was just a start.

*

Caroline's next project was to reunite left-behind children with parents who had gone to Australia in the years of the booming economy before 1841, when poor immigrant labour was desperately being sought but dependents were not. Just before Caroline had left Sydney, Governor Gipps had approved her request for the Colonial Government to bear the cost, or bounty, of bringing those youngsters to the colony.[16] Now Caroline started pushing for the British Government to make good on that promise. Whilst agreeing to the idea in principal, and even praising Caroline, the Colonial Land and Emigration Commissioners had reservations about the idea, and even suggested that Caroline had manipulated Sir George into an unwise position: "The Colonial Government have been led by the appeals of Mrs Chisholm, a lady who has distinguished herself by her humanity and her activity in connection with emigration, to promise a bounty for the introduction of these children."[17] The commissioners' concerns were three-fold: the organisation involved, the costs and the mortality rate on such voyages.

The logistics were certainly daunting. From her travels around New South Wales, Caroline had a list of some 211 abandoned children, more than 160 of them under 14 years of age. Just locating the children was an enormous challenge. They were from poor families whose literacy levels would not have been high, thus making communications by mail problematic. Then there was the difficulty of extricating them from the families with whom they had been living since they were abandoned. Not every child would have wished to make the journey, nor was every host family ready to give a child up. Some children had spent years with these unofficial foster parents, and now they were being sent to the other side of the world, to mothers and fathers they barely remembered. It must have been a painful emotional rollercoaster for many of them. Another obstacle was that almost all of the children were living in Ireland, scattered over twenty counties. At that time, there was "very little if any, shipping from Irish ports to New South Wales" so the youngsters had to be brought to London for embarkation, along with a handful living in England and Scotland.[18]

Then there was the issue of how many of the youngsters would actually survive the arduous voyage to the colony. The death rate on long sea voyages was still considerable, although, to the commissioners' credit, there had been some recent improvements. In 1838, the year that Caroline and Archibald took their two young sons from Madras to Sydney, almost five per cent of immigrants died whilst travelling from Britain to Australia, or, described in actual human terms, 679 men, women and children were buried at sea that year, on that one route alone. Children and the elderly made up the largest percentage of the deaths amongst the susceptible bounty passengers, who travelled huddled together, prey to disease and fever, in the badly ventilated bowels of the vessels. By 1845, albeit on the less travelled emigration route to South Australia, that rate had dropped significantly to just 0.62 per cent; of more than "641 souls, the only deaths were of three children and one infant".[19] The commissioners, though, did not give the figures for the busier route to New South Wales. Indeed, with a typically callous nineteenth-century disregard for the value of working-class life, they stated: "We believe that the passage to Australia may now be made by large bodies of the labouring classes, with less risk of death by disease than amongst the same number of persons living on shore in England."[20] Revealing something of a paradox though, they then went on to ascribe the improvement on the South Australian route to the reduced numbers of children making the journey.

The commissioners therefore had some justification for fearing the outcome of sending so many young people on a four-month

Dating from about April 1853, when Caroline was forty-five years old, this is an enlargement of a carte-de-visite, signed on the back by Caroline and probably taken when she visited Liverpool during her British lecture tours. It was found amongst the papers of her friend Elizabeth Rathbone in Liverpool. *(Courtesy of the Sydney Jones Library, University of Liverpool)*

Campbell's Wharf, Sydney, in 1842, in a lithograph by John Skinner Prout. Perched on the northwestern edge of what would become Circular Quay and in front of the Rocks, the wharf, named for merchant Robert Campbell, was a major focus of the colony's trading economy. From here the town spread south along George Street. *(National Library of Australia, nla.obj-135612733)*

Emigrants Leaving the Ship, Sydney Cove, by Thomas Picken, 1853. Thousands of bounty immigrants arrived in Sydney in the early 1840s, despite the downturn in the economy. After some four months at sea, mostly living in the bowels of the vessel, they were given only a few days to find work and lodgings before being ordered ashore. *(National Library of Australia, nla.obj-137053583)*

Sir George Gipps, Governor of New South Wales (1838–46), in a portrait by Eden Upton Eddis. Gipps was in charge of the colony during Caroline's first sojourn there. Sceptical of her motives and ability at the start, he became one of her strongest supporters, allowing her to open the Female Immigrants' Home and frank her own letters, and promising to help organise reunions for bounty children. Sadly, he died shortly after returning to Britain in 1847. *(State Library of Victoria)*

George Street in 1842, painted by Henry Curzon Allport. As it is today, George Street in the 1830s was Sydney's main thoroughfare. Along with its smart shops, post office and well-to-do private residences, though, the street, still mostly covered in dirt, was home to pubs, a gaol and markets. It was, in other words, a microcosm of the colony. *(State Library of New South Wales, ML 1111)*

The first Government House in Sydney, on the corner of Bridge and Phillip streets, painted by G.E. Peacock, 1845. When Archibald returned to Sydney in 1845, he would have seen the camels here. At the cost of £225, Governor Gipps had purchased three as an experiment; later they were put on display in the Domain. *(State Library of New South Wales, ML 658)*

A portrait of Roger Therry by Richard Read, 1834. Therry (1800–74) was an Irish barrister, judge, politician and writer. Along with his wife, Ann, he was one of Caroline's earliest friends and supporters in Sydney. He led the prosecution of the Myall Creek Massacre and *Carthaginian* cases. *(State Library of New South Wales, ML 180)*

John Dunmore Lang, in a sketch by Charles Rodius, 1850. A Scottish Presbyterian clergyman, politician and immigration activist, Lang (1799–1878) had a love/hate relationship with Caroline. Virulently anti-Catholic, he lambasted her for being a tool of Rome whilst also praising her "truly benevolent work". *(State Library of New South Wales, P2/10)*

Angela Burdett-Coutts (1814–1906), later 1st Baroness Burdett-Coutts, was one of the wealthiest women in England, having inherited her father and grandfather's banking empires. An acquaintance of Caroline's, she was also a considerable philanthropist, joining Charles Dickens in founding a home for "fallen women" called Urania Cottage, in Shepherds Bush, London. *(Alamy)*

Although this portrait of Caroline is unsigned and undated, it's believed it was painted in London in 1852, by Angelo Collen Hayter, and exhibited at the Royal Academy in London that year. Caroline would have been forty-four years old at the time. *(State Library of New South Wales, DG 459)*

Mount Alexander Gold Diggings, 1852, by R.S. Anderson. The 1850s saw the start of the gold rush in Victoria, and by the spring of 1854 Caroline's entire family was in Melbourne. Caroline visited the diggings within a few weeks of the Eureka Stockade rebellion. *(State Library of Victoria)*

Caroline's third son, Henry John Chisholm, had a successful career in the New South Wales Justice Department and rose to the rank of colonel in the Duke of Edinburgh Highlanders. *(Courtesy of Don Chisholm and the Australian Catholic University)*

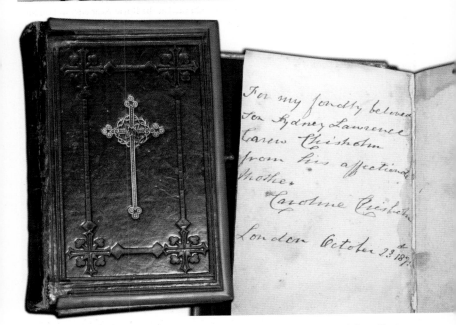

Caroline gave this prayer book (above left) to her son Sydney in 1871 and included an affectionate dedication (above right). *(Courtesy of Don Chisholm and the Australian Catholic University)*

This alabaster bust of Caroline was presented to her by Pope Pius IX, in Rome in 1853. It is now owned by Caroline's great-great-grandson Don Chisholm. *(Courtesy of Don Chisholm and the Australian Catholic University)*

A portrait of Caroline appeared on this five cents stamp issued by the Post Office in 1968. *(Caroline Chisholm, Famous Australians stamp series, 1968; designer: Alfred Cook, engraver: Lyell Dolan; © Australian Postal Corporation)*

Caroline became the first woman, apart from the Queen, to grace Australian paper currency. Her image appeared on the back of the five-dollar note, which was in circulation from 1967 to 1992.

journey across the oceans. To give the commissioners their due also, they did consider how best to keep a boatload of children safe, saying each ship would need to engage a matron, with proper assistants, a surgeon and a schoolmaster. The cost of the expedition was rising all the time, but between Caroline's urging and the governor's promise, there was not much that the commissioners could do except attempt to retard the process by insisting that Caroline and Archibald be responsible for finding the children.

For a variety of reasons, less than half the children were discovered or were available to travel. Nonetheless, near the end of 1847, the *Sir Edward Parry* set sail with a youthful cargo plus a few families and single women. It arrived in Port Phillip on 24 January 1848, before sailing on to Sydney. At the end of the voyage, some seventy-five children were reunited with their parents. The immigration agent in Sydney, Francis Merewether, described the boat as being in good condition on arrival, although two lives had been lost on the journey, a young woman and an infant.

During the next few years, when possible and as she discovered them, Caroline sent many more children to parents who had been desperate to retrieve them. One widow wrote back to Caroline, "They have arrived safely, all well; the eldest girl got well married; two of the boys I have got apprenticed; you have my most heartfelt thanks for your kindness in sending out my children, and you have my prayers night and day."[21] Whatever the rights and wrongs of the children's reunion programme, and those would have varied from case to case, the youngsters who arrived in Australia came to a land of plenty where there was little fear of starvation, unlike famine-stricken Ireland, which most of them had just left behind. Seen in that light, Caroline's efforts had clearly saved many young lives.

There was still more work to do, however, and fortunately Caroline was an avid multi-tasker. Whilst concentrating on these reunion projects, she was still pushing forward with her other objectives: to send a higher proportion of women to Australia and help poor families emigrate. She followed her meeting with Earl Grey in late 1846 with a letter to him dated January 1847, describing the "frightful disparity of the sexes, (men being out of all proportion in number to women)",[22] and requesting that respectable women be offered bounties to emigrate to the colony to rectify this problem. She then went on to detail what she saw as the three main effects of this inequality: "the gradual but certain extermination of those unfortunate tribes, the Aborigines of New Holland; ... the solitary and cheerless Hut of the unfortunate Emancipist living alone, or at times find two young men associated together".[23]

What is so revealing about this letter is not only her understanding and empathy with the plight of the Indigenous Australians — as mentioned earlier, nineteenth-century attitudes to non-whites were either barbarically indifferent or insensitively patronising; either way, it was highly unusual for a woman of the era to consider the effect of colonisation on Indigenous peoples — but also her total lack of offensive morality when apparently referring to possible homosexuality between "young men [who] associated together because they could not meet with respectable females to whom they could offer otherwise a comfortable home". Even appearing to reference homosexual behaviour would have been highly irregular in the conservative environment of the mid-nineteenth century, particularly for a woman. The fact that she recognised, and seemed to comprehend (albeit with a flawed belief that any homosexual behaviour by the young men resulted from lack of feminine companionship rather than natural preference) and even excuse the practice, confirms her as being a person more than a century ahead of her time. Until 1899 gay sex was punishable by execution in Australia; after that year it was commuted to life in prison. It was not until 1973 that South Australia became the first state or territory to decriminalise homosexual acts between consenting adults. Tasmania, the last state or territory to comply, was eventually forced to follow suit in 1997. There is a slightly euphemistic coyness in Caroline's writing, but certainly no embarrassment, and this in a letter not just to a peer of the realm but to a highly influential figure, whose opinion of her would be vital to her work. It argues an almost breathtaking self-belief.

Earl Grey's reply did not delve into the issues of either the Indigenous population or homosexuality; he ignored both. His answer, written by a minion, was highly appreciative of Caroline's suggestion for increased female emigration but inconclusive, passing her on to the Colonial Land and Emigration Commissioners. They did not pursue the idea.

Despite this setback, Caroline's experience and opinions were still highly valued in official circles. More than eighty years before British women were granted the vote, Caroline became only the second non-royal female to be invited to present her case to the government and its agencies. (Her predecessor, Elizabeth Fry, had campaigned to improve conditions in prisons, particularly for women; she had died in Kent in 1845). Though she was a lone woman in a man's world, Caroline was surprisingly successful. It was during 1847 that she was invited to give evidence before two select committees of the House of Lords considering the issue of emigration. In answering the questions posed to her, Caroline was able to give an accurate description of the work that she had been doing in New South Wales, including such detail as the types of contracts she had drawn up and wages and conditions for new settlers — business-minded as ever, she had obviously brought documentation with her. When appropriate, she also gave her views on, amongst other subjects, female emigration, the bounty system, availability of land for new settlers and transportation. One hundred and seventy years later, the written records of both committees show that she gave her responses in a reasonably succinct, unemotional style, with no signs of nervousness. For their part, the lords conducting the inquiries paid her the unusual compliment of not pandering to her sex, but treated her as they would any other expert witness.

The first committee, in April, was inquiring into "The Execution of the Criminal Law, especially respecting Juvenile Offenders and Transportation", whilst the second, in July, was on "Colonisation from Ireland", not just to Australia but also to the North American Colonies and the West Indies.[24] Caroline seems to have been something of a star of the second committee: her testimony was substantial, transcribed onto seventeen closely typeset pages. Her suggestion that an agency be established to augment the distribution of labour in the colony was taken seriously enough to be noted in the preface of the report. At least two other witnesses referenced her and there were two appendices extolling her work in Australia: one from 1842, by the immigration agent Francis Merewether, and the other from 1843 by the Legislative Council of New South Wales.

It was heady stuff. Caroline had won massive official recognition. Even if it didn't translate into government action, it still empowered her by emphasising her credibility on all questions of emigration to the Antipodes, and turning her into something of a minor celebrity. Without doubt, her sex was an advantage to her in this, as she was conspicuous: a man may have remained faceless amongst so many, but everyone knew Caroline. Following her modus operandi from Sydney, Caroline subscribed to the theory that the more public attention she gained, the more she could achieve, and she knew that meant keeping her name before the public. It seems also that she revelled in the publicity she received on its own account; she had never been shy about expressing her views. Her lack of reticence and willingness to court publicity made her an extremely unusual nineteenth-century woman (and Archibald possibly an even rarer man to allow his wife so much licence). Doing all this in the colonies was one thing, but now Caroline was making waves in London.

In the middle of 1847, Caroline published an open letter "Dedicated, by permission, to Earl Grey", titled *Emigration and Transportation*. It was priced at 3d a copy, or 15s per 100. She and Archibald paid for the printing themselves, and she later regretted that because of the high cost, the print-run had to be quite small.[25] This is a far more elegant piece than her *Female Immigration Considered*, written five years earlier, suggesting to some that Archibald may have helped with the actual wording. Whether or not she had a ghostwriter, the ideas encased within this twenty-seven-page public letter belonged entirely to Caroline, even to her custom of self-promotion. She reminded Earl Grey that his predecessor, Lord Stanley, had, back in 1844, thanked her for his services to the emigrants; only six months earlier, in her private letter to Earl Grey, she had said exactly the same.[26] The rest of the open letter covered many of her pet issues, such as female emigration. The main thrust, however, was an attempt to convince the Colonial Secretary that the British Government should pay to relocate destitute people from the United Kingdom to New South Wales, rather than consider reverting to convict transportation. Transportation to New South Wales had been effectively halted in 1840, but some wealthy landowners, such as Archibald Boyd and William Charles Wentworth, wanted it reintroduced because it provided free labour. (In the end, another 1400 male convicts were transported before 1850, when the practice was finally discontinued altogether.[27]) One of Caroline's main arguments encouraging the poor to emigrate was that they provided a better source of labour than did the convicts.

Her language in this letter is emotive, but it is undercut by sound economic theory:

> The demand for labour in New South Wales, Port Phillip, and South Australia, is urgent and increasing. Is it not a lamentable thought, then, my Lord, that deaths should daily result from starvation among British subjects, while in this valuable colony good wheat is rotting on the ground for the want of hands to gather it in ... that tens of thousands of fine sheep, droves after droves ... of fat cattle are annually slaughtered there and "*boiled down*," in order to be rendered into tallow for the European market, while the vast refuse is cast into the fields to be devoured by dogs and pigs, and yet no effort is made by England to provide for her struggling people by a humane system of colonisation?[28]

Maybe she had read something of early eighteenth-century economic philosophers on the benefits of rational self-interest. In effect, Caroline was suggesting a neat solution to the labour market shortage in Australia and the human catastrophe in Ireland.

Caroline was very aware of the distress in Ireland, both through her work finding the reunion children and through her correspondence with people who were desperate to emigrate but lacked the funds to do so. She quoted one man: "There is nothing here but hunger, misery, and death; all I can earn gives me only one meal a day, and the little ones would starve but for English charity." Another claimed, "It is easier for a gentleman to get into the House of Commons, than for a poor man to obtain 8d a day."[29] She contrasted that with a couple with four children in the colony, the man working as a farm labourer or shepherd, who could easily earn £25 per year plus rations and board, giving the family effectively £57 per year, enough to live on and save a little also. In monetary terms the colonial family was almost five times better off than its Irish counterpart, and that was supposing that an Irishman would have found employment for a full year. Caroline contended that the colonial working man could eventually turn his labour into capital and employ others: "Labour, it may be seen, will create capital; that capital will bring out emigrants, and find employment for them; thus, a self-creating and a co-operating system would, in a shorter time than is calculated upon, provide for hundreds of thousands."[30] She had a big vision. To Caroline, Australia was a vast blank canvas ready to be painted, and she was intent on choosing the correct pigments. As she went about her work, her interest in the cost of labour and its power to effect change would increase.

At the end of the open letter to Earl Grey, Caroline included eighteen of the "Voluntary Statements" that she and Archibald had collected across New South Wales during 1845–46. These promoted the idea that the paupers of England, Ireland and Scotland could become the yeomen of Australia. Never one to waste good material, particularly when it had taken substantial time and money to collect, Caroline used the statements again later that year when once more espousing the benefits of the colony in another short publication, *Comfort for the Poor: Meat Three Times a Day! Voluntary Information from the People of New South Wales, collected in that Colony by Mrs Chisholm in 1845–46.*

Despite her open letter to Earl Grey, and her previous welcome from the Colonial Office and the commissioners, however, Caroline's plans stalled. Her suggestion to both Colonial and British Governments for a system of "land-tickets" to help immigrants buy property in the colony was discussed briefly but then ignored. The powerful landowners in New South Wales were against it, as were the politicians in Westminster. The government was respectful and polite to Caroline, even at times encouraging, but not forthcoming. Caroline would need to find private support to bring her other schemes to fruition.

As the short European summer collapsed into the frosty days of autumn, Caroline had other concerns too. She was pregnant again with her sixth child, due in the summer of 1848. However, that would not stop her writing letters, contacting powerful supporters, publishing more material or forging ahead with her new pet project, the Family Colonization Loan Society.

CHAPTER 12

Cultivating Fame

1848–54

Charlton Crescent, Islington, London, 26 February 1850

He was beginning to regret that he had come. She asked him to sit, so he perched on the edge of a tattered, ancient couch covered in dark green cushions. The whole room smelt musty, in need of airing; his nostrils twitched. Yet, there was something about Mrs Chisholm. She seemed to accept his condescension as her due, but also had her own conceit, as if by having him in her home she was conferring some honour on him, rather than the reverse. If nothing else, there was character here. He might yet harvest more from this visit than he had expected.

The old woman who had opened the door to him edged herself into the apartment. Resting her hands for a weary moment on the back of an armchair, she asked if he would take tea. Her familiarity suggested she was something more than a servant. As though reading his mind, Mrs Chisholm smiled and said, "My mother." Then, "Mother, this is the famous author, Mr Dickens." And turning back to him: "Mother does enjoy your stories. We await each week's instalment of David Copperfield, *and read it avidly. When we have time."*

The mother murmured something in agreement. As he strained to hear her, there was a crash from above, a splintering of broken glass, followed by a penetrating squeal. The mother gave a tired nod and shuffled from the room. "She looks after the little ones so that I can do my work," Mrs Chisholm said. "The older boys are away at school."

Abandoning domestic matters, she leant across her desk — an island of order and cleanliness amid the chaos — to pick up a bundle of letters tied neatly with blue ribbon, and carefully freed them from their bonds before passing them across to him. He watched her, his writer's mind absorbing every detail. He took her likeness: she was a pretty, very diminutive, plump woman of from forty to fifty, with handsome eyes, though they had a curious habit of seeming to look a long way off.[1]

Now she was speaking to him, earnest, fired with her passion, her commitment to the struggling underclass of British society and its certain resurrection on the other side of the world: "These letters, you see, Mr Dickens, they tell ... they show ... how the merest person here can transform into a man or, indeed, a woman of worth, of substance. The British Isles are too full, but New South Wales is too empty. If the people will but emigrate, they will find good wages, good food and more than enough good land."

She spoke, he noted, almost with a classical rhythm as one used to commanding an audience. Her words then flowed almost without stop, for more than thirty minutes. Surprised by her knowledge, he caught something of her fervour. Eventually, he asked her to pause; he wanted to consider the letters from her immigrants without distraction. Picking up a quill, she became absorbed in some other matter, giving him the peace he desired to read and consider.

The letters all told much the same tale, of a realm of milk and honey, a halcyon, fair-weathered land of possibilities. He might find Mrs Chisholm a little too bourgeois — she was no Lady Herbert, even less a Lady Burdett-Coutts — but he liked her ideas. They matched many of his own thoughts and, yes, he could use some of these letters to illustrate them.

"Mrs Chisholm," he said. "You may know that I am about to publish my own weekly journal. I expect the first edition of my Household Words *to be ready within less than a month. I would like to include some of these letters within the journal. Do I have your permission to do so?"*

"Mr Dickens," she said, "what you suggest is an excellent idea. However ... before I agree, could you tell me how you would use the letters. Will there be an explanation? Might it be useful if I were to provide that elucidation. I am, you may know, in the habit of expressing myself as an author, with some success."

He had not expected such self-presumption. Was quite discomposed by it. Yet the notion took his fancy. It would be something different and provocative maybe, something from the source of immigration itself. Still, he was not about to let her dictate terms to him.

"A very kind offer, Mrs Chisholm. Very kind indeed; however, not quite what I had in mind for these letters," he said, holding them up as though their weight was worth the same in banknotes. He talked slowly, developing his ideas even as he spoke. "I shall title the article ... 'A Bundle of Emigrants' Letters' ... and, yes, I will present them with a full explanation of where they came from, as well as detailing your admirable plans for helping British emigrants discover the delights of Australia."

Mrs Chisholm opened her mouth, but he held up his hand to forestall her. "Maybe you would do me the honour to write short, colourful pieces about the colony for use in a later edition of Words? *Something from your own experiences. That, I believe, would be the greatest use of your talents and of immense interest to our readers. 'Pictures of Life in Australia'," he murmured. "Yes, that's what I'll call your piece, Mrs Chisholm."*

She looked uncertain, but he didn't give her time to argue, passing swiftly onto another topic that he felt sure would catch her curiosity: Urania

Cottage, the home for fallen women at Shepherd's Bush that he helped support. He wanted her opinion on whether such females, once reformed, would be able to start a new life on the other side of the world.

The promising exchange was interrupted. The mother, tottering under the weight of a hefty tea tray, struggled into the room, barely audible words, possibly some form of apology, dribbling from her lips. Her progress was impeded by two filthy-faced urchins, each attached by grimy little fingers to the back of her skirt. They let go to tumble together in a repulsive concoction on the floor. Serenely ignoring the children, Mrs Chisholm rose from her chair and offered him tea.

Pulling out his watch, he shook his head, black curled locks bobbing above his ears, high forehead slightly creased by raised eyebrows. "Unfortunately, ma'am, time is my enemy. I have already stayed longer than I had expected."

As he followed her along the narrow corridor towards the door, a feeble cry came from a room further up the hall. "A baby, Mrs Chisholm?" he inquired, mildly bemused.

"My youngest, Sarah, born about three weeks ago," she said. "I have been thinking, Mr Dickens, I could write about a bush dinner I was once invited to attend in New South Wales. It was cooked sir, by the son of the house! An interesting concept, don't you think?"

"Definitely, Mrs Chisholm," he said, putting on his thick great coat and depositing the bundle of letters into its large pockets. He shook hands with his hostess, hoping that she had not been touching any of her ill-kept, grubby children.

Stepping out into the darkening afternoon, his nose twitched again: there was snow in the air, cold but clean. The talk on immigration had been enlightening. The letters and Mrs Chisholm's written contribution would be useful. Mostly, however, he was thinking on the lady herself. His fingers itched for a quill.

The last frosty touch of winter's hoary hand was just beginning to retreat when Charles Dickens visited Caroline at her home in Islington, North London.[2] By then, Caroline had become a person of some notice. In the four years since she had returned to Britain, and despite giving birth twice, she had appeared before two government committees, advised hundreds of would-be emigrants about the Australian colonies, organised for families of convicts and left-behind children of settlers to be reunited in New South Wales, published details of life in the colonies, and now, not long before meeting Charles Dickens, had established the Family Colonization Loan Society to help emigrants fund their journeys to the Antipodes. This mostly high profile work had brought her notice in the press, and familiarity with members of the liberal intelligentsia, as well as powerful humanitarian politicians.

The meeting between Dickens and Caroline had been organised by Elizabeth Herbert, a friend of both Dickens and Florence Nightingale. Her husband, Sidney Herbert, later the first Baron Herbert of Lea, was, apart from his government duties — he became Secretary of State for War during the Crimean conflict — one of the founding committee members (and later chairman) of Caroline's Family Colonization Loan Society.[3] Grabbing the opportunity to bring Caroline and Dickens together, Lady Herbert wrote urgently to Caroline on 24 February 1850:

I saw Mr Dickens to-day and he has commissioned me to say that if you will allow him, and unless he hears to the contrary from you, he will call upon you at 2 o'clock on Tuesday next, the 26th. I told him about your emigrants' letters, and he seemed to think that the giving them publicity would be an important engine towards helping on our work, and he has so completely the confidence of the lower classes (who all read his Books if they can read at all), that I think if you can persuade him to bring them out in his new work it will be an immense step gained. He is so singularly clever and agreeable that I hope you forgive me for having made this appointment without your direct sanction, and for having also told him that I knew you wished to make his acquaintance.[4]

Following the meeting, Dickens reprinted a number of Caroline's immigrants' letters in what was basically a promotional piece that he wrote about the Family Colonization Loans Society, in the very first issue of *Household Words,* published on Saturday, 30 March 1850. The journal was sold at the low price of 2d. Never one to stint on words, Dickens devoted almost five pages to the letters and Caroline's plans for the society. Three months later,

A photographic portrait of Charles Dickens, from around the time he met Caroline Chisholm *(Alamy)*

Caroline co-authored, with the *Household Words* editor Richard H. Horne, another longish piece on her firsthand experience of life in New South Wales, including an extract about a settler's son cooking dinner. Horne's influence can be seen in the lighter, more casual prose of the pieces. (Probably as a result of working with the Chisholms, Horne eventually emigrated to Melbourne, where Archibald helped him find employment.)

Short, inexpensive publications about emigration and Australia were something of a fashion in the late 1840s and early 1850s in Britain. Samuel Sidney published at least three titles: *Sidney's Australian Handbook* (reprinted nine times), *Sidney's Emigrant's Journal* and *The Three Colonies of Australia*; John Capper brought out *The Emigrant's Guide to Australia*; Douglas Jerrold covered emigration in his *Weekly Newspaper*; and, of course, Dickens was writing about emigration in his *Household Words*. Dickens's interest in New South Wales, emigration and philanthropy was not just commercial; his enthusiasm for sending the poor to a land of opportunity appears to have been genuine. When he met Caroline, *David Copperfield,* one of his best-known works, was being serialised. Near the end of that story a number of the characters join together to emigrate to Australia, including Emily, who after an illicit affair has been on the verge of turning to prostitution to survive.

In a perfect example of art mimicking real life, Dickens was turning fact into fiction. During the 1840s, along with Baroness Angela Burdett-Coutts, he had helped established Urania Cottage in Shepherd's Bush as a home for "fallen women", mostly former prostitutes. The women were encouraged to reform their way of life and seek a fresh start in the Australian colonies. The Baroness, also a notable humanitarian, had become one of the wealthiest women in England after inheriting her grandfather's banking empire. Staying single until her late sixties, and thereby maintaining control of her wealth, she devoted much of her time and fortune to good causes.[5] Only days after meeting Caroline, Dickens wrote a note to the baroness displaying his caustic wit, at Caroline's expense: "I dream of Mrs Chisholm, and her housekeeping. The dirty faces of her children are my continual companions. I forgot to tell you that she asked me if it were true that the girls at Shepherd's Bush '*had Pianos*'. I shall always regret that I didn't answer yes — each girl a grand, down stair — and a cottage in her bedroom — besides a small guitar in the wash-house."[6]

Dickens went on to immortalise Caroline in *Bleak House* as the domestically myopic philanthropist Mrs Jellyby, a woman who spends her time writing letters on behalf of a new settlement and an obscure African tribe on the banks of the Niger River, to the detriment of her ill-kept and neglected children. The humorous caricature first made its appearance in the fourth instalment of the serialisation in June 1852, just over two years after Dickens and Caroline were introduced.

There is no evidence that Dickens had any further meetings with Caroline, although, considering that she wrote for *Household Words,* it seems likely that they would have encountered each other again. Nor is there any record of Dickens having met Archibald, though, reading *Bleak House,* one can imagine his opinion of Caroline's consort: "I never, to my knowledge, had the pleasure of seeing Mr Jellyby. He may be a very superior man, but he is, so to speak, merged — merged — in the more shining qualities of his wife."[7] Caroline's three older boys would also probably have been absent when Dickens met her, away at school. At home in Charlton Crescent then would have been four-year-old Sydney, born at sea, and his two younger sisters: two-year-old Caroline (named for both her mother and the baby that had died nineteen years previously) and the new baby, Sarah, who was then only a few weeks old and who would die within six months from a throat infection.[8] These were the dirty-faced children that so revolted Dickens and led him to parody Caroline.

For all Dickens's charitable concerns, particularly for females forced by poverty into prostitution, he had very little sympathy with women, like Caroline, who put their public work ahead of what he considered a female's first duty, the care and organisation of her own domestic sphere. In that, he was very much a man of his era, still subscribing to the rigidly restricted view of a woman's role in the world. In reality, though, the main difference between Caroline and the women Dickens admired, such as Lady Herbert, who had seven children, was that Caroline could not afford servants to take care of her offspring and run her home. Other female activists, such as Baroness Burdett-Coutts and Florence Nightingale, were, apart from being very wealthy, without husbands, let alone a dependent family.

In a society where class structure was paramount, it would have been difficult to pigeonhole Caroline. Her working-class origins were well hidden; she sat firmly in the upper middle class, occasionally frequenting the higher echelons of society. One of her truly impressive qualities was that, for the most part, people, whether they were poverty-stricken labourers or powerful ministers of state, appeared to take her at her own valuation. Charles Dickens was one of the exceptions.

*

Caroline's meeting with Charles Dickens came just as her Family Colonization Loan Society was actively seeking emigrants to send to Australia. Her objectives were simple. She believed that poor but hardworking families should be lent funds to help pay for their passage aboard safe and well-regulated ships. Once in the colonies, she expected the new settlers to start repaying the loans. Finding that the Colonial Office was prepared to listen and take cautious steps towards improving conditions on board emigrant ships, but was otherwise ignoring her schemes, Caroline had taken up the cudgel herself.[9] As always, she knew that her greatest chance of success was to excite the interest of the rich and powerful. In 1848, she had sought the support of one of the best-known peers of the realm, a parliamentarian, moreover, who was known for addressing a myriad of humanitarian ills and had earned the sobriquet of "the Poor Man's Earl", Anthony Ashley-Cooper, Lord Ashley, soon to be the seventh Earl of Shaftesbury.[10] He had already done much to improve Britain's appalling lunatic asylums (as they were then called); attempted to reform working conditions, especially for children and women in factories and mines; helped outlaw the use of chimneysweeps, or climbing boys; and sponsored the Ragged School system for underprivileged children. He was a man who could not turn his back on a good cause. Caroline's appeal to him was a stroke of genius: he was influential, knew the system, and where he led others would follow. It said much for William Jones's daughter that she had not just the confidence but now also the status that would allow her to consort with members of the social elite.

Establishing the society had been a slow process. She had initially approached Lord Shaftesbury in 1848 with her plan. In August the following year, she wrote him a letter about the need for such a society; in another, longer open letter in 1850 she clarified the proposal and set out the rules of the scheme. The second letter was published under the title: *The A.B.C. of Colonization. In a Series of Letters by Mrs Chisholm*. Lord Shaftesbury agreed to become the

Family Colonization Loan Society.
(ORIGINATED BY MRS. CHISHOLM.)

A PUBLIC GROUP MEETING

Of the Emigrants proceeding in the "Mariner," and others interested in Emigration, will be held at the

ROYAL BRITISH INSTITUTION,

Tabernacle Row, Cowper St., City Road,

On WEDNESDAY, FEB. 18, 1852.

The Chair will be taken at 7 o'clock, by the Rt. Hon.

The EARL of SHAFTESBURY.

A number of Noblemen & Gentlemen have kindly promised to attend.

ADMISSION FREE.

3, Charlton Crescent, Islington, Feb. 6, 1852.

A flyer advertising an early meeting of the Family Colonization Loan Society
(Museums Victoria)

first chairman of the society's London committee, which included other eminent gentlemen such as Sidney Herbert and Vernon Smith, the Member of Parliament for Caroline's home town, Northampton, who, disliking his common surname, retitled himself Robert Vernon when he became the first Baron Lyveden. Along with monetary contributions, their involvement gave the society the integrity and respectability it needed if it was to gain further sponsorship from the wealthy and, just as importantly, the trust of the poor. Amongst the donations subsequently received was a substantial £250 from the Countess of Pembroke; a similar amount came in from other sources, the total making the society financially viable and able to begin operations by early 1850.

Caroline realised that only better-off working-class and middle-class people would be able to save even part of the cost of their fare. Accepting these new criteria, she modified her scheme to suit. People wishing to emigrate, who had references proving them to be of good character, were encouraged to join the society at the cost of one shilling, then deposit further small amounts, from as little as one shilling at a time, until they had saved at least half the cost of their fare. The society set a full fare at £12, so it expected each adult to contribute at least £6; the discounted fare for children under fourteen years of age was £3, while infants travelled free. These were still not insubstantial amounts for some families; for example, a couple with two children older than seven years and two younger than seven years would still need to save up about £30 before boarding a boat. (Putting that into context, even more than a decade later — 1866 — the average annual earnings of agricultural workers in England was only £33 16s.[11])

By saving half of their fare, Caroline believed, the prospective emigrants would prove that they were both industrious and frugal. On that basis, the society would lend them, interest-free, the remainder of the fare, on the condition that it would be repaid within two years of them arriving in Australia. Indeed, the society's Rule No. 16 is one which twenty-first-century banking establishments could well take note of, stipulating "that no sums be advanced to parties beyond what they can easily repay within two years from the date of their arrival in the colony".[12] Not only was Caroline trying to ensure that the society incurred no bad debts, but she also wanted to make certain that the repayments were not too onerous for her clients. Continuing her reunion programme, she encouraged emigrants who had already settled in Australia to send money to the London committee as payment towards other family members being given passage on the society's ships.

Amongst the major differences between this and earlier schemes was that families were not to be limited in size, Caroline insisting that babies, young children and the elderly were all welcome, "for the eye of age is at times of more service than the strong arm of youth … No exception is to be made on account of age; the only voucher required will be a good character."[13] She was determined, too, that families should not be split up. She had, after all, spent much of the previous two years attempting to rectify this problem and had excellent knowledge of the damage done to both children and parents when they were separated for years. Nor was she thinking only of the youngsters: she noted that, too often, elderly parents left behind without immediate family ended their days in sad loneliness, either in front of an empty hearth or in the workhouse. She wholeheartedly believed that emigration should not destroy the natural cohesion of the domestic unit. That said, she did allow some family members, for example husbands or older children in their late teens or early twenties, to emigrate first so that they could contribute to the cost of bringing out the rest of the family, usually within the next twelve months.

Central to the entire operation was Caroline's vision that emigration should be of a collective nature. Rather than single families travelling alone, she insisted on groups of not less than three families banding together to share personal and financial responsibility for the journey, although sometimes she would allow a few single girls or men to join the family clusters. What was vital to Caroline was that each separate group should bond as a tight-knit unit rather than just be travelling companions. To achieve this, she insisted that each group of families should spend time together before they sailed, to get to know each other and develop special relationships. She believed that this would ensure that they cared for each other during the voyage and would encourage them to continue to work together, to the benefit of all, once they had reached their destination.

Forming close supportive clusters also made financial sense. An important safeguard against non-repayment of the loans was Caroline's insistence that each individual be responsible for the overall collective debt: "As each member of a group will have to pay his share of the *fees* due by any of its defaulters, this will brand such defaulters more deeply, and give additional security to the Society. If, for instance, a group consisted of twenty-one persons, and that one became a defaulter, each would have to pay a *sixpence* for his dishonesty; the insignificancy of the amount would only make his delinquency the more pointed."[14]

At heart, though, Caroline believed in the indelible honesty of ordinary people and argued it eloquently:

> The proposed repayment of the loan has been called *"The Forlorn Hope"* ... and, yet will it be said that the peasantry and the people of England, of Scotland, and of Ireland are so fallen, so destitute of still nobler and higher feelings, that they cannot be trusted with the loan of a few pounds? ... We exult in the intelligence of our people; we boast of our machinery and our science; but what is all this, my Lord, if our people cannot be trusted with a few pounds to convey them from want to plenty? If their principles are so bad and so utterly worthless ... it will be necessary to enquire into the causes that have so degraded them.[15]

Caroline planned that as each loan was repaid it would be repatriated to London to be lent to new groups of families, therefore allowing dozens of people to emigrate for much the same amount.

To establish the whole process, Caroline set up an Australian information centre in her home in Charlton Place, furnished a room as if it was steerage accommodation on board a boat, and held evening meetings for upwards of seventy would-be emigrants at a time. These meetings were often attended also by committee members, including Lord Shaftesbury and Sidney Herbert. Although quite relaxed, these get-togethers were treated as business meetings, not social gatherings, and no refreshments were offered.

Charles Dickens wrote about the first meeting attended by one emigrant, Richard Delver:

> An old woman of a homely appearance opened the door, and directed him up a remarkably narrow passage into a small room, fitted like a school, with benches and a tier of broad shelves in one corner, which he was told formed an exact copy of the berths or beds on board Mrs Chisholm's ships. ...
> He got into conversation with ... a pale thin young man, who was emigrating to be a shepherd, because he was not able to stand the work of a white-lead factory.[16]

Delver was a family man with a wife and two sons. He was also illiterate. At Caroline's suggestion, another pending emigrant, a bachelor and engineer, taught Delver to read, write and "cipher"; in return, Delver's wife, Maggie, made the man shirts and tended to his clothes.

As an excellent communicator, Caroline enjoyed personal interaction, and these meetings gave her yet another chance to shine. She would match single travellers, particularly girls, with like-minded family groups, and advise on what essentials each family would need for a four-month sea journey, as well as what they might need once they arrived at their destination, be it Sydney, Port Phillip or Adelaide. She also offered ideas on how families could best pool resources to save for their contributions towards their fares.

Caroline was becoming the darling of the press, and the progress of her society was reported in newspapers across the country, from *The Inverness Courier* in the north to *The Plymouth and Devon Advertiser* in the south, as well as in other major regional publications throughout Britain and in Ireland, such as *The Galway Mercury* and *The Dublin Evening Post*. When, finally, the society was ready to send its initial cargo of emigrants to Australia, no fewer than eight London-based papers and journals recorded the event.[17]

The first boat hired exclusively by the society was the *Slains Castle,* a 503-ton barque that sailed from Gravesend on 30 September 1850. It had been especially converted to Caroline's specifications for the voyage, giving the passengers ten per cent more sleeping space than was required under the British Government's Passenger Act. In what was probably a first for ocean-going vessels at the time, there was only one class — all passengers were to be treated equally, and they were even allowed to walk on the poop deck. Another innovation was separate bathhouses for males and females, although the water closets (toilets) were still flushed with salt water straight into the ocean. Alcohol was banned on board the ship for emigrants, but there were larger supplies of water than on other ships. Instead of the traditional dormitory-style accommodation, with little to separate couples or the sexes apart from thin curtains made from cheap materials, Caroline's passengers were housed in cabins. Married couples with young children were kept together, as were single women and single men, providing more privacy and security. The wooden berths were designed in such a way that they could be pushed back during the day to give more room. One contemporary was full of praise for the innovations aboard the society's ships: "The cabins, ranged on each side, were numbered, and resembled a ward in Greenwich or Chelsea Hospital ... By a space being left at the bottom, and the frame-work not reaching the roof by several inches, a free and perfect circulation of air was allowed in each cabin, besides, there being a small window covered by a piece of coloured cotton; thus, there were privacy, air, and light."[18]

The day before the vessel left port, Sunday services were celebrated on board by ministers of the Anglican, Wesleyan and Roman Catholic churches. The 250 men, women and children on board were "120 communicants of the Church of England, two Jewesses, and the others about equally divided between Wesleyans and Roman Catholics."[19] Caroline, of course, went aboard the *Slains Castle* to bid her emigrants Godspeed. It was an emotional farewell: "The moment for separation now arrived ... A young Jewess clasped [Caroline] in her arms, kissed her, and called her 'dear mother.' Other females wept aloud. The old women hung about her praying for the 'blessings of God to be her portion.' The men in silent grief grasped her hand; and the last cheer given was ... 'Three cheers for Mrs Chisholm's children!'"[20] For Caroline that particular salute must have been painful: her baby, Sarah, had died only a few weeks earlier.

The start of the journey was somewhat inauspicious, according to Archdale Low Whitby, one of the passengers, who was travelling with his wife, Eleanor, and three children, Archie, Frederick and Ellen. Archdale Whitby kept a day-by-day diary of the voyage, which lasted just over four months.[21] "Very few of us required Dinner today owing to sickness," he noted on 2 October 1850. There was a bit of excitement the next day when the *Slains Castle* laid anchor off Deal in Kent waiting for a fair wind. One passenger, a Mr Field, used a small boat to go ashore:

"It was generally believed that Field intended to bolt, so getting quit of his wife and family of three children," reported Whitby on 4 October. A search party was sent out; the man was found in a local pub and brought back to the ship. The next day the boat was under sail again.

By the end of November, the wind was squally and the barque was rolling in heavy seas. On 28 November, Whitby described a dramatic scene:

> The waves being like high mountains about us … at ¼ past 8 o Clock p.m. (Something wrong now we know … Captn Andrew a very good quiet man would at this time be comfortably playing Chess with the Doctor) … the Captn was heard with a voice like thunder giving orders for all hands … when all of a sudden "Crack Crack" … at the same time down came our Masts with a frightful crash carrying away part of our bulwarks — most miraculously none of us received any damage — it will be easier to imagine than describe the consternation which prevailed during this dreadful night — women crying and many waking their children up and dressing them so that they might be close to them, making sure we were all going to the bottom together.

Whitby went on to explain that the boat was taking water and, amid the fear, the captain ordered his sailors to sing their usual songs to alleviate panic, even as they desperately worked the pumps to keep the boat afloat. When the storm eventually passed, only a lower mast was left standing. The next five days were spent drifting as the carpenter, aided by some of the passengers, repaired the masts and sails.

Whitby's diary also details bad behaviour by both passengers and some crew, particularly at Christmas and New Year. On Christmas Day, Field, the man who tried to escape at the start of the journey, managed to get drunk and attempted a punch-up with another passenger. More importantly, the cook was likewise inebriated and tried to fight the carpenter. Both malcontents ended up in leg irons until they apologised to an extremely temperate captain. The day ended with passengers and crew singing songs. "We had for Dinner Soup de Bouilli [vegetable soup] and hard Dumplings consequently did not fair very sumptuously — We had nothing to drink but black water and tea — Our water by this time being very bad. Fortunately for us we had a filter which greatly improved it."

As the *Slains Castle* reached the Southern Ocean, Whitby recorded sightings of whales and albatrosses and, on 21 January 1851, only days before they made landfall, the first and only death on board, of Miss Emma Bishop, a twenty-six-year-old governess from Brixton, who had been travelling by herself. She died of dysentery,

a disease very prevalent on board just now. She was launched into the Deep at 8 Bells this Evening. It was getting dusk — The Captain read the burial Service, one of the apprentices holding by his side a lamp to see to read by, and although the Deck was thronged with spectators ... you might have heard a pin drop and the sea which a few hours before was raging mountains high was as calm as it could be.

Two days later Cape Otway was sighted: "Fine day with a good wind — At noon to our great delight we could see at a distance Cape Otway — [at] the cry of 'Land in sight' you may imagine all hands flew upon Deck ...We were amused this Evening by watching the Cape Otway revolving light."

The next day, 24 January 1851, the boat dropped anchor in Port Phillip Bay. A steamer took the passengers "some few miles up the River Yarra Yarra a pretty though narrow stream with trees on both sides which almost meet over head ... in Melbourne ... took up our abode ... at the 'Royal Exchange' Hotel, Great Collings Street, glad indeed to lay hold of some fresh provisions etc."

When the eager families arrived in Melbourne they were met, according to Whitby, by "Mrs Chisholm's Agents and others". Determined that arriving immigrants would not suffer the fate that had so distressed her in the early 1840s, Caroline had planned that immigration agents would be available to receive them. She also sent a letter to newspaper editors in each city where the boat was due to dock, commending the immigrants to their attention. She planned that in the future her agents would have tents erected as temporary residences for the new arrivals, whilst a larger tent would be set up as an employment agency. The agents were to give advice and collect the repayments from the loans that would be remitted to London. Caroline had attempted to top and tail the entire operation with her usual precision. To ensure even greater control, in March 1851 Archibald, who until then had been doing much of the society's bookwork in London, set sail for Adelaide, where, following his arrival in August he became the colonial agent and organised colonial committees and immigration agents at the major disembarkation points of Adelaide, Melbourne and Sydney. All seemed to be in place for a successful scheme. What could go wrong?

The *Slains Castle* was just the first of many society boats. The *Blundell* followed in May 1851, and the *Athenian* in September 1851. Within twelve months Caroline had sent close to seven hundred new settlers to the Antipodes. The society proved to be far more successful than a concurrent scheme organised by the British Government, as Eneas Mackenzie reported: "In twelve months, during a period that the government had been unable to fill several of their ships with emigrants to whom they gave a free passage, and when filled had only been able to obtain a class whom Earl Grey termed the refuse of workhouses, inferior to convicts, Mrs Chisholm had been able to collect families of the most industrious and frugal class."[22] It does beg the question as to whether Caroline's emigrants, most of whom seem to have been able to save some money towards their fares, were desperate people fleeing brutal poverty and, in the case of Ireland, famine and starvation, or whether they were more secure working- and lower-middle-class types, able to survive but looking for a better future — essentially economic migrants. For example, Whitby's command of written English, his records of longitude and latitude, and of other ships sighted, and his later behaviour — he made six voyages between England and Melbourne, as well as a side trip to New Zealand, between 1850 and 1892 — suggest that he was a man of good education and belonged to the more affluent middle class.

At least another sixteen vessels operated by the society sailed after the *Athenian*. The society's funds were boosted significantly in 1852, when the New South Wales Legislative Council, impressed by the society's achievements, voted to send £10,000 to the London committee to help it continue its work,[23] and in London "city merchants engaged in the Australian trade" also raised £10,000 to contribute to the running of the society.[24]

Each of the society's boats had its own characteristics and its own stories. The *Blundell* appears to have been a particularly lucky vessel: not only were its passengers granted free admittance to the

Great Exhibition at Crystal Palace in London before departure, but nearly all found employment immediately after arriving in the colony.[25] The third ship, the *Athenian,* was to become the first vessel to use a very crude form of air-conditioning. The surgeon on board, R. Bowie, Esq., fitted two perforated zinc tubes extending from the "stem to the stern" of the vessel and continuing up onto the deck. One tube carried off the used air while the other brought in fresh air, thereby ridding the bowels of the boat of the effluvia that inevitably resulted from so many people living, cooking and eating in close quarters.[26] The *Caroline Chisholm,* which sailed in 1853, included amongst its immigrants at least a dozen poor Jewish girls bound for Sydney and Melbourne and sponsored by "a committee of Jewish ladies" who were also looking to be of "assistance to poor Jewish families desirous of emigrating to the Australian Colonies".[27] At the time Jewish people made up about half of one per cent of the population of New South Wales, or about one thousand people.[28]

Gold fever had hit the colony in early 1851, initially across the Great Dividing Range near Bathurst in New South Wales and then, more substantially, at Ballarat, Castlemaine (then known as Forest Creek and the Mount Alexander Goldfield) and Bendigo in what would soon be the separate colony of Victoria. Millions of pounds were dug from the ground as city and bush dwellers alike downed tools and took to mining. The influx of hopefuls from across the globe was extraordinary, with Australia's population almost tripling in the twenty years from 1851 to 1871, from less than half a million to about 1.7 million people. In the light of those numbers, the tallies achieved by Caroline's society appear almost inconsequential. Records are vague, but most authorities agree that the society was responsible for bringing out some five thousand settlers between 1851 and 1855. There were also other private groups that sponsored emigration at this time, such as the Highland and Island Emigration Society and one organised by Caroline's old nemesis, John Dunmore Lang. Like Caroline's society, these were designed to transfer British subjects from the overcrowded Old World to the new, and none were totally successful or had longevity, for a variety of different reasons. Caroline's society at least appears to have been the longest lasting, and also set a completely new standard for shipboard travel for the steerage, or lowest-class, passengers. Just as importantly, many of Caroline's immigrants came to Australia to meet up with extended family members who had gone before them. It was a solid and highly successful family reunion plan that eventuated in many working- and middle-class groups putting down firm roots in the Antipodean colonies.

If, as a settlement programme, the Family Colonization Loan Society was moderately successful, in pecuniary terms it was a disaster, despite the generous injections of donated funds in 1852 and the fact that Caroline and Archibald both worked without pay. Some of the immigrants, particularly from the first ship, the *Slains Castle*, started, unasked, to make repayments, but they were ultimately in the minority. After arriving in Adelaide, Archibald, who was probably not cut out to be a debt collector, sought advice from the Advocate General; effectively, he was told that whether or not the contract between the society and the immigrants was enforceable in Australia was a moot point. More salient was the difficulty of finding defaulting immigrants, who had by and large slipped away into the interior of the colony. Many later arrivals headed straight out to the goldfields, their repayments to the society forgotten or ignored. Archibald apparently decided against legal action, and chose instead to remind immigrants of their responsibilities by advertising in the Adelaide newspapers.[29]

A few months later, at the end of October 1851, having established an immigration agent and local committee in Adelaide, Archibald moved to Melbourne to do the same. He discovered that, whilst some repayments had been made and almost £4000 collected from family members to bring relatives to Port Phillip, many thousands of pounds were still owed to the society by immigrants who had arrived on Caroline's boats. Once again, Archibald rejected legal action, in favour of making another appeal in the local newspapers, explaining that by not repaying loans the immigrants from the *Slains Castle* and the *Blundell* were denying others the same opportunity that they had been given:

> I only wish I could touch their hearts without wounding them. But I will not attribute the non-repayment of such loans to what, I am sorry to say, some ascribe it to. Some indeed have honourably fulfilled what was expected of them ... so I will lay the cause of the people not returning the loans to the excitement created by the gold discovery, the rush to the diggings ... forgetting in the feverish search for gold their obligations to the Society and their fellow men. Sure I am then they need not only to be told and assured, that mothers sigh here — children pine at home — ... to induce them to fulfil the very easy terms upon which they are asked and have agreed to refund the loans viz., "within two years from date of arrival, by eight equal quarterly payments." ... How gratifying it would be then ... if the immigrants who have received loans would but place the Society in a position to lend ... £5 or £6 each, and thus keep up a continued stream of emigration by family reunion ... If I press the repayment of the loans, believe me it is not on account of the party who may have originated

the plan ... [but on] ... the happiness and prosperity of
thousands of struggling people of near relatives ... deeply
interested in its success.[30]

This appeal was followed in *The Argus* with a heartfelt leader by
the newspaper's editors, calling on defaulters to make good their
promises of reimbursement of the loans made to them on such easy
terms and without which they could not have come to the colony:
"Ingratitude is a very detestable vice under any circumstances. But
it becomes double hateful when it bears the look of dishonesty ...
Every man who fails to refund his loan, keeps some other person
from coming out to the Colony; ... Surely, then it will not be
necessary to say another word on the subject."[31]

But it was. By November 1852, of the almost £3000 lent
to immigrants only £430 had been sent back to London.[32] By
1855 the immigration agent in Sydney would be saying that the
amounts collected were "too trifling to mention", with only £58
10s having been repaid in New South Wales by the end of that
year.[33] Ironically, when setting up the society, Caroline had posed
a question regarding the overall character of the British people,
particularly as it related to the loan repayments. She had written:
"It is a great moral problem yet to be solved, whether, with all our
religious, moral, social, and commercial advantages, we are rearing
rogues or honest men; if we are not doing the one, we are certainly
doing the other."[34] It seems that by 1855 she had her answer.

*

It would be some time before it became apparent in London that
funds from emigrating settlers were not flowing back to be reused
by the society. It is unlikely that Caroline was monitoring the

finances closely, particularly as her workload increased steadily. As well as preparing signed-up emigrants for their voyages, like a ravenous pied piper she was bent on feeding even more families into her vessels. The gold rush meant there was no lack of people wishing to migrate; what Caroline was intent on offering was a practical financial method to make that happen. From 1850 she organised and spoke at countless meetings and lectures to departing migrants, at gatherings in and around London, and then from 1852 she also took to the road, travelling as far afield as Birmingham, Liverpool, Northampton, Dublin, Glasgow and Edinburgh. Her talks were well attended, with reports of some two hundred people at one of her Northampton assemblies.

Everywhere she went the press followed. In Sydney, the newspaper editors had fallen into line behind her and now the same was happening in Britain; the London, Irish, Scottish and provincial newspapers gave her wide coverage. Caroline knew how to create controversy too, although she didn't always receive flattering reviews, which caused at least one spat between two newspapers in Scotland. *The John O'Groat Journal* attacked *The Edinburgh Advertiser*, complaining that "*The Edinburgh Advertiser,* in noticing the meeting, comments on the lady's personal appearance, says it is prepossessing, but has the bad taste to add, that 'it seems a little got up for effect.' Granting that it were so, which we are inclined to doubt, the labours of Mrs Chisholm for the benefit of society ... should have protected her from any paltry sneer."[35] The paper then went on to say that a committee under the auspices of the Lord Provost of Edinburgh had been set up to promote emigration from Edinburgh.

Like many a modern-day politician, Caroline may have organised her lectures to fit in with other business; in Glasgow, for example, apart from the town meeting, she toured a shipyard building a vessel to her personal specifications. In Edinburgh and Northampton, it is likely that she would have called upon Archibald's relatives and her own — she may even have decided to visit both towns because she knew that she would be offered free accommodation, no doubt an important saving. Although Caroline would not accept any direct personal payment, she did receive some of the fringe benefits of fame, for instance allowing railway companies to pay her travel costs as she journeyed across England, Ireland and Scotland.[36]

Caroline's lectures focused mainly on two issues: the workings of her society and what immigrants could expect from the Antipodes. She had visited both Hobart and Adelaide briefly, many years earlier, but she had never stepped foot in Victoria; her talks relied solely on her knowledge and personal experience of New South Wales. A few years later, she was to discover that whilst similar, the colonies were not facsimiles of each other. It was an assumption that was to cause her some consternation.

*

Two months after baby Sarah died in August 1850, Caroline had become pregnant again with her eighth and last child. Henrietta, known in the family by her second name, Monica, was born in July 1851, four months after Archibald set sail for South Australia — it would be another three years before he met his daughter. Monica was Caroline's fourth child in the six years since Archibald had returned from India to live with his wife. Apart from travelling to Australia to work for the society, his departure had the added benefit of being a failsafe birth control measure for Caroline. She was forty-two years old when he left. She would be forty-six when they met again and there would be no more pregnancies. Six of her eight children grew to adulthood, but they were not her main priority. In that, Dickens was right, but, unlike the fictional Mrs Jellyby, Caroline was no self-deceiver: she was aware of the effect her actions had upon her children, even to the extent of compromising their future prospects when finances were stretched.

By early 1851 both Caroline and Archibald were worried about money. Neither received any payment for the work they did for the society, and maintaining two households on opposite sides of the world only exacerbated the problem. Caroline had alluded to this in early August 1851, in a letter she wrote to *The Adelaide Observer* about Archibald's arrival there: "With our means, however, it would not be possible that this separation could continue for any length of time."[37] Now she had to make a decision on whether to continue her efforts on emigration or to support her sons' schooling.

When Archibald had left for Australia, he had stipulated that the three older boys were to remain at Sedgley Park School until the entire family set forth to join him. But the increasing monetary strain of the separation led Caroline to contravene those wishes. In April 1852, following two lectures in Birmingham, she visited her friend from Windsor days, Bishop William Ullathorne. Soon after, in a personal letter to the bishop, Caroline stated that she had not only been unwell, but was also so financially stressed that she had decided to withdraw the boys from the school.[38] She may have been feeling depressed after a recent illness and perhaps with Archibald away she desperately needed to communicate with a friend she felt she could trust. Even strong, confident people occasionally need a shoulder to help them through a tough period and, given Caroline's religious faith, it's not surprising that she turned to Bishop Ullathorne. She had known him for many years, he had always been one of her supporters and she no doubt felt that she could depend upon him and his advice. At the end of the note she mentions the burden of her work; it is one of the rare times when we see her let down her guard, her confidence slip.[39]

What made her decision to withdraw her sons from the school remarkable is that, knowing of her work with the emigrants and understanding her pecuniary difficulties, the church had offered to pay the difference between what she could afford and the actual fees for all three boys. Yet she rejected the offer. Caroline believed that the public would have greater confidence in her if she remained totally independent and to her that was paramount. Having taken the boys from school, she sent Henry, then aged thirteen, to Ireland and William, fifteen, to Rome (both boys were miserable — she probably collected Henry from Ireland in May 1852 whilst giving lectures there). Archibald Jnr, sixteen, she kept with her in London. Her letter to Bishop Ullathorne clearly reveals that she is willing to accept the collateral damage to her sons' futures, stating that "the following out of my vocation will I fear be a *lasting disadvantage* to them — and yet my Lord I dare not give up my work it hangs about me as a duty, and will not permit me to consider perhaps so much as I ought the sacrifices I am bringing upon others through their love, and obedience to me".[40]

Her attitude to her children remains one of the greatest mysteries of Caroline's character. Highly intelligent, dynamic, practical, humorous, articulate, sociable, attractive, a risk-taker, religious, charitable and caring — there are so many positive epithets to describe her, and yet it has to be acknowledged that she was, to a large extent, indifferent to her own children. One mitigating comment, however, comes from a direct descendant, Caroline's great-great-grandson, Professor Don Chisholm, who asserted during an interview in Sydney in 2016 that, despite everything, according to family lore, her children as adults maintained a close relationship with their mother, something they would not have done if they had felt neglected or disadvantaged or unloved.

*

On the other side of the world, Archibald was also concerned about their personal finances. Even so, he was still working for the society and, despite being unable to collect most of the monies owing, he had achieved some successes in Australia, such as establishing strong committees in both Melbourne and Adelaide that included churchmen, businessmen and members of the legislature. These men helped settlers send money home to bring out family members, checked conditions on ships arriving from Britain, attempted to ensure some care for new immigrants, and worked with Archibald to convince authorities to set up a reception centre in Melbourne. Archibald's commitment to and reasonable success in augmenting family reunions was probably the high point of his work for the society.

By mid-1852, however, he'd had enough. He sent a letter of resignation to the Melbourne committee. He was fifty-four years of age; he wasn't an old man, but he sounded tired: "The time has arrived when both Mrs Chisholm and myself may transfer our labours over to the joint Committees." He then went on to say that he was willing to continue in his honorary capacity until a replacement (who was to be paid) could be found, rejecting, however, any suggestion that he could continue himself, on a salary: "As Mrs Chisholm and myself have given our services ... gratuitously for so many years, I feel that ... our labours in this work should end in the same spirit in which it began, hoping that others, who have more leisure and means, will continue the operations of the Society, which we could not well do in justice to our children.'[41]

What is unusual in this letter, written in mid-1852, is that Archibald was tendering his resignation two years before Caroline joined him in Melbourne. She had initially expected to leave London in 1853, but was delayed mainly by the flood of emigrants needing assistance to reach the Victorian goldfields. Money was obviously foremost on Archibald's mind and the resignation could have coincided with the discovery that his three older sons had been withdrawn from Sedgley Park School. Maybe he hoped to conserve what he could to put towards their education in Australia. Whatever the case, his resignation was not accepted, as no suitable replacement could be found, so he continued his work almost until Caroline joined him in 1854.

In the meantime, Archibald was probably living a lonely and very restricted life on a pitiable income, using just a small part of his East India Company pension while sending the rest to Caroline and the children in London. He was paying thirty shillings a week for a small room in a boarding house. With the gold rush underway, it must have seemed that everyone was making money except him: anyone who wasn't at the goldfields was able to command a high wage whilst food and other commodities were expensive.[42] Although he had reached the rank of captain during his East India Company career, Archibald does not at this point appear to have been a dynamic leader of men or indeed a particularly adept organiser. From this distance, it is hard to be sure, yet the question of whether Caroline, in the same position, would not have had much more success in recouping the society's monies is inescapable. It seems likely that her talent, personable manner and acute ability to manoeuvre ordinary people as well as powerful officials, along with her undeniable determination, would have had far more impact than Archibald's more gentlemanly, lukewarm efforts.

*

By early 1852, Caroline had become one of the most recognised people, male or female, across the British Isles. As such, she had a part to play, a persona to maintain. Not only did she connect with the wealthy and powerful, her message was also aimed at the middle and lower classes, and they took note when she spoke. A portrait of Caroline, painted albeit by little known artist Angelo Collen Hayter, was hung in the Royal Academy in London; various likenesses and cartoons of her also appeared in such publications as *Punch* and *The Illustrated London News*; and *The Illustrated Magazine of Art* published a vivid description of Caroline following a meeting with her at her home in Islington:

> Most of our readers have doubtless seen many portraits of
> this lady ... Let them imagine a sedate, matronly lady, with
> eyes well set under a very capacious forehead — orbs that
> seem to "look you through" whilst addressing you — and
> withal a fascinating manner which at once seizes upon you,
> and induces you to prolong your stay ... We took our leave,
> convinced that we had seen by no means the least remarkable
> personage of these practical and wonder-working times.[43]

Caroline's determination to help her emigrants continued to reach into new and diverse fields. A pamphlet published in 1853, by Eneas Mackenzie, entitled *The Emigrant's Guide to Australia*, incorporated his *Memoir* of Caroline along with pronouncements from her on, amongst other issues, the culinary delights of the outback. The chapter on "Bush Cookery" came from an unpublished manuscript by Caroline and included a number of recipes: "The great art of bush-cookery consists in giving a variety out of salt beef and flour, minus mustard, pepper, and potatoes." After suggesting that both the meat and flour be divided into seven parts for the seven days of the week, Caroline provided a different technique for each day of the week: "*Tuesday* — Chop the meat very small; mix it with this day's flour, adding thereto a due portion of water; then form the whole into small dumplings, and put them in a frying-pan. This dish generally goes by the name of 'TROUT-DUMPLINGS'."[44]

Food was also a topic in a medical book published in 1853, at Caroline's request, by Jabez Hogg, a member of the Royal College of Surgeons of England. It was called *The Domestic Medical and Surgical Guide, for the Nursery, the Cottage, and the Bush* and may have been inspired by Caroline's friendship with Florence Nightingale. The dedication to Caroline reads in part: "To Caroline Chisholm who has reformed the system of colonial emigration, elevated the moral tone of a rising country, and indelibly written her name on the early historic page of Australia."[45] The tome is reasonably extensive, covering a variety of illnesses and diseases ranging from "stroke of heat" to "spitting blood" and "yellow fever"; it also explains the best way to build a bush shower, what constitutes various medicines and how to use them, how to stay well on a sea voyage, and how to maintain a healthy diet. Within the last category there is clear advice on who should consume what types of food: "*Broad and Windsor Beans* ought only to be eaten by those who have out-door exercise," and "*Chocolate* is very nourishing, but, on account of the oil which enters into its composition, it is difficult of digestion, and apt to disagree with delicate persons."[46] The book went into at least two editions.

Yet, despite the impressive patronage and backing Caroline had gained, she still had not won universal acclaim in Britain. Her detractors did not welcome her society or indeed her influence in government circles and amongst the liberal cognoscenti. Mutterings about her faith persisted, fuelled early on by John Dunmore Lang, who was in Britain until late 1849 and claimed once more, even before the society was underway, that Caroline was a tool of the Roman Catholic priesthood. Lang maintained in an open letter to Earl Grey that Caroline's motivation in wanting poor Irish girls to emigrate to Australia was "to supply Roman Catholic wives for the English and Scotch Protestants of the humbler classes in Australia, and thereby to Romanize the Australian colonies through the artful and thoroughly Jesuitical device of mixed marriages".[47] He insisted that even government migration schemes were ignoring the poor Protestant girls of England and Scotland, because the relevant ministers of state had paid too much attention to Caroline's suggestions on emigration: "I am well aware … your Lordship and the Lord-Lieutenant of Ireland were merely the dupes of an artful female Jesuit, the able but concealed agent of the Romish priesthood in Australia, who had thus adroitly managed to attach both your Lordships … to her apron string."[48]

Official figures tell another story altogether. There was a small but significant decline in the percentage of both major religions in Australia between 1851 and 1856. What makes it particularly interesting is that the drop, albeit minor, came at a time of massive population growth in the colony. The 1851 census shows that 30.4 per cent of the population was Roman Catholic, but that had dropped to 29.9 per cent by 1856. Similarly, in 1851, members of the Church of England made up 49.7 per cent of the population, but that receded slightly to 49.4 per cent in 1856.

In both cases, there were marginal increases of Presbyterians, Wesleyans, Jewish people and "Mahomedans, Pagans, and all other Persuasions", suggesting that the first inkling of multiculturalism was finally seeping through the barriers built by the original white invaders.[49] Whether the British Government was aware of these figures or not, the Colonial Secretary ignored Lang's concerns.

*

As 1853 dawned, Caroline was ready to rejoin Archibald in Australia. First, though, she had to collect her son William from Rome. She left London for Paris in the northern spring of that year. To Caroline, Europe was just another conglomerate of countries where the underprivileged and middle class were awaiting her message. Crossing the Continent, from France through Germany then south through Italy to the Vatican City, she made the most of her opportunities by holding lecture meetings along the way, and attracted large audiences. She spoke good French, though it is not known if she could converse in German; however, German immigrants had been settling in South Australia since 1838 and from 1850 until 1914 were the largest non-British or non-Irish group of European settlers in Australia. Moreover, gold fever had crossed the Channel and there was widespread interest in emigration to the Antipodean El Dorado. A few years later Caroline explained, almost with a certain amount of smugness, that "she had some difficulty in getting her name put into the papers [in France], but when it became known that she was in the country, numbers flocked to her to get her advice about emigration. She asked one of them why they wished to travel 16,000 miles when they were so fond of the Emperor [Napoleon

III], and the reply was — very good to fight under, but very bad to farm under."[50] There is no evidence that Caroline had any direct effect on emigration to Australia from Europe, but her single-minded determination and her unwavering belief in her ability to influence people remained her hallmarks.

About two months after leaving London, Caroline arrived in Rome. Sixteen-year-old William was enrolled as a second-year seminarian at Propaganda College, in training to be a missionary, but he had apparently been unwell and deemed unfit to continue his studies. Whilst in Rome, Caroline obtained an audience with Pope Pius IX. Although the small anteroom in the Vatican was filled with women, Caroline was the third person introduced. As she was about to make the usual obeisance on being presented, the Pope rose from his chair and took her arm: "Caroline Chisholm. Eccellentissima! [Che] perseveranza! Bravo!" — "Most excellent lady! Such perseverance! Well done!" — he said, while clapping his hands to demonstrate his approval of her work. "He told her that the plough was good for the country, good for men, women and children, and recommended her to persevere in her efforts to introduce agriculture into Australia. He said that railroads were missionaries of commerce and civilisation, but the most necessary thing was the plough should prosper."[51] The Pope then presented her with two mementos: a twenty-four-and-a-half-centimetre alabaster bust of herself and a gold medal. It is not known who made the Pope aware of her work, possibly her friend Bishop Ullathorne or, more likely, Cardinal Fransoni, who was in charge of Propaganda College and in regular contact with Caroline about William. The bust remained with the family until it was recently lent by Caroline's great-great-grandson, Professor Don Chisholm, to the Australian Catholic University in Sydney for permanent display, but the gold medal is missing, pawned in

Sydney in the late 1850s when Caroline and Archibald were in desperate need of funds.

Caroline and William returned to London in August 1853, to discover that news of her pending departure to Melbourne had spread throughout the city. In her absence, a testimonial had been held to raise funds to thank her and support her voyage back to Australia. Those behind the testimonial had held a meeting at the London Tavern, and the list of attendees was impressive, including Sidney Herbert and his wife, Elizabeth, and other parliamentarians, such as the Member for Northamptonshire, Robert Vernon, and Robert Lowe who, after being a member of the New South Wales Legislative Council for many years, had become leader writer of *The Times* newspaper before entering the House of Commons. Also there were the Governor of the Bank of England, Mr J.G. Hubbard, and various clergy. The subscription list included colonials, notably William Charles Wentworth; nobles such as Viscount Canning; and wealthy Jewish families, including the Montefiore and Rothschild families, whilst Florence Nightingale was amongst other friends and humanitarians who also contributed. The pounds came in from the well to do, the shillings from the ordinary people.

Punch magazine made its own contribution, a "carol" commemorating Caroline's work:

A Carol on Caroline Chisholm

Come, all you British females of wealth and high degree,
Bestowing all your charity on lands beyond the sea,
I'll point you out a pattern which a better plan will teach
Than that of sending Missioners to Tombuctoo to preach
Converting of the Heathen's a very proper view,
By preaching true religion to Pagan and to Jew,

And bringing over Cannibals to Christian meat and bread,
Unless they catch your Parson first and eat him up instead.
But what's more edifying to see, a pretty deal,
Is hearty British labourers partaking of a meal,
With wives, and lots of children, about their knees that climb,
And having tucked their platefuls in, get helped another time.
Beyond the roaring ocean; beneath the soil we tread,
Your're English men and Women, well housed and clothed and fed,
Who but for help and guidance to leave our crowded shores,
Would now be stealing, begging, or lie starving at our doors.
Who taught them self-reliance, and stirred them to combine,
And club their means together, to get across the brine,
Instead of strikes, and mischief, and breaking of the law,

This cartoon of Caroline appeared above the "carol" published in *Punch* in 1853.
(*Alamy*)

And wasting time in hearing incendiaries jaw?
Who led their expeditions? And under whose command
Through dangers and through hardships sought they the promised
    land?
A second Moses, surely, it was who did it all,
It was a second Moses in bonnet and in shawl.
By means of one good lady were all these wonders wrought,
By CAROLINE CHISHOLM'S energy, benevolence, and
    thought,
Instead of making here and there a convert of a Turk,
She has made idle multitudes turn fruitfully to work.
The ragged pauper crawling towards a parish grave
She roused — directed to a home beyond the western wave;
She smoothed his weary passage across the troubled deep,
With food, and air, and decencies of ship-room and of sleep.
There's many a wife and mother will bless that lady's name,
Embracing a fat infant — who might else have drowned the same,
A mother, yet no wife, compelled by poverty to sin,
And die in gaol or hospital of misery and gin.
The REVEREND EBENEZER I'd not deny his dues,
For saving Patagonians, and Bosjesmen, and Zooloos;
But MRS CHISHOLM'S mission is what I far prefer;
for saving British natives I'd give the palm to her.

And now that a subscription is opened and begun,
In order to acknowledge the good that she has done
Among the sort of natives — the most important tribe —
Come down like handsome people, and handsomely subscribe.[52]

And they did. In all, between £800 and £900 was collected
and given to Caroline. This time she was willing to accept the

money. When she had left New South Wales she had been given an expensive gift rather than coinage, but now it seems that she needed the cash — she may even have found it difficult to return to Australia without pecuniary assistance. Her four months' travelling in Europe would have been expensive and she would have still had to pay rent on the house in Islington and possibly pay a servant to help Sarah Laws look after the five children there. Then, too, the fares for herself and her children to Melbourne would have been costly. The Crimean War was underway and the government had begun commandeering vessels as troop ships, resulting in far fewer boats being available to make the Antipodean run and, in turn, inflated ticket prices. Caroline and her family were booked on the *Ballarat*. For her half cabin of 2.1 metres by 2.1 metres plus rations, Caroline paid £100. Tickets for the four boys — Archibald Jnr (now eighteen years of age), William (seventeen) Henry (fifteen) and Sydney (seven) — cost £40 each for second-class accommodation, taking meals with Caroline, whilst tickets for the girls — Caroline (six) and Monica (three) — cost £21 apiece.[53]

When the *Ballarat* sailed for Melbourne on 14 April 1854, it was just short of eight years since Caroline, Archibald and their four sons had arrived in Hull. The intervening period had not just added two (living) daughters to the family and enlarged Caroline's girth, it had also proved what was possible with aspiration and determination. Only a few weeks before her forty-sixth birthday, Caroline stood in rarefied seclusion atop an extraordinary summit. Britain, midway through the Victorian era, was settling into its glorious years as the world's pre-eminent empire, and boasting that the sun would never set on its flag. Caroline stood out against its conformity. A woman of humble beginnings, married to an unremarkable soldier, had without guile or guilt, pervaded the nation's consciousness. She had used the most modern technology of her time to do it, the train, the newspapers and the telegraph carrying her ideas to the north, south, east and west of the kingdom. Now she was leaving on her own terms.

It was a challenging time for her campaigns. At least two of the Family Colonization Loan Society's boats, the *Robert Lowe* and the *Caroline Chisholm,* both kitted out according to Caroline's specifications, had been requisitioned by the British Navy as troop carriers, and the chairman of the society, Sidney Herbert, was now Secretary of State for War, and therefore more concerned with the conflict and Florence Nightingale's nurses than Caroline's emigrants. Nevertheless, Caroline's departure was reported across the country, particularly in London, in such papers as *The Times* and *The Illustrated London News*, which devoted three-quarters of a page, including an illustration, to her farewell. Some twelve years later, Caroline and Archibald would slip back into London with virtually no one aware of their return. Before then, however, there were the Victorian goldfields to tame.

CHAPTER 13

A Golden Land

1854–58

En route to the Victorian goldfields, October 1854

She inhaled deeply, filling her lungs with air and savouring the pungent scent of the eucalypts, freed by the heavy downpour just passed. "Can you smell that?" she asked the young man next to her in the dray, having mopped her eyes and forehead with a plain piece of linen. "It is the aroma, the essence of the Australian bush that I have kept in my heart all those years at home … Home?" She questioned herself now as though the inconstancy of her soul had only just occurred to her. "I no longer know what I should call home." She pondered a moment then inhaled again. "Yes, this is how I remember it. Do you?" she asked the boy again.

Her son beside her shook his head, damp brown curls swaying beneath his dark brown hat. "No, Mama," said Archibald Jnr, "but there is something familiar in all this," his arm arcing towards the bush beyond the dray.

The driver, seated in front of them, lashed the reins with more show than effect, whooping for the horses to giddy-up. Turning a grizzled face to Caroline, he addressed her with little deference. "We'd best look for a camp in the next few miles," he said, "before we reach the Black Forest, otherwise we might get stuck for the night. The mud'll be up and there be wombat holes as big as wheels, an' worse. They say Mad Dan Morgan is back this-a-way again, too."

There was a wicked glint in the driver's eye that Caroline disliked. She wouldn't be held captive to fear. She looked to the sky: the rain may not have passed, but there were still a good few hours of daylight left. She said they should go on.

The driver gave a derisive snort. "As yer wish."

"Are you sure, Mama?" asked Archibald. "Papa said that I was to keep you safe."

"We keep going," said Caroline.

The heavens darkened. To the east, a crack of lightning was followed by thunder. They smelt the storm before it hit with fury, but it didn't last long. A pale rainbow hung upon the moist sunshine, the heat rose again. Eventually the dray plodded into the grey-green shade of the Black Forest to be met by a raucous avian cacophony of cawing and screeching. Much to Caroline's chagrin, she realised that the driver had been right. In dry weather, the track, with its holes, tree roots and narrow bends crisscrossing in all directions, would have been treacherous enough, but the heavy rain had created a river of mud that was all but impassable. They would have to walk.

Leading the horses and dray, the disgruntled driver pushed through a small opening in the vegetation to a patch of higher ground and claimed it for their camp site. No one argued. As they settled onto the grassy verge, they missed, at first, the figure crouching in the shadows next to a fallen tree. "Hello there, where you be travelling?" asked a thin voice.

The driver let forth an oath, swung round looking for his gun, but Caroline had the man's measure.

"I am Mrs Chisholm, with my son Archibald," she said. "We are heading for Bendigo. You seem unwell. Can we help you?" she asked.

"Wrong way. 'Tis a pity," he said trying to stand, lurching forward and all but collapsing at their feet.

Whilst the driver built a smoky fire, Caroline sat the man down and had his story from him. Not much older than her son, he had been at the diggings for the past five months but had found little there apart from dysentery and loneliness. He'd dug up only a few pounds of gold, not enough to live on once he'd paid for his licence and food. Others did well, he said; maybe he just wasn't cut out to be a digger. He'd sold everything, even his tent, and now had only 1s 9d left in his purse, so he was heading back to town to find a job before he starved.

"Have you no family here?" asked Caroline.

"No, I came out alone," he said, "to make my fortune." She sat him next to the fire, put a dry blanket around his shoulders and gave him tea and damper to eat. Exhausted, he fell into a heavy slumber almost as soon as he had finished the best meal he'd eaten in days.

A little while later, crawling under the dray to sleep on the sodden earth, Caroline winced as she manoeuvred herself onto a blanket with a shawl for a pillow. It had been almost a decade, she thought, since she had last slept so rough, and she was not as supple as she had been then.

Morning brought bright sunshine and the cheerful birds' chorus. Whilst he ate more tea and damper, Caroline asked her new acquaintance about the goldfields. Wouldn't the government be wise to help the diggers secure land for their long-term livelihood, she asked.

He disagreed. "I didn't come out here to farm. I'm town bred. I came to find gold. Trouble is," he said draining his mug of tea and holding it out for a refill, "they don't give us a go. They charge us £1 to work a claim … that's £1 each month whether we find gold or not. Mark my word, there'll be trouble soon." He stopped, a little rueful. "I'm sorry, ma'am. You've been kind to me. I shouldn't be carrying on to you."

He dragged himself to his feet. "Thank you, Mrs Chisholm, and to your son too, for all your kindness." He nodded to Archibald. "I hope all goes well for you at the diggings." Handing back the blanket, he bade them farewell, "I should head off now, I still have a long walk ahead."

Cautiously he limped away, picking his path through the muddy track.

They struck camp and Caroline climbed back into the dray. There was little talk as the horses dragged them mile over weary mile. The road hardly improved, but at least it was visible in the sunlight, and beginning to harden again. Every now and then they passed a farmhouse or a hamlet with a few log buildings and a pub, or a cart coming in the other direction.

It was early afternoon the following day when they descended, finally, towards Bendigo Creek. Spread out before them was a startling ugliness. It was as though a giant miscreant, an enemy of nature, had ripped the vegetation — trees, grass, scrub, all of it — from the slopes either side of the struggling rivulet, leaving a barren, ulcerated landscape. Hundreds of men pounded the lifeless ground, desperate for a Midas incarnation.

Slowly Caroline's party made their way down, stopping occasionally to ask the way to the Gold Commissioner's lodging, where they had been promised accommodation. The sounds of the bush receded and were replaced by the rattle of the miners' cradle, the crunching and scraping of the shovel and the thud of pick hitting sand and rock. The miners they passed hardly raised an eye from their labour, let alone evinced any interest in their progress.

As they advanced, an international tent city spread out before them across the valley, with flags proclaiming allegiances to Great Britain, nations of Europe, and America. The larger tents run by shopkeepers were selling everything from ladies' stays to grog; off to the side, shunned by the rest of the miners, was the Oriental camp. The commissioner's man welcomed Caroline and offered her what passed for a room in a rough-built cabin. Archibald, uncomplaining, acted as his mother's aide de camp, whilst Caroline at once began questioning the diggers. Some had heard of her, some had even travelled in her boats; others had no idea who she was and a few thought her questions impertinent. None of them wished to give *details, saying there were already too many of them and they wanted to keep others from invading the diggings.*

Two days she spent in Bendigo. She talked land and homely comforts, the reunion of wives and children; the men talked of gold, anger at the government, licences and suffrage. She had an idea for sheds to accommodate poor travellers to the fields. They shrugged: it could be useful but wasn't essential. It would help bring family to the diggings, she said. The men were ambivalent. If she wanted to help, they said, could she keep the Chinese away? That made her angry.

The diggers went back to work. Caroline went back to Melbourne.[1]

With Caroline's return to Australia in the winter of 1854, her celebrity began to fade. The day she arrived in July that year, she was proclaimed in the press as "Our Benefactress" and a large gathering of people initially turned out to welcome her off the steamer that brought her ashore from the *Ballarat*. In what could have been a harbinger of her influence in the colony, however, there was a delay of some hours and many people left. In the end, it was a smaller, albeit vocal, crowd that cheered her onto dry land.[2]

For all her experiences of Sydney and New South Wales, this was the first time that Caroline had visited Victoria. When she arrived, white settlement in Melbourne was less than twenty years old, having been founded by John Batman in 1835. Just as importantly, the newest graduate of the Antipodean colonies had gained its individual status just three years earlier in 1851 and was behaving with all the brashness of a teenager finally let off the parental leash. As in the early days of Caroline's sojourn in New South Wales, there had been a massive population influx: in 1841 the non-Indigenous population of what was to become Victoria was less than 12,000 people; by 1854, just thirteen years later, that had grown to 237,000, or, put another way, had increased by more than 2000 per cent.[3] Of course, not all the people flooding into Victoria were from overseas; thousands also came from across Bass Strait, the Tasman Sea and the Great Australian Bight or overland from New South Wales.

The reason, of course, was gold. The same day *The Argus* welcomed Caroline it also reported news from Ballarat of a group of Germans digging up £2000 worth of gold. The early years of the gold rush saw a booming economy in Victoria, but as the numbers of diggers increased and the easily accessible gold began to run out, unemployment grew, particularly in Melbourne. There was a dip in the economy, although it was not all doom and gloom — the bigger population led to a building boom as the city expanded, tradesmen were in demand and their wages were high.

Just as the main reason for the migration to the two colonies of New South Wales and Victoria was different, so too were the immigrants. A decade earlier, when Britain's paupers were given free bounty passage to Sydney, they came for a lifetime, seeking at least a living wage and perhaps, ultimately, their own plot of land. A large proportion of those arriving in Melbourne in the early 1850s, on the other hand, were opportunists, intent on finding the quickest route to riches via the goldfields. Inevitably, most would settle in the colonies, but from the beginning they were more focused on making money and were bolder when dealing with authority. As some investment was necessary to travel to the fields and start digging there, many in this new generation of international immigrants were middle class, slightly better off financially and more educated. Amongst the many labourers and farmers there were clerks, accountants and engineers. In effect, they were far more capable of looking after themselves.

Similarly, the typical response to their surroundings of those just landed in Port Phillip Bay was far less romantic than that of the New South Wales immigrants; instead of a eulogy about the beauty of Sydney Harbour they were more likely to write an unflattering description of the Yarra, as with this visitor, describing her journey from the port to Melbourne in 1852:

And now the cry of "Here's the bus" ... I had hoped ...
to gladden my eyes with the sight of something civilized.
Alas, for my disappointment! There stood a long, tumble-
to-pieces-looking waggon, not covered in, with a plank
down each side to sit upon, and a miserable narrow plank it
was. Into this vehicle were crammed a dozen people and an
innumerable host of portmanteaus, large and small, carpet-
bags, baskets, brown-paper parcels, bird-cage and inmate,
&c., all of which, as is generally the case, were packed in a
manner the most calculated to contribute the largest amount
of inconvenience to the live portion of the cargo. And
to drag this grand affair into Melbourne were harnessed
thereto the most wretched looking objects in the shape of
horses that I had ever beheld. A slight roll tells us we are
off. "And is this the beautiful scenery of Australia?" was my
first melancholy reflection. Mud and swamp — swamp and
mud — relieved here and there by some few trees which
looked as starved and miserable as ourselves. The cattle we
passed appeared in a wretched condition, and the human
beings on the road seemed all to belong to one family, so
truly Vandemonian[4] was the cast of their countenances ...
On we went towards Melbourne — now stopping for the

unhappy horses to take breath — then ... arriving at a small
specimen of a swamp; ... "The Yarra," said the conductor. I
looked straight ahead, and innocently asked "Where?" for I
could only discover a tract of marsh or swamp, which I fancy
must have resembled the fens of Lincolnshire, as they were
some years ago, before draining was introduced into that
county. Over Princes Bridge we now passed, up Swanston
Street, then into Great Bourke Street, and now we stand
opposite the Post-office.[5]

Caroline arrived in a Melbourne that was thriving on the wealth
only recently dug from the soil. Apart from streets of shops, there
were schools, churches, libraries and even art galleries being built.
Australia's first telegraph line had been erected between Melbourne
and Williamstown the year before and the first passenger railway
was about to start operating between Port Melbourne (then
called Sandridge) and Melbourne's Flinders Street Station. The
University of Melbourne would open the next year. The city had
an immigration reception centre (which Archibald had helped
establish) and there was also an extensive tent city south of the
Yarra called Canvas Town. Residents there paid a rent of five
shillings per tent per week; the shelters were set out in rows
to form streets which, it was believed, were better signposted
than the thoroughfares in town. Whilst there was undoubtedly
unemployment and poverty in Melbourne, by 1854 it was not on
the same scale that had so distressed Caroline in Sydney in the
early 1840s, and possibly it was better managed. Her first action
on arriving was to ensure that the immigrants that had landed
with her off the *Ballarat* could be lodged at the Government
Immigration Barracks. Unlike the old days in Sydney, though,
there was no need for her to hunt up jobs for them — indeed, it

was a measure of the ebullient state of the economy, or the lure of the goldfields, that within a week and a half all had moved out of the barracks.[6]

Caroline's interest in the Family Colonization Loan Society seems to have washed away on the voyage to Melbourne. A few days after her arrival, she did write an open letter to *The Argus* newspaper asking immigrants to repay money they owed the society; however, there is little evidence of her ongoing interest in the society after that time.[7] About eight months before she arrived in Melbourne, Archibald had finally found a replacement to take over his role as secretary of the society and had left to start a business. Following his and Caroline's exit from the London committee, and with fewer of the society's boats arriving in Port Phillip Bay, the Melbourne committee eventually petered out. Although she was still interested in immigration, Caroline began championing a new cause: the need to make land available to new settlers — land that in Victoria was comprehensively tied up by the squattocracy.

At the start of her residence in Melbourne, Caroline assumed that she would be fêted in the way that she had become accustomed to during the past fourteen or fifteen years in Sydney and London. That expectation was fuelled about six weeks after her arrival by a large public soirée held to officially welcome her to the southern capital. Although only tea and cakes were served, it was a substantial affair, with the mayor along with leading politicians such as Dr Palmer, the Speaker of the Legislative Council, and senior clergy attending. An orchestra and a renowned songstress, Mrs Tostar, performed twice before the start of several speeches, the longest, according to the newspapers, being made by Caroline herself. She had no qualms about accepting admiration for her work or acknowledgement of the good that she had done. As reported in *The Argus*, she began by saying that it was pleasant to receive accolades: "Many gentlemen, if they were in her place that evening, would say that they were quite over-whelmed, and that they were utterly undeserving of these praises. For her part, she would say that she deserved about half the ratio that had been uttered in her favour. (Cheers and laughter.) She would rather that they charged her with egotism than that she should mislead them."[8] They were the words of an exceptionally confident woman who had grown not only to expect the tributes but who also recognised her own contribution to society. She was, maybe, sounding more like a politician of the twenty-first century than a philanthropist of the nineteenth. Even 160 years later few charity workers, male or female, would be quite so bombastic about their achievements.

In one final grand public gesture towards Caroline, led by both the local newspapers and the remaining members of her society's Melbourne committee, it was suggested that another testimonial be presented to Caroline, particularly as it was known that she and Archibald were far from wealthy. More than one newspaper editorial submitted that without financial distractions Caroline would be much more able to continue her humanitarian efforts.[9] (Initially, there was also acclaim for what Archibald had done in Australia for the Family Colonization Loan Society and the family reunions of poorer immigrants; his name was mentioned once in the articles but then slipped from notice.) It was decided that a substantial cash amount should be gathered for Caroline, from both government and private sources. After four divisions in the Legislative Council, a vote was carried by a majority of twenty to three to award Caroline a gratuity of £5000, conditional on private subscriptions raising another £2500. The gift was to be made the following year, in 1855.[10]

The money was most welcome. After years of working for little or no pay, and with only Archibald's East India Company pension to support them and their six growing children, the Chisholms were broke. Following his resignation from the society, Archibald had tried to bolster the family's fortunes by opening a warehouse called Chisholm & Sons, off Flinders Lane East. Its business was to provision the stores on the goldfields. The family lived on Flinders Lane too.[11] Archibald's business skills, however, were questionable. He would have had little experience in running a going concern, and years of working altruistically, allied with his more reticent personality, could hardly have stood him in good stead for the cut and thrust of a commercial enterprise. So, despite the warehouse, the family's finances desperately needed an injection of funds.

Setting aside her previous reticence regarding financial assistance, Caroline asked the testimonial committee for an advance on what they were intending to collect on her behalf. They gave her a "small sum of money to put them in a position of earning their livelihood".[12] This allowed Chisholm & Sons to open a retail shop on the northern end of Elizabeth Street, a better location for picking up passing trade, particularly diggers on their way to the goldfields.[13] The family moved there as well. It must have been incredibly difficult for a proud woman like Caroline to go cap in hand for money, even though she, and most others, were well aware that what she was asking for was only a soupçon of the amount that she and Archibald had expended over the years on their charitable endeavours. Indeed, *The Argus* newspaper pointed out that the Chisholms were now poorer than many of the immigrants that they had helped in the past. Apart from the advance, there was no reporting of the balance of the testimonial, either private or government, being presented to

Caroline, but it is likely that she did receive it, as the Chisholms later had money to start another business. By then, though, stories of rebellion and conflict on the goldfields were dominating the news, to the exclusion of many other events.

*

In the spring of 1854, just three months after she had arrived in Melbourne, Caroline took to the road again. She may have felt that because of the generous testimonial already given, and the promise of more to come, she should advance some new cause for the colony in addition to her campaign to free up land. Alternatively, she may have been reacting to targeted criticism from the writer William Howitt, who claimed that she was ignorant of the conditions in Victoria and had therefore, whilst living in Britain, deceived would-be immigrants into believing that the colony was some sort of pauper's paradise. Howitt, another contemporary of Dickens, had arrived in Melbourne with his two sons on the same boat, the *Kent,* as Richard Horne, in 1852.[14] In his published letter from Bendigo in April 1854, he was scathing about the deception that he claimed Caroline had practised upon susceptible British workers. He described her lectures promoting emigration to Victoria as "most mischievous, because totally untrue ... Had these people come out with a fair statement of the truth of things, nine-tenths of them would have succeeded. It was the fallacious picture which disgusted them."[15] Howitt agreed that there were some good wages to be had for the right workmen, but he insisted that that advantage was outweighed by the three great evils that Caroline's ignorance had hidden: the inability to buy small landholdings for farmers, the ruggedness of travel to and from the goldfields and on the diggings themselves, and the excess of drunkenness throughout the colony. Possibly even more wounding was his attack on Archibald: why, asked Howitt, when he had been resident in Victoria for so many years, had he not informed his wife as to its true nature?[16]

Nor was Howitt's the only criticism. A speaker at a large meeting of jobless immigrants in Melbourne in November 1854 claimed that unemployment was rife, that most could not find work within the first six weeks of arriving, and that, however benevolent a person she might be, Caroline had injured the colony: "Those who advised persons to come here inflicted a serious evil if they did not advise them also to bring six months' provision with them."[17] Acting in accordance with his constituents' views, the Member of the Legislative Council who had spoken in favour of these workers at public rallies was J.P. Fawkner, one of the three members who had voted against the public testimonial to Caroline.

Caroline had always been quick to respond to criticism in the past. This time she ignored the attacks. But maybe concerned that she had, indeed, been responsible for misleading information, she paid a flying visit to the goldfields in late October and early November 1854. Leaving Archibald in Melbourne to run the business with William and Henry, along with a young Irish widow, Mrs Ann Gately Clinton, to look after the children, Caroline departed with her eldest son, eighteen-year-old Archibald Jnr.[18] A pair of horses were offered to her for the journey, but she paid for the dray and driver herself; some of her accommodation was at the Gold Commissioner's expense, and elsewhere locals assisted her with lodgings. She later claimed that by paying her way she remained independent and would otherwise be considered a "servant of the state".[19] The moot point, obviously, was that without the money she received as a testimonial, she would have been unable to go.

The trip took her through the treacherous Black Forest to the diggings at Bendigo, some 150 kilometres northwest of Melbourne. In the short time that she was absent she also visited Kyneton, a prosperous town on the way to the goldfields, and diggings at Castlemaine, Forest Creek and Simson's (near present-day Maryborough). Unlike the settlers of New South Wales, the diggers were not interested in long-term goals so much as their immediate problems on the goldfields, including the cost of licences and finding the increasingly elusive pay dirt. Caroline never fully appreciated what was important to the diggers, as opposed to what she thought they needed to be successful citizens of the colony.

Returning to Melbourne, Caroline held a public meeting to address two of "the three great evils" Howitt had accused her of perpetuating. (The one she didn't mention was the drunkenness of the diggers, but by then Chisholm & Sons was advertising and selling both wine and spirits, so she may have felt it was a ticklish subject.) Discussing the rough conditions travelling to and from and in the goldfields, she asserted, "I have always told people coming to this colony they would have to rough it, and I think it is rougher now than it was."[20] This issue was one that she was to address with some success within twelve months. Regarding the lack of available land, she castigated the government and set out a plan: "The great grievance of the diggers is that they cannot get the land ... This ... requires to be immediately remedied. *(Renewed applause.)* ... I want to see the lands unlocked ... The energy and activity of the people is beyond anything ... If the land in the neighbourhood of Simson's diggings were sold in garden allotments, and in farms of a hundred acres, we should soon have a fine body of yeomanry in the district." She went on: "I never could — I never would have recommended any man to come to this country if I did not think this possible, and that it would be done soon."[21]

William Howitt was delighted when he heard that she had visited the goldfields and even more so that she had admitted her fault. He described it as "the honest and noble confession of an heroic nature".[22] He did not, however, comment on Caroline's claim that the diggers were mostly intelligent men who would do so much better farming than rushing around from one digging to the next, or her statement that the diggers "enter their blankets at night, more like dogs than men".[23] Clearly she thought the steadiness of a home and farm far preferable to the adventure of living rough and taking a chance on the future.

At the meeting in Melbourne, Caroline spoke at length and with energy. Her investigations, however, had been vastly inferior to the ones she had conducted in New South Wales almost a decade earlier. There she had spent the better part of four years travelling across the colony, meeting and talking to hundreds if not thousands of men and women about the minutiae of their lives, their living conditions and their ambitions. In forensic detail, she had compiled evidence of what was good, what was bad, what was necessary and what needed altering to improve their circumstances. Without doubt, through her own hard work, she made herself an expert on the subject. By contrast, this time she had spent only a few days moving from one goldfield to another and into the local towns, certainly talking to whomever she met, but without engaging at the detailed level of her earlier ventures. On such a shallow examination, she could not have understood the nature of the goldfields or the diggers as she professed to do, nor should she have offered professional opinions as she had in the past. Maybe she could not see past her own view that all immigrants would inevitably require farmland, maybe she did not see the difference between Victoria in the 1850s and New South Wales in the 1840s, or maybe she was no longer really interested — after so many years she may simply have been tired and in need of a rest from her work. Whatever the case, Caroline totally missed the burning issue that was about to bring revolution and death to the goldfields.

During her Melbourne speech she mentioned land nine times, but licences only twice, and then only in relation to the cost of land. Almost as an afterthought, and only at the end of her hour-long talk did she make a glancing, almost out of context, though very positive, reference to male suffrage, saying, "The diggers are an orderly class, and if universal suffrage should be adopted anywhere in the world, it is here."[24] That comment, though, was sandwiched between her constant references to the land question.

The availability of land was a concern for the diggers, but nowhere near as burning an issue as the cost and injustice of the mining licences. Across Victoria, diggers paid £1 each month for a gold licence that entitled them to work a plot of earth measuring 3.6 square metres. Many miners lost most of one day of each month queuing at the Gold Commission's headquarters to buy the certificate. The diggers felt the cost of the licence was exorbitant, and their anger was fuelled by agitators who derided it as a tax and asserted that there should be no payment without a say in government. Opposition to the levy dated back to 1851, almost immediately after the licence had first been imposed. By 1853, growing unrest resulted in the Red Ribbon Agitation in Bendigo, when more than twenty thousand miners signed an anti-licence petition. By 1854, in the months leading up to Caroline's visit to the goldfields, the issue had become red raw. *The Bendigo Advertiser* alluded to the disquiet when reporting Caroline and Archibald Jnr's trip: "Mrs Chisholm herself is, no doubt, undecided as to what steps she will take in the direction of the diggings, as, from their unsettled character, they are scarcely all that she could desire for her protégé."[25]

It is simply stunning that Caroline could have lived in Melbourne in the spring of 1854, visited diggings and gold towns, attended receptions and spoken to diggers and the press, and not have been aware of the intense fury that was only a few weeks from exploding. It seems that she simply ignored it. That was strangely unlike her. Until this point, Caroline's success derived partly from her ability to always have her finger on the pulse of events and then exploit that insight to achieve her goals. The impenetrable bubble in which she appears to have encased herself at this time, and her seeming and unusual lack of empathy for the underdog, suggest that she either thought she understood more than the locals, had lost any real interest in the difficulties of the immigrants at the diggings, or was simply too tired or too unwell to be seriously bothered with the issue.

Events on the goldfields came to a head in November. On the day when *The Argus* reported on Caroline's public lecture in Melbourne, 11 November 1854, some ten thousand miners gathered at Bakery Hill, opposite the government encampment, to create the Ballarat Reform League. It demanded the end of the licences and full adult male suffrage by secret ballot. These demands were not dissimilar to those of the English Chartist Movement, which had been effectually cauterised in 1848. The former Chartists and radicals leading the miners' movement came from disparate backgrounds across the British Isles, America and Europe but, despite any differences in nationality, religion or class, they had found common purpose in the Antipodean goldfields. By the end of the month, at the Gold Commissioner's request, reinforcements of both troopers and police had been sent from

Melbourne, and the miners had elected a more militant leader, Peter Lalor, who had arrived in the colony just two years earlier aboard the *Scindian,* one of Caroline's society's boats. He ordered a stockade to be built on the Eureka lead-mining site and had armed men swear allegiance to a blue flag bearing the white stars of the Southern Cross constellation, which was said to have been designed by a Canadian miner, Henry Ross. It became known as the Eureka Flag.

At about three o'clock on the morning of Sunday, 3 December, almost three hundred soldiers and police marched towards the stockade, outnumbering the miners by about two to one. No one is certain who fired first, but the result was brief and brutal. At the end of the one-sided battle that lasted little more than ten minutes, at least twenty-two miners were dead, along with six police. Peter Lalor escaped, although his arm was later amputated as a result of his injuries. Of the 120 miners detained, thirteen were brought to trial in Melbourne. All were acquitted. The Ballarat Gold Commissioner was removed from his post, to be quietly reassigned to an insignificant position elsewhere in Victoria.

The resulting inquiry and report led to a number of changes, most of which the miners had demanded, including the abolition of gold licences, to be replaced by an annual certificate and a tax levied on the value of the gold they collected. Even more significantly, by November 1857, full suffrage, with a secret ballot for every white male over the age of twenty-one, had been legislated. As had another, far from admirable, demand by the miners: the introduction of restrictions on Chinese immigration, an early herald of the abhorrent White Australia Policy.

Caroline seemed totally divorced from the stirring events that had occurred. She was still overlooking the issues of the miners' licences and male suffrage, as though she were living in a parallel universe, and, unlike earlier, she now seemed to disregard the land rights of the Indigenous people. She took up her pen within days of the Eureka Stockade uprising to criticise the governor, Sir Charles Hotham, and his government's financial management, and to suggest that the bloodshed had to do with the need for land rather than rights:

> Sir ... When we consider the rich and beautiful country God has given to us — a country that waits only for the plough to give us wheat — the vine to give us wine — the olive to give us oil — every luxury and comfort that men can desire is within our reach, only waits our bidding. Gold lies at our feet, and yet with all these advantages we are on the verge of national insolvency, and the lands of our people are stained with blood.
>
> May the frightful and sorrowful position we are in induce us all with one spirit to co-operate in bringing about a more creditable state of things. Let us cast aside all party feeling or class interest: — let us retrench, economise ... Let us fling to the wind the wild fallacy that public works carried on with borrowed money is fitting employment for newly arrived immigrants. We have too long indulged in taxing ... We have become ... a nation of consumers, instead of producers. We must alter our system, if we wish to recover character: and if Sir Charles Hotham is a wise man, he will at once call to his assistance that first minister of finance, the Plough.[26]

The crucial democratic values that evolved from the Eureka Stockade cannot be denied, but nor can the congenital belief in the value of home and land ownership that has pervaded Australian culture since before Federation. From her early days in New South Wales, and then again in Victoria, Caroline stood up to the squattocracy, championing the idea that it was not just a necessity but a right of all free people to have the ability to own their own plot of ground. It is a discussion that still resonates in twenty-first century Australia.

*

Caroline's expedition to the goldfields did at least result in one significant scheme. It was her own, original idea, although to some extent it was based on the immigration depots she had established in the 1840s in New South Wales. She decided that a network of shelters needed to be built along the major routes to the goldfields, to provide temporary accommodation for travellers. To garner support for her plan, she adopted her usual strategy of writing letters to influential figures in the community, government and the press, and holding public meetings. Though she had some success with the newspapers, it wasn't surprising, with all that was going on in the goldfields, that she received much less publicity than she had in the past. Nevertheless, her idea found favour with the community and the government, which offered to fund it up to a value of £3800.

Caroline's "Shelter Sheds" — later known as "Chisholm's Shakedowns" — were built on Crown Land, at a distance of one day's walk from each other. Each shed was designed to accommodate families, as well as up to thirty single men and ten single women, and had stabling, a shed for carts, two cookhouses and two washhouses. Wood, water, candles and basic rations were sold on site at set rates by station keepers, who had their own house next door. A bed for a night cost 6d for each adult and 3d for each child. Wood and water for cooking cost another 6d per

A poster advertising the Shelter Sheds set up by the Chisholms in Victoria
(Museums Victoria)

adult, or 3d for a child. Tickets for the sheds were sold in both Melbourne and Britain. Caroline was prescriptive about the costs because she was very conscious of not competing with the various stores and established inns along the tracks.

The first ten sheds were constructed along the 120-kilometre route from Melbourne to Castlemaine, at Essendon, The Gap, Gisborne, Keilor, Keilor Plains, the Black Forest, Woodend, Carlsruhe, Malmsbury and Elphinstone. Tenders were called to start the work in April 1855 and the shelters were ready by Christmas that year. Caroline headed the society set up to establish and manage the sheds.[27] The society secretary was her old friend and early biographer, Eneas Mackenzie, who since 1853 had held a position as Under Secretary with the Victorian Government (at a salary of £450 per year).[28] Caroline found married couples to run the sheds. Much of the following year she spent travelling backwards and forwards along the route, checking that they were operating to her expectations. Disappointingly, although the ten sheds built along the Castlemaine route were successful and well maintained, no others were commissioned. There is no firm reason as to why, when the Castlemaine sheds were so useful, that more were not built on other routes. The most likely explanation is that by late 1855 Caroline's health had become an issue and without her committed enterprise, the government failed to continue the programme.

There is something about Caroline's determined focus on her Shelter Sheds that suggests that she was striving for relevancy in a changing world. Certainly, whilst she struggled to excite the powerful and the elite with her vision for the sheds, as well as land reform, there were no ongoing consultations with the prominent lawmakers of the day, as there had been in earlier years in Sydney and London, and no invitations to appear before select committees. If anything, her various, still energetic letters in the press, particularly regarding land and immigration, were mostly ignored in government circles.

*

With her Shelter Sheds, writing her letters to the press, and lobbying the government to free up land, Caroline had enough work to keep her busily based in Melbourne. She also took over her husband's ongoing work with family reunion. Throughout the previous few years, Archibald had let first his home and then his business be an address through which newly arrived immigrants could contact family or friends. Advertisements in the Melbourne newspapers during the 1850s indicate that Caroline first assumed this responsibility whilst living in Flinders Lane and continued it in Elizabeth Street.

When the Chisholms received the balance of the testimonial money in 1855, it made a significant alteration to their lives. The family kept the Elizabeth Street store and added to it a warehouse and retail business just around the corner in A'Beckett Street. Archibald, along with Archibald Jnr and Henry, had other plans too: they wanted to quit Melbourne for what they probably considered a more promising opportunity in a rural setting. They bought a well-known mixed business in Kyneton, northwest of Melbourne, previously owned by Joseph Rogers and Robert Harper.[29] Rebranded Chisholm Brothers, the business may have been an attempt by Archibald to ensure that his sons had a future with an ongoing income. The name change was significant: the Melbourne stores had been called Chisholm & Sons, so now, presumably, Archibald was hoping that his boys would take over most of the work, giving him a chance for a quieter life as an overseer.

The purchase of the new business in Kyneton meant that the family was split in two once again, and that they reverted to maintaining two households, a costly exercise. For the next few years, Caroline lived mostly in Melbourne, in A'Beckett Street, with, possibly, William running the city store, whilst Archibald Snr, Archibald Jnr and Henry were in Kyneton working in the new shop. The three younger children, Sydney, Caroline, and Monica, were also most likely in Kyneton, with the governess and housekeeper Mrs Clinton, although it is possible that they may have remained, at least some of the time, at Caroline's home in Melbourne, with Mrs Clinton looking after them.

It was about this time that Caroline first experienced the ill health that would remain with her, in varying degrees of severity, for the rest of her life. She suffered from some sort of kidney trouble, but it is unclear what illness she had or how it manifested itself. This affliction may have been the reason why she was unable to spend more time at the goldfields during the previous year; however, that is speculation, as there is no indication that she was unwell at that time. Being within easy reach of a city doctor may have kept her in Melbourne whilst most of the family moved to Kyneton; on the other hand, she may simply have wanted to continue her work with the Shelter Sheds, which required regular travel between Melbourne and Castlemaine.

In 1855, Kyneton was a thriving centre of some two thousand people. A local correspondent for the Melbourne *Argus* writing in December that year was fulsome in his praise for the township: "The principal buildings are the steam flour and saw mill, hospital, Bank of New South Wales, and National School — all of excellent design and substantial masonry, built of the blue-stone that abounds here."[30] The correspondent went on to describe the four houses of worship servicing members of the Church of England, the Independent, Wesleyan and Roman Catholic churches; a Mechanics' Institute; schools; and a new printing press. As well, Kyneton had two newspapers, *The Kyneton Advertiser* and *The Kyneton Observer*.[31] The correspondent continued, "I may add that Kyneton is situated on the Campaspe, fifty-eight miles from Melbourne, on the main road to Castlemaine ... Bendigo, &c, and (in the style of the old geography books) is celebrated for its salubrity, rich soil, and plentiful supply of good water."[32]

After ten years in London and Melbourne, Kyneton must have felt like the perfect tree change for Archibald and the children. The Chisholms' shop, on High Street, opposite the Limerick Hotel, was a nineteenth-century version of a supermarket, selling, according to its advertising, an eclectic mix of items, ranging from iron bedsteads, lanterns and Cork butter to sperm whale candles, ladies' bonnets and cases of brandy. Caroline would have had ample opportunity to visit her family while supervising the construction and operation of her Shelter Sheds. Kyneton was about two-thirds of the way to Castlemaine, so no doubt she combined Shelter Shed business with visits to the family; in January 1857, she mentioned in a letter to *The Argus* that she had travelled through the Black Forest six times the previous winter, the forest being much closer to Kyneton than to Melbourne.[33]

If its numerous newspaper advertisements are anything to go by, the business in Kyneton was prosperous for a time and the Chisholm men were well received in the town. Archibald became a magistrate and, despite his evident compassion, was none too lenient with his sentences, such as the penalty he imposed upon an unhappy villain named William Simmons, who received one month's imprisonment with hard labour for stealing a leg of mutton.[34] Even greater recognition lay ahead for the Chisholm name, of a kind that was out of reach for Caroline.

The town of Kyneton, Victoria, in the mid-1800s *(State Library of Victoria)*

In 1856, with all the passion and optimism of a juvenile society, Victoria's colonial leaders introduced one of the keystones of the modern democratic process, the secret ballot. Having agreed to hold a secret ballot following the events at the Eureka Stockade, the lawmakers grappled with how to instigate it effectively. The idea of a secret ballot was not new — it went back to the days of ancient Athens and Rome. In the modern era, its revival began in France with the 1795 Constitution following that country's revolution, but there it was a haphazard affair, voters writing the name of their preferred candidate on a ballot paper at home or picking up one from a candidate's supporters in the streets. Such a system could easily be abused. The system that the men of Melbourne created, and which became known as the Australian ballot and has since been copied throughout the democratic world, ensured the ballot would not be contaminated. The two most important provisions were that the government would control the printing of official ballot slips and it would employ dedicated, impartial electoral officers to oversee the whole election process. Another essential and now widely adopted innovation was the introduction of private booths in which voters would fill out their ballot papers.[35] These measures were trialled in the vote for Victoria's first elected bicameral government, held in 1856. Only white males over the age of twenty-one who met certain property conditions were entitled to vote, however.

Prior to the election, when names were sought for men to represent the Kyneton Borough, which also included Woodend and Malmsbury, in the new Legislative Assembly, Archibald was asked by more than one hundred local men to stand for the seat. He declined. It may have been that at fifty-eight years of age he wanted a quieter life. If elected, he would have been expected to travel regularly to Melbourne and fight for a range of causes, and he may well have had enough of that. Without doubt, financial concerns would also have played a part, as Members of the Legislative Assembly did not at this point receive any remuneration.

Undaunted, the citizens of Kyneton turned to Archibald Jnr, asking him to represent them in his father's stead. The younger Archibald did not qualify to vote, let alone to stand for the seat, on at least two counts: he was under age, being only twenty, and he did not meet the property requirements, given that the Chisholm Brothers business was probably owned either by his father or in partnership with his brothers and it is unlikely that they held the freehold.[36] Residency was not an issue as it is now, but if it had been it may have also invalidated him, as his official address was 12 A'Beckett Street, Melbourne, where Caroline was living at the time, rather than Kyneton. Despite these prohibitions, Archibald Jnr accepted the nomination, his supporters either not knowing or caring about the rules.

Archibald's two opponents were another non-resident, Robert Nadir Clarke, and a forty-five-year-old local businessman, George Walker Johnson, a married man with eleven children, who was a freemason, chairman of the local Agricultural Society, a member of the Kyneton cricket club and of both the hospital and National School boards.[37] Proving that politicians and voters may change but the issues rarely do, two topics being hotly debated on the hustings that year were the availability of land and education funding. Robert Clarke ran a rather quiet campaign, but there was definitely acrimony between the other two. Johnson attacked Archibald for his youth, his place of residence and his religion, whilst Archibald ridiculed Johnson for his mode of speech and lack of education.[38]

Only 540 men were eligible to cast their ballots in the Borough of Kyneton on 7 October 1856. Voting was not compulsory, so not everyone turned up at the polling booth in the Police Barracks on Mitchell Street. The votes, particularly from the smaller towns, were counted early, and it appeared at first that Archibald was ahead in the hamlet of Malmsbury, but it was not to last, particularly when Archibald displayed a reticence alien to most modern politicians: "[At] 3 p.m. some uneasiness began to be felt by the friends of Mr Chisholm as to his return, and therefore requested him to record his own vote, but this he would not do, as he thought it did not look handsome in a candidate to vote for himself."[39]

The final results were announced at about 6 p.m. Robert Clarke had received 31 votes, and Archibald 123, but George Johnson had won the poll with a resounding 244 votes.[40] Archibald had lost the election, but he had not disgraced himself, particularly considering that he was a twenty-year-old newcomer to the area. The following year, he was asked to consider standing for the next election but he declined. One benefit of the campaign was that it raised awareness of Chisholm Brothers, as large advertisements for the business often ran alongside election reports in newspapers.

*

For a little while, it seemed as though the family was finally on a stable financial footing — the Australian-born son, Henry, now going on for seventeen years old, even had enough money to invest in bank shares.[41] The prosperity was not to last. Either the sons, like their father, were not good businessmen or maybe the profits just didn't go far enough to cover all eight members of the family, particularly when they were spread across two households. The next monetary crisis, though, was still a little way into the future.

In the following year, 1857, Kyneton bestowed another honour on Archibald Snr. The new Governor of Victoria, Sir Henry Barkly, was taking a spring tour of the colony and planned to spend a night in Kyneton. Archibald, who continued to sit on the magistrate's bench, was asked to officially welcome him to the town. It was a big event. According to *The Kyneton Observer*, public buildings, hotels, shops and private homes were covered in bunting and banners proclaiming "Advance Victoria" and "Speed the Plough". As the governor approached the courthouse he received a gun salute and hundreds of people crowded around to catch a glimpse of him and hear Archibald's welcome. That evening the local manager of the Bank of New South Wales held a dinner at his home above the bank for Sir Henry and a selection of town luminaries and their wives. Archibald, and possibly his eldest son too, would have been amongst the guests, but there is no mention of Caroline attending either the daytime welcome or the dinner. Of course, she may have been absent, but that is highly unlike her, and there is evidence that she was in Kyneton a few days later.[42] The inference is, of course, that Caroline's star was waning, and the newspaper did not rate her a mention amongst so many significant townspeople and guests — something that would have been unimaginable only a few years earlier.

Although she visited Kyneton often, Caroline continued to live in Melbourne. Her second son, William, however, was about to move on. Now almost twenty years old, he was married on Monday, 20 April 1857, by the Bishop of Melbourne, James Goold, to an Irish girl at St Francis Cathedral.[43] Susanna McSwiney's parents were listed on the wedding notices as Denis McSwiney, Esq. and Margaret Madden from County Roscommon. The young couple lived in Collingwood after the wedding, and William left Chisholm Brothers to work with his best man, James Mayne, a wine and spirit merchant in Melbourne.[44] It may have been at this time that the Chisholms' Melbourne businesses were sold; certainly, there is no evidence of Archibald or either of his other sons moving to Melbourne to manage them.

Once William had left, there seemed to be little reason for Caroline to maintain her lodgings in Melbourne, and yet she did so until the end of the year. She was unwell again with a reoccurrence of her kidney problem and that may have prevented her moving or, as mentioned earlier, she may have wished to remain close to her doctor. Then, too, she was still overseeing the Shelter Sheds, continuing in a small way with family reunions and giving advice to new female immigrants. The main issue that interested her at this time, though, was the availability of land. By means of a letter-writing campaign and her involvement in the Victorian Land League, she tried to convince the government to free up land for small farms.[45]

After all her years of hard work and frenzied activity, now, with Archibald and the children settled some one hundred kilometres from her, Caroline finally had time to herself to think, question and formulate ideas rather than just react to events. The results of her ruminations reflected her deep-seated radicalism and keen understanding of the human condition. She had always refused to conform to the nineteenth-century ideal of what a woman should be, rejecting the domestic sphere for a life of striving to achieve what she could for as many people as possible. In doing so she had been immensely successful. Now that she no longer had the physical strength to continue as she had once done, nor very possibly the desire, she was ready to move on to a more cerebral form of activism, considering and expounding ideas and promulgating them through the press. Some of her propositions were many decades ahead of their time and resonate strongly today. Where in the past she had simply insisted that all religions should be treated equally, now she took that notion further, attacking the institutionalised bigotry of the day and extending it to include ethnicity. In effect, Caroline was putting forward the idea of multiculturalism, a century and a half before the term was coined.

Responding to the gold miners' complaints about Chinese diggers in the goldfields, the Victorian Government had introduced, amongst other retrograde measures, a £10 immigration tax on the Chinese, who were also denied any of the arrival assistance offered to white people. Despite these rejections, the Chinese continued to settle in Australia and by 1857 there were well over 25,000 living in Victoria.[46] Caroline made her position clear near the end of a long letter about immigration sent to the editor of *The Argus* and published in June 1857:

There is one great question, Sir, which at present affects us
deeply, and which, I must confess, I have closely watched,
and that is, the question of Chinese immigration. With
respect to the Chinese, I cannot help apprehending that our
neglect in providing shelter of some sort for them may some
day cause a sweeping calamity. The excitement against the
Chinese may be looked upon in some measure as a political
dodge, in order to divert attention from the land question …
This immigration cannot be stopped; … there will be no
rest until man is recognised as man, without distinction of
colour or clime.[47]

It was a topic that she was to return to a few years later in New
South Wales, but in Victoria at that time it won her few friends,
the government refusing even to discuss the issue with her.

As 1857 drew to a close, Caroline's health continued to
deteriorate. She decided to leave Melbourne for Kyneton to live
full time with her family. Her farewell dinner at the Duke of Kent
Hotel in Lonsdale Street was a very different affair from the one
organised to welcome her to Melbourne three and a half years
earlier. This one was attended by about only forty people, with
few persons of note to excite mention in the press. After toasts
and speeches, Caroline responded that she was deeply gratified by
the speakers' praise, and that it was the tonic she needed because
her exertions on behalf of immigration in Victoria had not been
suitably backed up by the legislature. Reports in both *The Argus*
and *The Age* described her speech as "complaining", making her
sound petulant because the government had not complied with
her wishes on the questions of immigration and land.[48] After
almost twenty years of dedicated working towards her vision of
settlement in Australia, it must have been difficult for Caroline

to acknowledge that her time of influence and innovation may have passed. With the Australian colonies growing up, the style of immigration changing and a new assertiveness from the white constituency taking hold, she would need to redefine herself if she wanted to remain within the public sphere.

Caroline was about to face the most grievous years of her life. She was desperately ill, seriously impoverished and would soon endure the heartache of losing a loved one. Yet with passion, intellect and humour, she would not only manage to find the strength to return to public life, but also make a major contribution to Australian' society by influencing the way people would think and vote on the big questions affecting the colonies.

CHAPTER 14

The Female Radical

1858–66

**Temperance Hall, Pitt Street, Sydney,
Tuesday, 10 December 1860**

The quivering glow from the gas lamp illuminated the clock to the side of the stage. Caroline glanced at it. Seven-thirty. Still fifteen minutes until she was supposed to start and already the hall was full to bursting. From her vantage point above, Caroline looked down on hundreds of naked male heads. What gratified her most, though, were the hats: each one marked a woman, and she was surprised at how many she could see.

She recognised some in the crowd as they looked up to the stage, caught her eye, smiled. Many of the men had been at her first lecture some five months ago. She wondered whether they had brought their wives this time, or if all these women had decided to attend tonight of their own volition. If that were the case, it showed some courage: females were rarely seen at political talks. The thought tickled her sense of humour. I wonder if they think of me as a woman, or just an oddity, she mused.

The clock ticked on. Still ten minutes to go. The room was overcrowded now, hot, stuffy; the lights in the wall sockets flickered. More than one woman looked to be wilting. Caroline had an idea. She called her sons to her and sent them scuttling to find chairs in nearby rooms to put on the stage. Then, lifting her voice above the din, she spoke. "Ladies, Ladies," her voice imperative, piercing the confused babble. "It is such a warm evening. It is cooler up here on the stage and we have chairs for your comfort. Please, ladies, join me," she said, throwing out her arm invitingly.

There was silence, and stillness. Caroline's eyes alighted on two women she knew. She called them by name, insisting that they venture on stage. They were hesitant, possibly embarrassed by the idea of such a public display. Eventually one and then the other stepped up; there were cheers from some sections of the male audience. Other women followed until Caroline found herself at the centre of a female arc. The women formed an impressive and colourful background, seated neatly in their fulsome crinoline skirts, one touching the other, spread out behind her.

Looking out at her now mostly male audience, Caroline noted that one or two wore mildly bemused expressions. She wondered if they understood the significance of what they were witnessing. Caroline did. The colony was in the midst of a fiercely contested election, but one in which only men could vote. Here tonight, hundreds of them had turned up to hear the issues discussed by a woman. Not only that, but whilst they were left to gather on the floor of the hall, a sisterhood, deprived of any political power, had risen above them, as though the women had now taken control.

Caroline knew it was only an image, and one that would not be sustained, not this time at least. Still, it was a beginning.

She stepped forward to begin her talk. She would enjoy this evening.[1]

In Melbourne, during the previous few years, Caroline had drifted, but 1858 was to become something of a watershed for her and her family. It blossomed with hope. Having settled into Kyneton life, Caroline's health improved a little. When the Chisholms were invited to a neighbour's wedding, their daughters, Caroline, now ten years old, and Monica, seven, both served as the bride's attendants whilst Caroline was invited to make a speech to the happy couple. Kyneton was certainly a small town compared with Melbourne, but Caroline's family was well liked there.[2]

In March, William's daughter, and Caroline's first grandchild, was born in Melbourne and christened Josephine. Unfortunately, Caroline was unwell again and may not have attended the celebration. By the end of May, when she should have been celebrating her fiftieth birthday, she was suffering a serious reoccurrence of her kidney problem, leading doctors to suggest that she relocate to Sydney to benefit from the warmer climate. So, by the middle of the year, Caroline found herself back in the town she had quit more than a decade earlier. With her were her husband and their three youngest children, with Sydney, now twelve, joining the girls. Archibald Jnr, now twenty-two, and Henry, nineteen, stayed in Kyneton to dispose of the business as best they could, whilst William, twenty-one, remained in Melbourne with his wife and baby daughter.

The relocation ushered in probably the most difficult time to date in the lives of both Caroline and Archibald. The journey from Kyneton to Sydney in winter would have been long, arduous and painful, particularly if, as was likely, they travelled overland by coach. Their finances were again precarious: the Kyneton business was not as prosperous as it should have been, and until it was sold they remained short of money; in the meantime, if they spent whatever they received from the store, they might have very little to fall back on in the future. Those financial concerns, though, were secondary to the issue of Caroline's health. By the time the Chisholms arrived in Sydney, she was extremely ill.

Archibald booked the family into the Post Office Hotel, in George Street, and called upon an old friend, Dr William Bland, to attend Caroline. A man whose very surname was a paradox, William Bland was then almost seventy years old and nearing the end of an extremely full and eventful life. Born in London, the son of a doctor, he was appointed a naval surgeon in India at the precocious age of twenty-three. The following year, during an argument in the officers' mess, he killed a man in a duel. Convicted of murder, he was sentenced to seven years' transportation to Sydney and arrived as a convict in 1814. Within eighteen months, Bland had been pardoned and had set up a lucrative private medical practice. A couple of years later, at the age of twenty-eight, he married Sarah, the twenty-year-old daughter of an evangelical missionary. It was not a happy union. When Sarah ran off with an officer of the East India Company, Bland decided that this time legal action was preferable to guns. The court agreed, awarding him damages of £2000, but before he could collect the settlement the officer absconded, possibly with Sarah, who also vanished from the colony. Not long afterwards, Bland spent another year in jail for writing satires that insulted the then governor, Lachlan Macquarie. Over the next forty years, however, Bland became an upstanding member of society: a doctor, landowner and member of the Legislative Council. Although he still had an uneven temper, he was a man who liked to involve himself in the issues of the day. He also had an exceedingly kind heart and was a considerable philanthropist.

Bland knew Caroline from her early days in Sydney, and came at once to her aid. These were dark days, with Caroline almost penniless and desperately unwell. At one stage, when even Bland thought she could be in her final hours, she overheard a bizarre conversation. Her surreal sense of humour was revealed in her recounting of the conversation at a later date:

> I was so far gone at one period, that a clergyman asked the doctor, in my presence, how many hours he expected I could survive. He remarked to the doctor as he stood by, as he supposed, my dying bedside, that as I was a strong-minded woman, he was sure he would be excused if he asked him how many hours he thought I could live — that he had a pressing engagement at Parramatta, and he would not like to be absent, as he would have to superintend the ceremonies at St Mary's.[3]

We don't know Bland's reply, but presumably the clergyman did go to Parramatta because Caroline had not done with life yet.

Whether it was Bland's talent or Caroline's determination or a combination of both, she slowly improved, the inflammation to her kidneys abating. It would take a long time for her to recuperate and she would never be quite well again, but at least she had survived. Caroline was effusive in her gratitude to Bland, describing him as "that venerable and venerated medical gentleman, Dr Bland, who in the most liberal and kindest manner attended me, without expectation of fee or reward".[4]

Whilst still recovering, Caroline sent two notes to another old friend, Catholic priest Father John Therry, the first one asking him to visit her and the second requesting a loan. "Can you for a short time lend me fifteen or twenty pounds?" she wrote simply.[5] There is no record of his reply, but it is likely that he acceded to this request, as not long afterwards the family moved into a small house amongst the workers' cottages in Albert Street, Redfern, in the city's south, where the rent was cheap. Archibald found work in a drapery shop, and the three children were enrolled in a new government school opened just two years earlier on what was then Cleveland Paddocks.[6] The school, made of temporary prefabricated galvanised iron, had more than two hundred pupils.[7] In later life, one of Monica's friends wrote a memoir that included her impressions as a child of both Caroline and Archibald: "Major — he was so called — Chisholm remains in my recollection as a gentleman perfectly refined in manner and appearance, thin and pale and sad-looking ... I remember her ... as a stout florid-complexioned woman, winning of manner and of soft speech ... The family ... were in very poor circumstances."[8]

After starting with such optimism, 1858 had become a difficult year and it had still not ended when Caroline and Archibald received devastating tidings from Melbourne: twenty-one-year-old William had died suddenly after a short illness. Like salt being poured on an open wound, the tragedy was compounded only a couple of months later, in January 1859, with news that William's daughter, ten-month-old Josephine, had also died, and had been buried next to her father in Melbourne's General Cemetery. About three years later, William's widow, Susanna, took Holy Orders, becoming a nun with the Sisters of Charity and eventually moving into a convent in Woollahra in Sydney. As her religious name, Susanna adopted Joseph, possibly in memory of her baby daughter.[9] To lose a son and a grandchild at the end of that terrible year must have been an inconceivable sadness for both Caroline and Archibald.

As yet, they had received no financial help from their sons in Kyneton — presumably selling the business proved more difficult than buying it. It was at this time that Archibald pawned the gold medal given to Caroline by Pope Pius IX some six years previously. Although still receiving his major's pension, that was worth only £292 per annum and the cost of looking after Caroline and relocating to Sydney with the younger children would have eaten into it considerably. Even with his income from his work in the drapery shop, there would have been barely enough to support the family; he was probably receiving only ten to twelve shillings per day.[10] Nor, at sixty-one years of age, was he likely to improve his earning power or have the stamina to attempt new ventures.

With Caroline recovering slowly and confined to home and Archibald's long hours in the shop, it was unlikely that either of them made contact with other Sydney friends from the early days. Caroline must have found it irksome to be back in the city where it had all begun and be a captive of her indisposition and poverty. The city had matured and advanced in the twelve years that the Chisholms had been absent. Like Melbourne it had grown. In 1838, the inhabitants had numbered some thirty thousand non-Indigenous white people, predominately men; by 1860 that population was edging up to almost double that number. Physically, Sydney was still the jewel of the colony according to the visitor John Askew: "The view of Sydney from part of the harbour is without a parallel. Tiers of fine buildings seem to rise one above another, like the seats in an amphitheatre, and towering above them all is the tall spire of St James's Church"[11] More importantly the city had clean water, gas lighting and excellent fresh food: "All the fruit ... are much superior in flavour to those produced in England. I never knew how delicious a really good orange was, till I tasted one in Sydney. During the orange season, they can be bought in the market for 2d and 3d per dozen."[12] The downside, though, was that enduring challenge of Sydney, to wit, the cost of housing: "A perpetual source of dissatisfaction with the working-people was the insane manner in which the landlords raised the rents of their dwellings. The news of a new gold-field, or the finding of a large nugget at any of the mines, or any other species of prospective prosperity, sent up the rents. In some instances as much as 6s per week."[13]

In such circumstances, Archibald's wage would barely have kept a roof over their heads or put food on the table, let alone paid for Caroline's medicine, clothes and shoes for the growing children, or other family requirements. Despite still being far from well, Caroline realised she had to contribute too. She did some work for a confectionary and gave lessons in English to "China Men, at 1s and 6d per lesson".[14] She would have been able to manage both jobs from her home. Many of the Chinese who had arrived for the gold rush ended up as market gardeners on the outskirts of Sydney.[15] As in Victoria, there was considerable anti-Chinese sentiment in New South Wales. In 1861 the state Legislative Assembly passed a "Chinese Immigration Act to Regulate and Restrict their Immigration into the Colony". Much like the Victorian legislation of 1855, it levied £10 on each new Chinese arrival and a similar cost on the captains of the boats for every Chinese adult brought to New South Wales.[16] During a public lecture in 1860, Caroline spoke of her Chinese students with respect and said that she was opposed to the anti-Chinese legislation. It was an unpopular stance, showing again that she was not one to pander to the crowd.

Back at the beginning of 1859, though, she was still struggling with her health and finances and lectures were far from her mind. Across all the contours of her career, what had sustained Caroline the most was her faith. She had not cast her religion aside, yet it seems that its representatives in Sydney had abandoned her, for a time, at least. When Jabez King (J.K.) Heydon, the publisher of the Sydney *Freeman's Journal*, and like Caroline a convert to Catholicism, visited her at home in May of 1859, he was troubled by her condition, both physical and financial, and deeply concerned for her religious isolation. In a letter to Father Therry he wrote, "I was greatly shocked yesterday, on calling on the celebrated Mrs Chisholm ... to find her in the deepest distress from sickness and poverty. Although extremely ill from disease of the kidneys and unable to get out, no clergyman has visited her for about four months."[17] Caroline was obviously upset at being ignored by the clergy, particularly now when she most needed them. Yet her reaction was not bitterness. Instead she analysed what had happened and why, and then she sought a solution. She still had an extraordinary ability to rise above the petty and the banal, to find a way of addressing a problem that was, she would have realised, not just pertinent to her, but to so many others as well. In this case her manner of dealing with it was inspired, allowing her to vent her feelings, earn some money and promote her ideas and passions.

Through the latter part of 1859, as her health slowly improved, Caroline penned a novelette, *Little Joe*. It appeared in eleven instalments in *The Empire* newspaper between Boxing Day 1859 and 15 May 1860. A moralising story full of ill-concealed homilies in the guise of conversations between characters, it highlighted the clergy's failure to frequent their poor parishioners. Caroline ascribed this absence to what was then called "State Aid", whereby the government rather than the people paid the clergy's wages. That was only one of the issues that spilt from her pen: her other main concern, land for the poorer settlers, featured strongly, as did the honour and love of the working class compared with the brutal indifference of the capitalist. The story itself is about a young boy, Joe, orphaned at the start of the narrative and taken in by a kindly, though impoverished widow with children of her own. Joe's adventures bring him into contact with jovial and caring ordinary people, a wealthy man who learns to put humanity ahead of profit, and a villain whom Joe betters with the help of his friends and supporters. It is hardly a rollicking tale, nor is one left in suspense at the end of each instalment, but it twists and turns enough to hold some interest, gives a fair description of everyday life in the late 1850s, and must have been well received as *The Empire* ran so many chapters. The end of the last instalment is ambiguous: it may have been the completion of the tale or, possibly, Caroline may have intended to continue writing but, as so often happened with her, became distracted by other events.

One of those disruptions would have been the arrival in Sydney during 1859 of her two sons, Archibald Jnr, now twenty-three, and Henry, twenty, with the proceeds from the sale of the Kyneton business, after all the debts had been paid. The funds meant that the Chisholms were able to rent a larger home in a slightly better area closer to the town, Stanley Street in East Sydney, and with both boys working, the family's finances improved further — Archibald Jnr took a job as a clerk and Henry found a position with the New South Wales Civil Service.[18]

*

Almost as though she knew that time was now running out, Caroline, with her health and finances improving, went on the political offensive. This time it wasn't in the latent guise of letter writing, but full force in front of hundreds of people in a series of lectures in Sydney between the winters of 1859 and 1861. It was as though committing her thoughts to paper whilst writing *Little Joe* had not been enough: she needed to give physical vent to her ardent views. Her initial decision as a young woman in

Northampton to turn charity into a lifetime career had defined Caroline as being deeply concerned with the destitute and disadvantaged. Her initial attempts at philanthropy had focused on helping young girls and women, but as the years passed and her experience of the world dilated, so too did her convictions, resulting in a fervent belief in the need for a democratic society in which everyone should share. In effect, she was advocating that quintessential Australian maxim of a "fair go".

Caroline did proselytise, but not at all in a religious sense. She prayed and practised as a Catholic herself, but had absolutely no interest in converting anyone to Rome. She probably didn't see the point, believing that apart from a belief in a god and living a good life, the style of one's observances was immaterial. Caroline's interest in conversion was to do with social equity, and that included females being liberated from domestic bonds and being allowed to play a greater part in a society that had hitherto excluded them. Her lectures fomented much interest, not just because she presented aberrant theories, but also because, and despite the respect she received, she was a curiosity, a woman inhabiting the male domain. It was unheard of for women to talk at public meetings, let alone be bold enough to be the focal point of the gathering. Even ten years later in London, when Mrs Peter Taylor was chairperson of the first public suffragette meeting, she was mocked as being not only ridiculous but immoral as well.[19]

Caroline spoke, of course, about land and immigration, but she broadened her agenda to include, amongst other issues, her support for further electoral reform, the eight-hour day, the value of the press, the avarice of landlords (which she had experienced) and the future of women. She was not the only one advocating fundamental change and there is little doubt, judging by the

A poster advertising one of Caroline's lectures in Sydney, in 1861 *(Museums Victoria)* reaction she received, that she spoke to sympathetic audiences, but she was alone in promoting women's rights.

In her very first lecture, on a variety of topics including "the land question", she addressed her own peculiarity, defending her right as a woman to speak on serious matters. A report in *The Empire* explained how she countered her detractors: "They forgot this, that real property can be bequeathed to posterity in a variety of ways, whilst the mental property of ideas and experience can only be conveyed by constant and personal teaching. Why then should the ideas and experience she might possess be lost to the public through any want of fashion and form in her as a lady."[20] Caroline was taking aim at two targets here. When she mentioned "bequeathing real property" she would have been highlighting the fact that a married woman in New South Wales was still barred by law from owning or inheriting anything — until 1879 the husband was the sole beneficiary. The insistence on female intellectual ability was another spear aimed at a complacent male audience, and one that would only reach its target some twenty-five years later, when first Melbourne University and then Sydney University finally began to admit women students. Both universities were founded in the 1850s.

In the same lecture, Caroline advanced the idea of female suffrage. The year before, 1858, in New South Wales, all white men over the age of twenty-one had finally won the right to vote in a secret ballot, without any property conditions (interestingly, their counterparts in the United Kingdom would wait another sixty years, until 1918, to receive the same benefit). Indicating how comfortable she was with public speaking, Caroline first launched a satirical attack on her male audience, asking, as *The Empire* reported, "What had they, the men of Australia, done towards advancing the political and social interests of the country, and yet they called themselves the 'lords of the creation'?" The reaction was laughter and cheers. Then Caroline made her point: "Undoubted, they had a great deal yet to do before the political system of this country could be placed on a firm and satisfactory basis. Some people imagined that vote by ballot would lead to the enfranchisement of ladies, and they appeared to look upon such a result with apprehension. But under a proper and enlightened system she believed that such a contingency would be more advantageous than otherwise."[21] Whilst the concepts were radical, the language was not, allowing her audience to ease into the philosophies rather than be bludgeoned by them. Even so, there was no laughter or cheers this time, and she passed directly on to her next subject.

It is possible that amongst the crowd that night there was a young girl who had arrived in Sydney a few years earlier aboard one of Caroline's Family Colonization Loan Society boats. Maybanke Anderson (née Selfe) would, some thirty years later, be a leader of the women's suffrage and education movements in New South Wales.[22] Australian male attitudes to female suffrage in the 1850s and '60s can best be explained by what happened in Victoria a few years later, when the wording of an electoral act allowed women to vote in the 1864 general election, which they subsequently did. The male legislature, however, then decided that the act had been a mistake and they revised it the following year to once again disenfranchise women.

Caroline's first lecture was held in the voluminous Prince of Wales Theatre in Castlereagh Street. About four hundred people were present, but were almost lost in an auditorium big enough to hold up to three thousand. Although her other talks were to be free, Caroline shared the profits from this one with the theatre's manager. Taking Caroline back to the days of the height of her influence in New South Wales, the lecture was attended by not just her friend Dr Bland, but also by several prominent politicians, including Jack Robertson and Charles Cowper, who would both become premier of the colony, and would promote the liberalisation of the male franchise and reformation of the land laws.[23]

Caroline's second lecture was held some eighteen months later in the early summer of 1860, in the middle of the election campaign for the lower house, the Legislative Assembly. Her topic, land reform, was the defining issue on the hustings, with both sides, in modern terms, seeking a mandate for their policies: either to maintain the status quo for the wealthy squatters or free up the land for the less affluent. The talk was held in the Temperance Hall in Pitt Street and attracted well in excess of the four hundred people who came to the first lecture — *The Sydney Morning Herald* described it as a "very large audience". Stuffy and hot, the room was so crowded with members of both sexes, that before she commenced Caroline invited as many women onto the stage as would fit. It was certainly more comfortable there, but it was likely that Caroline, skilled at engendering publicity, was also making a strong visual statement about the need for female involvement in politics and the crucial questions of the day. Much of this lecture was a reworking of arguments that she had put previously, including an attack on that bastion of conservatism, elitism and the squattocracy, the all-male Australian Club, which even today does not accept women members.

At the end of the two-hour talk, a vote of thanks was proposed, the speaker jovially commenting that Caroline herself should stand for election. She answered the suggestion seriously, and it was in reply to this that she described her opposition to any anti-Chinese legislation. Perhaps reflecting widespread scepticism that a woman would ever stand for parliament or that there would be support for Chinese immigration, only one of the three Sydney newspapers that covered the lecture, *The Empire*, reported these comments. The single person of note to attend this lecture, and draw praise from Caroline, was her old adversary John Dunmore Lang. Although there was no evidence of any closer contact between the two in the following years, this was obviously an olive branch, both offered and received. At the end of the lecture, both were hailed by a vocal audience with three resounding cheers.

The 1860 election was won by Caroline's supporters, Jack Robertson and Charles Cowper. The following year, much to her delight, Jack Robertson pushed through his land reform legislation, giving up the premiership and changing from the Legislative Assembly to the Legislative Council to achieve it. In the following year, 1862, Victoria passed similar laws. Caroline has never been credited with any part in bringing these laws to fruition; however, undeniably, her constant campaigning in both colonies did influence the establishment of more equitable land laws. Australia in 1860 had tossed off most of its convict shackles; now it was wriggling out of its colonial fetters. It would be another forty years and more before it stood as an independent, inclusive nation, but like white male suffrage, the land reform laws were crucial to its development.

There were to be two more lectures from Caroline, both focusing substantially on social issues and improving the quality of life for the working class. In what may have been a first, Caroline even raised the still fractious issue of equality in housework. In February 1861, she spoke at a church hall on the corner of Abercrombie Street, Broadway, to the St Benedict's Young Men's Society, of which her son, Archibald, was the president. This talk was on the early closing movement not of hotels, but of shops. It was not a large audience but many of those in attendance were female.[24] Although her husband, Archibald Snr, no doubt worked long hours at the drapery, she addressed the subject principally from a woman's point of view. A few days previously at a similar meeting, a man had blamed women shopping "after tea" for the reason that stores remained open until ten o'clock at night. Caroline threw the responsibility right back onto the men. *The Sydney Morning Herald* reported what she said: "The gentlemen — husbands — instead of doing much of the work at their homes — work that the husbands alone ought to do — they left it at an early hour for their business, and spent their evening hours in other places than their homes, and consequently the time of the wives was taken up in doing the work referred to … They had to defer shopping till the evening."[25] Raising various other arguments, she also suggested that it was dangerous for women shop assistants to go home alone late at night. She said instead that the free evening could be better spent either improving their minds or — another radical proposition for the time — enjoying some well-earned recreation. (Caroline did not, however, address the inevitable reduction in pay that early closing would have incurred for shop assistants, only maintaining that work was always more fruitful in the morning.)

Her fourth lecture, "Our Home Life", was held again at the Temperance Hall in Pitt Street and listened to by at least six hundred people. It was a meandering talk that highlighted many of her past experiences and achievements, along with current social concerns in Sydney. She spoke passionately about homelessness and child prostitution, unemployment and workers' wages. Attacking the high cost of rents for crowded, substandard dwellings, she referred to a report by Henry Parkes, later known as the Father of Federation, before claiming that "The houses in Sydney appropriated to the working classes were ... utterly unfit for homes. In one case seventy human beings were herded together in a house of six rooms."[26] On a personal note, which brought a laugh from the audience, she claimed that "she was paying too high a rent; and her rooms were so small that she could not walk in them with crinoline (laughter). It was a monstrous thing ('Crinoline'). (Renewed laughter.)"[27] She ended this last lecture with an ardent eulogy on democracy, which in 1861 was still approached with considerable suspicion by many people:

> You have of late heard a great deal about democracy ...
> It has since been represented to you as a sort of monster
> whose cravings nothing can satisfy ... and you may be a
> little startled when I can assure you that you are all possessed
> with more or less of this spirit. For a man that wants to
> support himself and his family in an independent manner
> is considered a terrible democrat. A man that wants a bit of
> land and a cottage of his own, that he may not be moved
> about at the will of another man, is looked upon as a
> monstrous and most unbearable democrat. A man who wants
> liberal and equitable laws is put down as a dangerous and
> awful democrat. A man who may wish to see the salaries
> of high officials reduced, and that taxes may be lessened is
> viewed as a most meddling and mischievous democrat ...
> Because you dare to advocate and to seek for the rights of
> man, you are counted as "howling idiots", as "ignorant and
> needy" democrats. This is in fact the height, weight, and
> depth of your Australian democracy.[28]

That glowing rhetoric, decidedly radical and eloquent, was to be the final words that Caroline delivered in public. Few could doubt that they emerged from a deep belief in the rights of all people, whatever their condition, sex, creed or ethnicity, or that she had a clear vision for a future Australia based on egalitarian principles. It's difficult to imagine that Caroline's lectures didn't have a substantial effect across the colony. They were certainly well attended by both sexes and by prominent politicians of the day. The fact that at least three newspapers, including two of the major dailies, *The Sydney Morning Herald* and *The Empire*, reported on all four lectures suggests that they were considered of genuine interest, mostly covering topical issues of the day. Then, too, the newspapers would have effectively disseminated Caroline's words and ideas further afield, across Sydney and the bush. For the most part the press supported much of what she said. A month after the first lecture, *The Empire*, established by Henry Parkes, left no doubt about its opinion of her writing in its editorial: "If Captain JAMES COOK discovered Australia, if JOHN MACARTHUR planted the first seeds of its extraordinary prosperity — if LUDWIG LEICHHARDT penetrated and explored its before unknown interior — CAROLINE CHISHOLM has done more: she has peopled — she alone has colonised it in the true sense of the term."[29] As in London, Caroline's friends and supporters in Australia included many from the liberal elite, including power brokers such as Henry Parkes, Jack Robertson and Charles Cowper. It may be unrealistic to claim that Caroline's support for women led directly to the suffragette movement of the 1890s, which would result in Australia becoming only the second country in the world to allow women to vote and the first to give them the right to stand for parliament; yet she was probably the one who started the conversation in the public arena. Once it had begun, there would be no going back.

*

Giving up public life possibly for financial reasons, Caroline went back to where her philanthropy had started and opened another girls' school, but this was not a charitable endeavour. Unlike in India, she charged tuition and boarding fees, no doubt in an effort to alleviate the financial pressure on her family. The scheme had the added benefit of enabling her to supervise the education of her daughters, Caroline, now fourteen, and Monica, eleven. Most likely, Archibald joined Caroline and the girls at the large home she had leased on Stanmore Road, Newtown, and named Rathbone House, after her friends Elizabeth and William Rathbone, whom she had met whilst lecturing in Liverpool, England, in April 1853.

After placing a series of advertisements in all the Sydney papers, Caroline officially opened Rathbone House school on 1 July 1862. It was a major project for someone with her indifferent health, but she threw herself into it wholeheartedly, promoting it as an "educational establishment for young ladies" which sought to "combine a sound education and intellectual improvement with the social, domestic and practical duties of life".[30] It wasn't cheap; in grave need of funds, Caroline may have traded on her own celebrity when setting the fees.[31] Insisting on payment in advance, she charged fifty guineas a quarter for boarding pupils above ten years of age and forty guineas for those below ten years. Given the views that she had so recently espoused, it appears somewhat ironic that only the wealthy, including the squattocracy, would have been able to afford these fees. Her need of financial security for once overrode her values.

According to her advertisements, Caroline offered her students the subjects of English, Grammar, Composition, Geography, Arithmetic and Writing, as well as two of the following options:

French, Music, Dancing and Drawing. There was no extra charge for such items as stationery, books, washing, bedsteads, bedding or cutlery, and girls who wished to remain at the school during vacation time could do so without extra charge.[32] By comparison, an inner-city boarding school for young ladies, advertising in the same newspaper and including the same educational basics as Caroline's school but with Latin and Italian instead of Music, Drawing and Dancing, charged only £15 (just over fourteen guineas) per quarter.[33]

Within twelve months, Caroline had moved her school to a building on the Cooks River in what is now Arncliffe. She named her new house Green-Bank, this time after the home of the Liverpool Rathbones.[34] Publicising the change, with no alterations in prices, Caroline described a sylvan setting for her young charges that sounded more like a resort than a school: "The Rooms ... are spacious, lofty, and well ventilated, and the out-buildings are excellent. There are about twelve acres of Pleasure Grounds and Gardens attached, with a fine, large, and open Orchard of Fruit trees, intersected by wide and shady walks. There is also a good Bath-House adjoining the House, where the Young Ladies will have the further benefit of Sea-Bathing, as often as may be deemed desirable."[35] By late February 1864, though, Caroline was running the school alone. Archibald had taken their daughters to Britain, possibly to provide them with a more established education.[36] Although there is no evidence, Sydney, not yet eighteen years of age, may have travelled with his father and sisters, also for the benefit of his education.

Caroline continued to advertise her school in the Sydney newspapers until late April 1864, just two months after Archibald had departed. From that date on, there is no mention of Green-Bank, in the newspapers or indeed in any letters in the newspapers from Caroline either.[37] The school possibly closed for financial reasons, particularly if Archibald was absent, or because of the state of Caroline's health — the kidney disease had continued to trouble her intermittently. It may also have prevented her from travelling to Britain to join Archibald. She was, however, also waiting for the outcome of the New South Wales Legislative Assembly decision on whether or not to provide her with a substantial testimonial of £3000 in recognition of her immigration work; it is unlikely that she would have left whilst this was still being debated and she had some chance to influence the outcome.

The idea of a gratuity had been initially raised in parliament in 1862, and supported by, amongst others, Jack Robertson and John Dunmore Lang. *The Empire* newspaper had campaigned even earlier on Caroline's behalf, from 1859 onwards. Initially wanting a public testimonial, by 1862 the newspaper reverted to suggesting that the government should give her a substantial gratuity, and it published at least three poems and two extensive articles lauding her work with immigrants and her overall contribution to the colony. One poem was written by renowned Australian poet Henry Kendall, whose sister, Jane, worked for Caroline, teaching music at both her schools.

Caroline Chisholm

"A perfect woman, nobly planned,
To warn, to comfort, and command."[38]

THE Priests and the Levites went forth, to feast at the courts of the
    Kings;
They were vain of their greatness and worth, and gladdened with
    glittering things;

They were fair in the favour of gold, and they walked on, with
    delicate feet,
Where, famished and faint with the cold, the women fell down in
    the street.
The Priests and the Levites looked round, all vexed and perplexed
    at the cries
Of the maiden who crouched to the ground with the madness of want
    in her eyes;
And they muttered — "Few praises are earned when good hath been
    wrought in the dark;
While the backs of the people are turned, we choose not to loiter nor
    hark."
Moreover they said — "It is fair that our deeds in the daylight
    should shine:
If we feasted you, who would declare that we gave you our honey
    and wine."
They gathered up garments of gold, and they stepped with their
    delicate feet,
And the women who famished with cold, were left with the snow in
    the street.
The winds and the rains were abroad — the homeless looked vainly
    for alms;
And they prayed in the dark to the Lord, with agony clenched in
    their palms,
"There is none of us left that is whole," they cried, through their
    faltering breath,
"We are clothed with a sickness of soul, and the shape of the shadow
    of death."
He heard them, and turned to the earth! — "I am pained," said the
    Lord, "at the woe

Of my children so smitten with dearth; but the night of their trouble
    shall go."
He called on His Chosen to come: she listened, and hastened to rise;
And He charged her to build them a home, where the tears should be
    dried from their eyes.
God's servant came forth from the South: she told of a plentiful land;
And wisdom was set in her mouth, and strength in the thews of her
    hand.
She lifted them out of their fear, and they thought her their Moses
    and said:
"We shall follow you, sister, from here to the country of sunshine
    and bread."
She fed them, and led them away, through tempest and tropical heat,
Till they reached the far regions of day, and sweet-scented spaces of
    wheat.
She hath made them a home with her hand, and they bloom like the
    summery vines;
For they eat of the fat of the land, and drink of its glittering wines.[39]

The Empire also produced a small book entitled *What Has Mrs Chisholm Done for the Colony of New South Wales?*, which was released for sale in the Spring of 1862, priced at one shilling. The book's title referred to the question asked by Thomas Holt during the testimonial debate in parliament. A former friend and supporter of Caroline's, Holt was a wealthy pastoralist, company director and benefactor. Despite that, he had questioned her commitment to New South Wales, suggesting that she had neglected it for Victoria and was now "weary of well-doing". It brought a stinging and fulsome reply from Caroline, also published in *The Empire* that year, in which she went into great detail on her past activities. By the end of the year, Thomas Holt had apologised, saying that he would not intentionally cause Caroline pain and that he was referring to her work in Britain when she had sent so many immigrants to Victoria instead of New South Wales. It was a flare-up that lasted only a short time, but it indicated that Caroline was jealous of the way her legacy would be viewed and, whilst she could, would do her utmost to ensure that neither she nor her work would be misunderstood or devalued. She was, after all, doing what she had done best for the past twenty years: attracting attention to herself and turning the press to her purpose.

The matter of the testimonial dragged on for four years as a result of significant resistance within the government to presenting any gratuity to Caroline, many of the members of parliament questioning the value of her past service to the colony. With a persistent group of Caroline's supporters refusing to give up, the debate went into committee. The £3000 was eventually whittled down to £500 — at one stage one member even suggested £300. A vote to award the money in the government estimates was finally passed at the end of March 1866. With the typically agonising slowness of government, though, another vote on the estimates bill was set for debate in November, meaning that Caroline would receive nothing before then. In the meantime, however, Henry Parkes, amongst others, organised quietly for the Colonial Treasury to pay her half the amount, £250, immediately. That payment was only revealed when several members sought again to reduce the testimonial when it was brought up during the estimates bill in November.[40]

Many newspapers were outraged at the treatment that Caroline had received from the government, papers like *The Tumut and Adelong Times*, which serviced the further reaches of the colony, where many of Caroline's immigrants now lived. It

claimed that she was "deserving of a far greater recognition".[41]
The *Freeman's Journal* described the final amount as "niggardly
justice ... Well would it be for Mrs Chisholm if she could afford
to reject this paltry sum and let future historians of Australia tell
how unworthily statesmen had in earlier days repaid the efforts of
those who had laboured well and worthily in her cause."[42]

Of course, Caroline would not have been able to do so:
she needed the money. It is possible, however, but unlikely,
that she may have received some funds when Sarah Jones died
in March 1859. Sarah's will stated that all her land, houses,
tenements and other properties be sold and the profits divided
amongst her five daughters, of which Caroline was named the
youngest.[43] This does not lay to rest the question of Caroline's
parentage. Caroline was an extremely well known woman in
Britain and achieved recognition far in advance of her roots,
so it's not surprising that Sarah Jones named her in her will.
As to the money, there is no evidence that Caroline received
anything either in Australia or later in Britain. Any funds, of
course, would have gone to Archibald, but one imagines that
he would have handed them over to his wife for her use. There
have been suggestions that she used the inherited funds to set
up her school, but without proof this issue remains a mystery.
It is equally likely that any money she garnered from her first
lecture, and from Archibald and her two working sons, was put
towards the school.

In late 1864, Henry, then twenty-five, married Kate Heffernan
at St Mary's Cathedral. In a mark of the way Caroline had slipped
from public view, the announcement in *The Sydney Morning
Herald* described Henry as "the son of Major Chisholm, late 30th
Regiment M.N Infantry", but made no mention of Caroline.[44]
The following year she would have welcomed her second

grandchild, Henry's son William, no doubt named for his brother who had died seven years earlier in Melbourne.

Ironically, during the mid-1860s one of the boats originally commissioned by Caroline's Family Colonization Loan Society and named after its founder, the *Caroline Chisholm,* was being used as a passenger vessel on the east coast. Thus, although Caroline herself was rarely heard from during her final two years in Sydney, her name was constantly in the shipping sections of all the local newspapers.

With Henry now married, Archibald Jnr found rooms for Caroline in the house in which he lived, in O'Connell Street in the city. She was happy there, and her health improved, as she wrote to her friend Elizabeth Rathbone in Liverpool: "I am sure you will be pleased to hear that I am getting better; every day this last week I have been able to go out for a walk twice a day".[45] The location was perfect for her, being close to her sons' offices. Although she was mostly confined to home, she had a window and made good use of it — she could see her boys when they "pop[ped] to the bank and other offices several times in a day".[46] Maybe just as vital to Caroline's wellbeing was what else she saw from her room: it was close to *The Empire* and *Herald* offices and, as she wrote, "[I] am quite in the way of seeing my old friends." Then, too, it was not far from the Legislative Assembly, so that when the house met, she wrote, she would be able to watch the debates.[47] Caroline may have been infirm and out of the public eye, but she was not about to quit her interest in the world, just yet.

Shortly after receiving the first half of her New South Wales Government gratuity, Caroline departed Sydney, probably with her eldest son, Archibald, on 9 June 1866, aboard the *Maid of Judah*. Her name was found in the shipping lists in *The Empire*; the only other reference to her leaving was made two days later when *The Sydney Morning Herald* reported that it had mistakenly omitted to mention her name in the passenger list. It's likely that Caroline always intended to join Archibald back in Britain. Throughout their marriage, they had endured long separations. This would be the last. There is no evidence as to whether she was contemplating returning to Australia once her daughters had been educated or whether she had decided to live out her life in the country of her birth. There is, however, every indication that she was not giving up on the colony and was pleased that her sons had settled there.

Caroline was fifty-eight years old when she slipped out of Sydney, leaving the men in government still arguing over her worth to the colonies. For almost half her life, since arriving as a young matron of thirty, she had pursued a single overall goal, the advancement of poor settlers in the colony, and been both a buttress and a visionary for the development of Australia. She had found a wide canvas, already dabbed with different hues — those of the original Indigenous people; the first settlers with their brutal penal codes; and the free settlers looking to escape a constrained, hungry, tired Old World for the raw vitality of this new one. In 1838, the colony had been at a crossroads. Its rapid development with an influx of thousands of immigrants was fuelling a critical humanitarian crisis.

Bringing new perspective, Caroline set to work on this canvas with her own composition in mind. Deliberate, unhurried and effective, she singlehandedly changed the attitudes of the colony's powerful governing elite to the plight of the desperate bounty immigrants. She gave thousands of new settlers the chance to establish themselves in jobs and on land throughout New South Wales. Having sketched out her vision, she returned to Britain to encourage and send out thousands more of the families and friends of the earlier settlers, as well as hardworking lower- and middle-class immigrants — all people she knew would have a better life in Australia. Again, to make her plan work she co-opted the government leaders to her cause. She added the final touches to her image of Australia by insisting that land and multi-culturalism be considered, along with the rights of all people, especially women.

It had been a remarkable career. Acting from morality and love, also and undoubtedly with humour and hubris, she had left an indelible mark upon the colony. She had seen many of her ideas take effect, though it would be many years before her other, more radical concepts would be accepted.

For close on forty years, Caroline had been a nomad. That Saturday in early winter, when her ship finally weighed anchor and set sail through the Sydney Heads, she may not yet have realised that it would be for the final time.

CHAPTER 15

The Final Journey
1866–77

Barclay Road, Fulham, London, March 1877

The curtains across the bay windows had been pulled back to let in the timid spring sunshine. There was only a hint of warmth in it, but Caroline was inordinately cheered by the sight of sunlight spreading across the patchwork quilt that covered her bed. She looked outside to where clumps of daffodils swayed in the breeze, their golden-crowned heads smiling bright. She had always loved them, always seen them as tokens of a new beginning. She shifted position slightly, trying to make herself more comfortable. The effort brought on a shuddering series of coughs and gasps for breath that left her exhausted and aching. She didn't think that she could stand much more of this. If God was ready for her, she was almost ready to go.

Her coughing brought Monica into the room. The sight of her daughter worried Caroline. At twenty-six, Monica should have been a married woman with her own family, not nursing her old, invalided mother. Making an effort for her daughter, Caroline drank the medicine that Monica tenderly held to her lips. She pretended that she felt better for it, then sent Monica from the room again, saying that she wished to rest.

As she lay back on her pillows, laughter wafted in from the footpath outside, children on their way to the common to play — a happy sound. With her eyelids drooping now against the daylight, Caroline's mind drifted back across the years. She thought she heard again the giggles of little girls skipping along the beach in Madras. She had tried to prepare them for a better future. She wondered how they had turned out in the end, if she had made a difference.

She sighed deeply, feeling a certain contentment. She had no such doubt about her immigration work. "They needed me," she whispered, although she was the only one listening. She thought back on all those rough journeys through the bush, the months at sea and days on thundering trains, the contracts and letters she had written, the meetings and committees and lectures. Chiefly, though, she remembered the people. The wealthy and powerful who had assisted in her work — there had been some good men and women — but mostly she thought about the poor and the needy, the ones she had helped to a better life. So many of them had been heartfelt in their thanks to her for giving them a future.

If she had a regret, it was for her children. She had dragged them along behind her, perhaps showing less concern for their welfare than a mother should have done. Even so, they had grown up well, becoming fine men and women. She supposed that she had Archie to thank for that. Indeed, Archie had been the perfect husband: she could not have achieved even a quarter of what she had done without his support. Kind, uncritical, compliant Archie — she owed him so much.

Clouds covered the sun; the room grew chilly. Her mind drifted back to that big warm southern land and the immigrants. She had been vital to them back then, especially the women, but what about now? Was her work only as fleeting as the sunshine on a cold March morning in London? She knew it wasn't. She had given them not just a good start, but a fair start. They would thrive, as would their children and their children, right down through the ages. There would be changes: democracy was coming; it was inevitable. She smiled as she remembered someone at one of her lectures suggesting she should stand for parliament. Maybe one day there would even be a lady governor in Australia. Anything was possible.

Part of her wished that she could live forever, to see what would become of the land she loved. She knew, though, that her time was drawing near, and her body had had enough. She was pleased, though, that her sons were in Australia: that meant that part of her would remain with them, live on in the colony and be part of its destiny.[1]

Liverpool, spreading inland from the Irish Sea, was, in 1866, a microcosm of Britain's urban industrialisation. It was one of the wealthiest cities in the country, even for a short time challenging London for the title of the richest, yet its schizophrenic confines housed the elegant and the sophisticated alongside the brutal and the desperate — the Brownlow Hill workhouse, for instance, with its degraded inmates numbering up to three thousand, surviving pitilessly only miles from visionary Oriel Chambers, a revelation of stone and glass, the world's first metal framed glass–curtain-wall building — a forerunner of the New York skyscrapers twenty years later. On the water, the Prince Albert docks were the focal point of Britain's own influx of immigrants. In a portent of the reverse post–World War II immigration more than a century later, Liverpool, with almost half a million inhabitants, was a European melting-pot, hosting large numbers of Scandinavian, German, Greek, Irish and Jewish people.

This is where Caroline landed on 23 September 1866, to be reunited once again with Archibald.[2] Compared with Sydney and Melbourne, Liverpool would have felt crammed and noisy, but the streets would have been teeming with bustling energy. After eight years living in the mild Sydney climate, Caroline may have found the autumn weather decidedly cold and the city's environment almost alien: the wind blowing in off the Irish Sea and the weak sunshine; the damp, hushed pinks of verbena and phlox, and the gentle calls of sparrow, greenfinch, robin and thrush, so soft and muted after the startling sounds and blazing colours of the Australian bush.

Caroline and Archibald settled into a home on Brookland Road, in the Old Swan district of the city, about five kilometres from Greenbank, home of their friends the Rathbones.[3] As noted earlier, the friendship between Caroline and Elizabeth Rathbone probably dated back to when Caroline was lecturing in Liverpool in 1853, and they seem to have remained close. In a letter from Sydney, in 1865, Caroline thanks Elizabeth for her "motherly kindness to my children", before going on to say, "Oh how much I long to see you to thank you for your sympathy."[4] Elizabeth's husband, William, came from a renowned philanthropic family. A wealthy merchant, and politician, he had, amongst other endeavours, established public baths and washhouses to help fight a cholera epidemic in the city in the 1830s. Before arriving in Liverpool, Caroline had apprised Elizabeth Rathbone of her desire to live close to the docks so that she could visit ships and be within easy reach of would-be emigrants seeking information about the Australian colonies.[5] There is no evidence, however, that Caroline ever engaged in any such activity in Liverpool. She may have been too ill or, once again, too distracted to do so, but the fact that she even contemplated continuing her work pays tribute to her indomitable spirit.

This would be Caroline and Archibald's final reconciliation. They had parted so many times and for so many years during their marriage; that was now ended, and they would spend their final years together. For a short time, Archibald Jnr was the only child, albeit a grown-up one, at home with them in Liverpool. When Archibald Snr had arrived in Britain in 1864, he had initially taken the girls and Sydney to visit relations and friends before seeing to their education. Caroline Jnr, eighteen years old in 1866, was being taught by the Marist Sisters at Elm Villa Convent, "a pretty little house with a garden on Holloway Road" in Highgate, London, whilst Monica, now fifteen, had been sent to a convent school in Belgium, where the fees were not too high, and Sydney, twenty, was most likely in Ireland, also extending his studies.[6]

Less than a decade earlier, Caroline had been famous throughout England, Ireland and Scotland. Not just the London newspapers but, largely due to her lecture tours and the interest in emigration, the regional and small-town press had regularly reported her thoughts, as well as the progress of her Family Colonization Loan Society. Now, though, when she returned to Britain as a private citizen, there were no reports and no comments. It was as though she had never existed. All that was to change briefly, however, as a result of a bizarre episode.

In early 1867, an audacious trickster, Henry Philip Dashwood Arthy, was convicted in London's Bow Street Court of having defrauded the Royal Bounty Fund using false pretences and sentenced to ten years' penal servitude.[7] Six months earlier he had petitioned the British Prime Minister, Lord Derby, pretending to be Caroline. He stated in his letter, "I was the original founder of the present government system of emigration to Australia." He further claimed that "Caroline" was now a widow, suffering ill health and in need of funds to educate her grandchildren in Australia. The British Government paid the imposter £100 before the deception was discovered. The real Caroline gave a deposition to the London court disowning the letter, noting that she was still at sea when it was sent, and rebutting any suggestion that she was a widow. The report of the court case and its resolution was published in newspapers up and down the country, thus spreading the word that Caroline had returned.[8]

Almost as quickly as the story had surged, it died. Soon after, however, financial issues brought Caroline back into the spotlight fleetingly. Unsure if they would receive any more money from New South Wales, and with Archibald's pension yearly losing value, the Chisholms were once again living in extremely straitened conditions. In May 1867, the British Government awarded Caroline an annual pension of £100 "in consideration of the valuable and disinterested services rendered by her to emigrants in New South Wales".[9] Civil List pensions were reported in all the newspapers. Some of these publications had not forgotten Caroline's commitment and energy in her heyday, and like their colleagues in Australia were scathing of the government's parsimony. *Lloyd's Weekly London Newspaper* wrote, "There are thousands in this country who bless her for her brave work in the cause of emigration; and there are tens of thousands who revere her name in Australia ... This time Lord Derby has selected most worthy objects; but he ... has been niggardly to Mrs Chisholm."[10] Other papers simply reported the award without comment, like *The Northampton Mercury*, which added only that she was "a native of Northampton".[11]

*

Not unlike many other notable people who fade from public life as they reach their eventide, a gentle dusk began to envelop Caroline. Her close friends and family were aware of her plight but few others were. With the glare of fame turned off, she was sheltered from any unwanted intrusions during her final years with Archibald. In 1869 the couple moved to Highgate in London. It's unlikely that Caroline had ever fully recovered from the kidney disease that had so incapacitated her in Australia, and now she was suffering from a new ailment, dropsy, an old-fashioned term for oedema, possibly even cerebral oedema.[12] Whatever the cause, she was extremely unwell, and on the point of being bedridden. Sydney, now twenty-three, had already returned to New South Wales and Archibald Jnr, thirty-three, was planning to join him. It is possible that Caroline's sons left Britain without realising just how unwell she was at that time, particularly as such intimate details may not have been shared with them. As a family, too, they had been used to travelling from one side of the world to the other, so the boys may have expected to visit their parents again. Before he left, Archibald Jnr visited family in Scotland. A cousin later wrote to his father, "You will all feel heavily the departure of dear Archie for the Colony ... and the more so considering

Caroline in old age *(courtesy of Don Chisholm)*

the frail state of his dear Mother's health ... and you yourself not being over strong ...This is indeed a world of many sorrows."[13]

Not all the Chisholms were sorrowful, though. Henry, thirty, was still in Sydney and progressing well with his civil-service work and growing family — by then he was the father of three children: William, four, Mary Ellen, two, and a newborn, Archibald Frank. As for the girls, Caroline's namesake, her oldest living daughter, was now twenty-one and, despite suffering from what was probably fibrositis, was married that year to Edmund Gray, the son of Irish Member of Parliament Sir John Gray. The couple settled in Dublin but found time to visit her parents. The last child at home was the youngest, eighteen-year-old Monica, who, having returned from the convent school in Belgium, was helping to care for her mother.

Caroline, Archibald and Monica maintained a quiet life, never losing touch with the family members in Australia. Archibald Jnr married Anne Loder at the end of winter in 1870. Ironically, the advertisement in the Sydney newspapers attempted to pay homage to both his parents and ended up something of a melange: "Archibald, eldest son of Major and Mrs Caroline Chisholm, Strathglass, Invernesshire, Scotland, to Anne Jane, second daughter of the late Henry Loder, Esq., of Sydney".[14] The following year, Anne gave birth to twin girls; sadly the younger one, Letitia Isabella, died three months later.[15]

Though Henry was well established in Australia, it seems that Sydney, after returning to the city for which he was named, suffered some kind of reversal at work and was possibly sacked from his job. He wrote to his parents about his disappointment. Caroline may have been confined to bed, her body wretched and disobliging, but her mind was still as ebullient as ever. She wrote back to her son: "I do not believe in chances, but I have faith to think you are going through special training to fit you for your future — good metal stands the heavy crush when the inferior would fly into fragments … Cheer up Sydney, the sun will yet shine on."[16] It was a remarkably positive homily from a woman wracked by pain and confined to bed, a prisoner of her own body, who was forced to exist in one small dark room, without even the funds to alleviate the dreariness of each succeeding day. By this stage Caroline may have realised that she was unlikely to see her three sons again. It is probable, though, that she supported their choice to make their lives in Australia. After all, she had spent most of hers promoting the many advantages of living in the Antipodes, so it must have seemed only fitting that her descendants would be born and grow up in that sunshine land on the other side of the world that she knew offered so much promise.

*

The years slipped away. Then tragedy struck, in Sydney and most unexpectedly, at the end of January 1875. Just five years after his wedding, Archibald Jnr died of rheumatic fever. He was thirty-nine, and was survived by his wife, Anne, and their two daughters, Caroline and Jean. It must have been devastating for both Caroline and Archibald. They had now lost both the sons born in India, along with their two baby daughters, who had died within six months of birth, as well as two of their granddaughters. Of Caroline's eight children, only four remained. More fortunately, at this time Sydney's luck improved. He became a clerk for a stock and station firm and married Isabella Loder, the sister of Archibald's widow. Henry, now the oldest, was forging ahead making a solid life for himself in the New South Wales Justice Department.

About this time, Archibald wrote to Henry on two matters that were probably preying on both his and Caroline's minds. He asked Henry to try to locate the gold medal Caroline had received from Pope Pius IX back in 1853 — as mentioned earlier, Archibald had pawned it in Sydney when the Chisholms had been desperate for funds. It seems that it was never found. The other concern was for the couple's unmarried daughter, Monica, who in 1875 was twenty-four. With Caroline now bedridden for a number of years, Archibald, at seventy-seven, was becoming aware of his own mortality as well as hers, and was worried for Monica's future. Since returning to Britain, Caroline and Archibald had been existing on his meagre pension and her small annuity, the total being a paltry £392 a year. Archibald explained to Henry that when both he and Caroline died, Monica, as his dependent, would be entitled to only £60 per annum (from the Madras Military Fund); he hoped that their friends might, in the eventuality that she remained unmarried, make representations to the government to award her at least half of her mother's pension too. He wrote that he was leaving letters to that effect addressed to Henry and various friends.[17]

In mid-1876, with the aid of their two daughters, Monica and Caroline, and the latter's husband, Edmund Gray, Caroline and Archibald moved to better accommodation in Barclay Road, Fulham. Her daughter Caroline later recounted how, as her mother was carried from her dark room, she was told to close her eyes. Once outside the house she opened them and, looking up, exclaimed, "Oh, thank God for the beautiful sky!"[18] It was also as she was being transported to this new home that, as mentioned previously, she asked to stop the carriage so that she could see the latest fashions in the shop windows.

The Fulham residence was only slightly larger, but had a much better outlook. After years of lying in a dark room, Caroline was now ensconced in a bed next to a bay window, giving her light, air and sunshine. It was there, only a few months later, on 25 March 1877, that she died. The death certificate recorded "Senile Softening of Brain 6 years, Bronchitis 14 days".[19] She was sixty-eight years old.

As the press announced her death, gave particulars of her funeral — she was to be buried in the Billing Road Cemetery, in Northampton — and spared room for eulogies, Caroline's demise reverberated around the two nations that she loved. Her passing was mentioned in every nook and cranny of the British Isles; similarly, in Australia there were reports from Rockhampton in the north to Fremantle in the west and south to Hobart. *The Argus* in Melbourne provided one of the most eloquent tributes:

The name of Caroline Chisholm carries us back to times
in which civilisation was not yet wedded to sympathy,
to times when a cruel economy was predominant in the
best governed countries in the world, to times when the
homes of millions of the poor in Europe suffered a painful
dissolution, and the colonial problem threatened to defeat
enterprise and set aside experience. Forty years ago Australia
was an unknown land to politicians, travellers, and traders.
The penal settlements had darkened a prospect which never
was singularly bright, and had covered with shame and
obloquy a reputation already worsted by the terrors of the
unknown. The unhappy emigrant to the far-off island found
poor comfort in the knowledge that it was the largest in the
world, that its climate was generous, that it was free from the
track of the panther, and knew no blight from pestilence. He
felt that it was a place of banishment, that the dreary regions
which one day might be his own never could be his solace,

that it might be his fate to perish untimely in the dread ordeal before him, and sink in the struggle far from home and kindred. With the unhappy women who were driven out, the terrors were still greater. The journals were filled with tales of appalling woe, of starvation on board ship, and a ruin worse than death on shore. It seemed hardly possible that evils which Governments had vainly endeavoured to suppress should be utterly borne down by a woman; that a system which a Cabinet Minister dared not have attempted should be developed to perfection by the unaided exertions of an English lady.[20]

Afterword

Archibald survived Caroline by only five months, dying on 17 August 1877. He was buried next to his wife, beneath the same tombstone, at the Billing Road Cemetery, in Northampton. The graveyard is a little more than seven kilometres from Wootton, the village where Caroline's father, William, was born in 1744 (and which is near the Caroline Chisholm School, opened in 2004). It was almost as though, after all their years of travel, Caroline and Archibald had finally gone home to where it had all started for them as a couple, just after the Yuletide in 1830.

Caroline and Archibald left four living grown-up children divided by half a world: the two boys, Henry and Sydney, in Australia, and the two girls, Caroline and Monica, in Dublin and London. Following the couple's deaths, several of Caroline's friends, including Florence Nightingale, petitioned the government on behalf of Monica.[1] In the Civil List Pensions of June 1878, she was awarded £50 per annum "in recognition of the services rendered by her mother, Mrs Caroline Chisholm, 'The Emigrant's Friend'".[2] That amount was additional to the £60 entitlement that Monica received from Archibald's pension from the East India Company. Sometime after that, Monica married

Maurice Gruggen and they moved to Moosomin, Saskatchewan, in Canada, to take up farming. From letters written by Monica, it appears that she paid for the upkeep of her parents' grave for many years, but when her farming venture faltered, she was unable to continue. Monica had no children, nor does it appear that she ever returned to Britain. In her last recorded letter, dating from 1929, she was still in Canada and mentions her own and her husband's ill health. She was seventy-eight years old at that time.[3]

Monica's letters also reveal a little of her older sister's undulating life. At the time of her marriage in 1869, Caroline's husband, Edmund Gray, was something of a hero, having received an Irish bravery award, the Tayleur Fund Gold Medal, for helping rescue the crew of a schooner sinking off Killiney Bay the previous year. Strangely, Caroline Jnr is thought to have witnessed the event, although she had not yet met Gray.[4] Her husband became an Irish newspaper proprietor, politician and a Member of Parliament in the British House of Commons, who was, notably, in favour of Home Rule. He also became Lord Mayor of Dublin and later High Sheriff of the City of Dublin. Despite this stellar career, Gray, a heavy drinker and asthma sufferer, died at forty-two years of age, after a short illness. He had been a very wealthy man, probate showing that he left Caroline Jnr an estate of some £90,000, the equivalent of being a multi-millionaire today. One of Monica's letters refers to Edmund Gray's wealth, saying that he also had "a lovely house in Dublin and a seaside house — when my sister was Lady Mayoress of Dublin she was very popular and the Corporation presented her with a lot of diamonds."[5] Unfortunately, Caroline Jnr's fortune did not last. She married again, to a Maurice O'Connor, and according to Monica "lost everything during her second marriage". Caroline Jnr died in 1927 at the age of seventy-nine. Her first marriage had produced at least two children: Mary, on whom there is little information, and Edmund Dwyer-Gray, who migrated to Australia, finally settling in Tasmania. He became a farmer and a journalist, joined the Labor Party, hyphenated his name to help his election prospects (the change moved it up the alphabetically listed ballot papers to capture the 'donkey vote'), and rose to become state treasurer and briefly, in June 1939, premier of Tasmania. Though he married, he and his wife did not have any children, and he passed away in December 1945.[6]

Caroline's family and descendants continued to thrive in Australia. Although her eldest son, Archibald, died at a relatively young age, both his daughters grew to adulthood. Jean married Edward Gerber, whilst her sister, Caroline, married Dr Frederick Langton and produced a large and successful family of doctors.

Henry and Sydney also remained in New South Wales. Little is known about Sydney, except that he married and had no children. Henry was undoubtedly the most successful of Caroline's offspring. He was appointed a police magistrate at both Yass, on the state's Southern Tablelands, and at Wollongong, on the coast south of Sydney. At the same time and, no doubt influenced by his father's career, Henry became a colonel in the Duke of Edinburgh Highlanders and helped found the Highland Society of New South Wales. He died in 1923 at the age of eighty-four, leaving his widow, Kate, and six children: William, Mary, Archibald, Henry, Edmund and Caroline.

Fittingly, it is the descendants of Henry, the successful Antipodean son, who have done the most to keep Caroline's story alive. They are still living in Australia, contributing mightily to the nation's social fabric. There are at least three generations of Chisholms, including, today, three successful brothers, Caroline's great-great-grandsons Robert Chisholm, a retired journalist; Professor Richard Chisholm AM, Adjunct Professor of Law at the

Australian National University and a retired judge of the Family
Court, who was also a founding member of the Aboriginal Legal
Service and of the children's rights group Action for Children;
and, the eldest brother, Professor Don Chisholm AO, Professor of
Medicine at St Vincent's Hospital, Sydney, the Garvan Institute
of Medical Research and the University of New South Wales,
who works primarily in the treatment and research of diabetes.
Don Chisholm's son James is on the international board of the
Hunger Project, whose mission is to make hunger throughout
the world obsolete, whilst his daughter Sarah, like her great-
great-great-grandmother, Caroline, began her work by aiding
female immigrants and newly arrived refugees in New South
Wales. Sarah, too, looked for practical solutions, helping establish
social enterprise projects whereby new arrivals could settle into
their surroundings and access paid work. Like her forebear, her
prime objective was to give the women respect and autonomy.
More recently, Sarah has been involved in environmental
social enterprise. Expressing her motivation, she could be
channelling Caroline when she says: "The world's resources and
opportunities are not always accessible to a range of people in our
communities. Some struggle to access basic human rights and
decent opportunities. I have always believed that something has
to be done to address this. I see some amazing work being done,
at other times, I realise that there is still so much more to do."

*

In every epoch, there are exceptional travellers, individuals who
help reconfigure and reshape their world until what they stand for
becomes the touchstone of a humane or equitable society. Caroline
Chisholm was one such person. The breadth and scope of her

achievements would be exceptional today; in an era when most females were confined to domestic banality with little say in their own lives, they were truly extraordinary. Her initial mission was to free vulnerable women from their cruel dependency on men, to give them choices and opportunities for self-determination, the chance to work for decent wages in fair conditions. In doing so, she demanded a new level of safety and respect for women, indeed for all workers. In her early years in Sydney, Caroline widened the scope of her activities to eventually aid some eleven thousand men, women and children — finding them employment, saving them from destitution and helping to create thriving country communities. Later she was to instigate family reunion schemes whereby left-at-home relatives in Britain could join their kin in Australia to put down roots in the New World. There are many successful families across Australia today that owe their place in society to the start Caroline gave their forebears. Yet, notably, Caroline also acknowledged the Indigenous inhabitants of Australia as the "original owners of the land", a recognition that would take 145 years and the 1992 Mabo decision to finally be enshrined in law.

By instigating the *Carthaginian* case, Caroline underlined that boat captains and surgeons should be responsible for the wellbeing of their passengers and, moreover, owed them a duty of care. That was a significant victory for impoverished immigrants, who previously had had no legal redress against the brutality many had to endure on the long voyage to Australia. Similarly, during her Family Colonization Loan Society days, Caroline insisted that boat surgeons were well paid and, hence, experienced medical practitioners. Challenging the British Government's Passengers Act, she introduced a new standard of travel for steerage class, whereby immigrants had reasonable cabins, washhouses and cooking space and were entitled to good food and water; she also made some attempt to ensure that they had clean air below decks and, most importantly, privacy. Her plans were to define a new style of travel for long-distance passenger ships. She set standards that were eventually to become minimum requirements under law.

In an issue that still chimes today with the great Australian dream of owning your own home, one of Caroline's most consistent and passionate campaigns supported the rights of everyone to purchase their own land. In addition to the Shellharbour experiment, she lobbied continuously during her appearances before select government committees in both Sydney and London, during her public lectures and, repeatedly, for years, in letters and articles to newspapers on both sides of the world. She was not the only one advocating the freeing up of land, but she was a powerful and well-known voice, and her efforts undoubtedly rallied support to the cause. Before she left Australia in 1866 she had her reward, with both New South Wales and Victoria legislating in favour of small landholders.

Many of Caroline's most radical ideas showed a vision far in advance of her time. Whilst many twenty-first century societies still struggle with ethnic divisions, she supported multiculturalism decades before the word was even invented, clearly understanding the modern concept of "unity in diversity". At a time of determined anti-Asian sentiment, Caroline wrote and spoke of the need to welcome Chinese immigrants and treat them as an integral part of the community. For Caroline, what mattered was not a settler's past but the innate morality of their character, their ability to be positive, to work and achieve results. She found no cause to discriminate against any person because of the god they worshipped or the colour of their skin. She believed in inclusiveness, and saw creeds and ethnicities as part of the vast, delightful patchwork of humanity. Equally, she espoused the benefits of democracy, universal suffrage and fairer working conditions. In the 1850s and 1860s she defied the conventions that kept women bound to a private domestic life, speaking out in public lectures to argue that all women should have full self-determination and, even, eventually be enfranchised.

Despite her avant-garde ideas, Caroline made no revolutionary demands; instead, the key to her success was her ability to encompass intellectual, practical and compassionate considerations while expressing a robust self-belief that instilled confidence in others and encouraged them to see beyond myopic conventions. Caroline had an unequivocal, ebullient faith in the future of the colonies. She knew that a truly hardworking, eclectic community would eventually produce a proud, successful society full of heart and soul. Our generation, and future ones, should recognise her part in shaping a flourishing, egalitarian and, most importantly, humane Australia. We are all in her debt.

Endnotes

Introduction

1   Samuel Sidney, *Sidney's Emigrant's Journal and Traveller's Magazine, Second Series,* Wm. S. Orr and Co., London, 1850, p. 271.

2   Ibid.

3   Captain Archibald Chisholm was with the East India Company, not the British Army. The title of captain outside the East India Company was honorary.

4   Postage in the colony was expensive: a half-ounce letter sent from Sydney cost 4d to Parramatta, 7d to Windsor or Campbell Town, 10d to Bathurst and a shilling for three hundred miles; see Margaret Kiddle, *Caroline Chisholm,* Melbourne University Press, Melbourne, 1950, p. 23.

5   Governor Gipps wrote to an English friend that Caroline had overrated the powers of her own mind; see Sidney, *Emigrant's Journal,* p. 271.

6   Caroline Chisholm, *Female Immigration Considered, in a Brief Account of the Sydney Immigrants' Home,* James Tegg, Sydney, 1842, p. 5.

7   Thomas Callaghan, *Callaghan's Diary: The 1840s Sydney Diary of Thomas Callaghan of the King's Inns, Dublin, Barrister at Law,* Francis Forbes Society for Australian Legal History, Dream Weaver Publishing, Sydney, 2005, p. 116.

8   Ibid., p. 168.

9   Mrs William Parkes (Fanny Parkes, née Byerly), *Domestic Duties; or, Instructions to Young Married Ladies, on the Management of their Households, and the Regulation of Their Conduct in the Various Relations and Duties of Married Life,* Longman, Rees, Orme, Brown and Green, London, 1828, p. 30.

10 Mrs Ellis (Sarah Stickney Ellis), *The Daughters of England, Their Position in Society, Character and Responsibilities*, D. Appleton and Co., New York, 1843, p. 6.

11 Samuel Sidney, *The Three Colonies of Australia: New South Wales, Victoria, South Australia; Their Pastures, Copper Mines and Gold Fields*, Ingram, Cooke and Co., 1853, London, p. 135.

12 Mary Hoban, *Fifty-one Pieces of Wedding Cake: A Biography of Caroline Chisholm*, Lowden Publishing Co., Kilmore, Victoria, 1973, p. x.

13 Elizabeth Windschuttle, "Feeding the Poor and Sapping their Strength: The Public Role of Ruling-Class Women in Eastern Australia, 1788–1850", in Elizabeth Windschuttle (ed.), *Women, Class and History*, Fontana/Collins, Melbourne, 1980, p. 53.

14 Anne Summers, *Damned Whores and God's Police*, Penguin Books Camberwell, Victoria, Australia, 2002, p. 51.

15 Carole Walker, *A Saviour of Living Cargoes: The Life and Work of Caroline Chisholm*, Wolds Publishing Ltd, Leicester, UK, 2010.

16 Eneas Mackenzie, *Memoirs of Mrs Caroline Chisholm, with an Account of Her Philanthropic Labours in India, Australia, and England; To which is added a History of the Family Colonization Loan Society; also the Question, Who Ought to Emigrate? Answered*, Webb, Millington and Co., London, second edition, 1852, pp. x, 152.

17 Kiddle, op. cit., p. xxiv.

18 Callaghan, op. cit., p. 169.

Chapter 1: Love Child

1 Walker, op. cit., p. 186.

2 Max Roser, "Life Expectancy", published online at OurWorldInData. org; retrieved from: https://ourworldindata.org/life-expectancy/

3 Jane Randall, *Women in an Industrializing Society: England 1750–1880*, Basil Blackwell Ltd, Oxford, 1990, pp. 38, 40.

4 Faramerz Dabhoiwala, *The Origins of Sex: A History of the First Sexual Revolution*, Oxford University Press, New York, 2012, p. 181.

5 "Philogamus", *The Present State of Matrimony: Or, the Real Causes of Conjugal Infidelity and Unhappy Marriages*, John Hawkins, London, 1739, pp. 11, 10.

6 Dabhoiwala, op. cit., p. 92.

7   Edith Pearson, "Caroline Chisholm, 'The Emigrant's Friend', 1808–1877", reprinted in Rodney Stinson (ed.), *Unfeigned Love,* Yorkcross Pty Ltd., Sydney, 2008, p. 171.

8   Ibid.

9   F.K. Prochaska, *Women and Philanthropy in Nineteenth-Century England,* Oxford University Press Inc., New York, 1980, p. 9.

10 *The Works of the Rev. John Wesley, in Ten Volumes,* vol. VII, J. & J. Harper, New York, 1826, p. 152.

11 Eneas Mackenzie, *Memoirs,* p. 2.

12 Pearson, op. cit., p. 172.

13 Ibid.

14 Eneas Mackenzie, *Memoirs,* pp. 3–4.

15 Walker, op. cit., p. 178.

16 Ibid., p. 177.

17 Pearson, op. cit., p. 180. Pearson's essay about Caroline is based on, amongst other sources, an interview with her daughter, also named Caroline. The younger Caroline would have been about sixty-six years old when Pearson wrote her essay. The younger Caroline said that her mother was sent to live with an "older woman" and related the story of a thief being frightened away by Caroline and the older lady throwing coal at him (see page 28). It is not known why Caroline was sent away from home. The older woman may have been her natural mother, or an early school teacher or a widow in need of help. It was not unusual for middle- and upper-class women to send their children from home when they were young.

18 Walker, op. cit., pp. 184–86.

19 Pearson, op. cit., pp. 180–81.

20 D.K. Shearing, *Education in the Peterborough Dioceses in the Century Following the "Glorious Revolution" 1688,* PhD Thesis, Institute of Education, University of London, 1990, pp. 285–86.

21 Reverend Henry Venn, *The Complete Duty of Man or, a System of Doctrinal and Practical Christianity. With Prayers for Families and Individuals,* William Collins, London, 1829, p. 375.

22 James Fordyce D.D., *Sermons to Young Women: Two Volumes in One,* third American edition from the twelfth London edition, M. Carey, Philadelphia, 1809, p. 19.

23 Pearson, op. cit., p. 173.

24 John Moran, introduction to *Little Joe,* by Caroline Chisholm, Preferential Publications, Ashgrove, Queensland, 1991, p. iii.

25 Joan Perkin, *Women and Marriage in Nineteenth Century England,* Routledge, London, 1989, p. 3.

26 Eneas Mackenzie, *Memoirs,* p. 144.

27 Pearson, op. cit., pp. 180–81.

Chapter 2: Marriage and Faith

1   Walker, op. cit., pp. 16–20.

2   International Clan Chisholm Society, www.rampantscotland.com/clans/blclanchisholm.htm

3   Walker, op. cit., pp. 16–20.

4   Caroline Chisholm, letter to Bishop Ullathorne, Bishop of Birmingham, quoted in Walker, op. cit., pp. 114–15.

5   Mary Wollstonecraft, *A Vindication of the Rights of Woman, with Strictures on Political and Moral Subjects. With a Biographical Sketch of the Author.* A.J. Matsell, New York, 1833.

6   Eneas Mackenzie, *The Emigrant's Guide to Australia with a Memoir of Mrs Chisholm,* Clarke, Beeton & Co., London, 1853, p. 6.

7   *Saturday Review,* 12 November 1859.

8   Wollstonecraft, op. cit., p. 10.

9   Helena Michie, *Victorian Honeymoons: Journeys to the Conjugal,* Cambridge University Press, Cambridge, 2006, p. xiii.

10 Renton Nicholson, *The Swell's Night Guide; or, a Peep Through the Great Metropolis, under the Dominion of Nox: Displaying the Various Attractive Places of Amusement by Night,* H. Smith, London, 1846.

11 A Lady, *A Manual of the Etiquette of Love, Courtship, and Marriage,* Thomas Allman, London, 1852, p. 11.

12 Perkin, op. cit., p. 276.

13 Sarah Stickney Ellis, *The Wives of England, their Relative Duties, Domestic Influence, and Social Obligations,* D. Appleton & Co, London, 1843, p. 20.

14 Dr William Acton, MRCS, *The Functions and Disorders of the Reproductive Organs in Childhood, Youth, Adult Age and Advanced Life Considered in their Physiological, Social and Moral Relations,* John Churchill, London, 1863, p. 101.

15 Family Planning Association, London, "Contraception: Past, Present
    and Future", www.fpa.org.uk/sites/default/files/contraception-past-
    present-and-future-factsheet-november-2010.pdf

16 Hoban, op. cit., p. 413.

17 Most easily shown by the will of Caroline's sister Harriet, who died
    in 1872. She left bequests to her local Wesleyan Chapel as well as to
    various nieces and nephews, including one niece married to a Church
    of England minister, and one of Caroline's sons, Henry, who was a
    Catholic. Walker, op. cit., p. 153.

18 Raymond Apple, "The Jewish Emigrants from Britain: Australia and
    New Zealand", in Gabriel A. Sivan (ed.), *The Jewish Emigrant from Britain
    1700–2000: Essays in Memory of Lloyd p. Gartner,* Jewish Historical
    Society of England, Israel Branch, Jerusalem, 2013.

19 Artemas Bowers Muzzey, *The English Maiden, Her Moral and Domestic
    Duties,* Tallboys, Clark & Wilson, London, 1842, p. 153.

20 *The Old Limerick Journal,* vol. 40, 2004, p. 25.

21 Sir John Philippart, KGV and KPS (ed.), *General Index to the First
    and Second Series of Hansard's Parliamentary Debates forming A Digest of
    the Recorded Proceedings of Parliament, from 1803 to 1830,* Baldwin &
    Cradock, London, 1834, p. 303, "Petition from Northampton, against
    any further Concession to the Catholics, the object of the Petitioners
    being to secure as completely as possible, the Integrity and Safety of the
    Protestant Establishment in Church and State, 1829".

22 William Whellan & Co., *History, Gazetteer and Directory of
    Northamptonshire,* Whittaker & Co., London, 1849, p. 185.

Chapter 3: Life and Death

1   In writing this scene I referred to the following sources: Irvine Loudon,
    "Deaths in Childbed from the Eighteenth Century to 1935", in *Medical
    History,* vol. 30, no. 1, 1986; and Anonymous, *Plain Observations on the
    Management of Children during the First Month, Particularly Addressed to
    Mothers,* Underwood, London, 1828, pp. 1–15.

2   Geoffrey Chamberlain, "British Maternal Mortality in the 19th and
    Early 20th Centuries", *The Journal of the Royal Society of Medicine,* vol. 99,
    November, 2006, p. 2.

3   Ibid. In fact, a former naval surgeon, Alexander Gordon, had discovered
    the same link some fifty years earlier, but his findings had been so badly

received that he had been hounded from his practice and forced to return to the navy to find work.

4   Monica-Maria Stapelberg, *Through the Darkness: Glimpses into the History of Western Medicine*, Crux Publishing, London, 2016.

5   Walker, op. cit., p. 27.

6   Loudon, op. cit., p. 29.

7   Walker, op. cit., p. 31.

8   Parkes, op. cit., p. 286.

9   Whellan, op. cit., p. 172. There is no indication that Caroline or Archibald (who would have received her property and any income and monies along with her hand in marriage) maintained any financial association with this or any other property in Northampton in later years, whilst there is evidence that William, a hog jobber like his father, was still resident there in 1849.

10 "Mr De Ville of Mrs Chisholm Organization deduced from Phrenological Examination, Brighton 29th July 1833". Signed by James De Ville. Brighton Jan. 30th 1833, Papers relating to Caroline Chisholm, 1833–ca. 1854, Collection State Library of NSW, Call Number Ac19/Folder 1.

11 T.M. Parssinen, "Popular Science and Society: The Phrenology Movement in Early Victorian Britain", *Journal of Social History*, vol. 8, no. 1, 1974, pp. 1–20; see JSTOR, www.jstor.org/stable/3786523

Chapter 4: India

1   The depiction of Madras is based on James Welsh, *Military Reminiscences; Extracted from a Journal of Nearly Forty Years' Active Service in the East Indies,* Smith, Elder and Co., London, 1820, pp. 5–7; and Julia Maitland, *Letters from Madras. By a Lady During the Years 1836–1839,* John Murray, London, 1846, p. 18.

2   Walker, op. cit., p. 33; and *The Asiatic Journal and Monthly Register for British and Foreign India, China, and Australia Vol. XII New Series January–April 1834,* Parbury, Allen & Co, London, 1834, p. 209. Archibald received his promotion on 8 April 1833.

3   Maitland, op. cit., p. 18.

4   Ibid., p. 19.

5   Ibid., p. 19.

6   Eneas Mackenzie, *Memoirs*, p. 7

7   Maitland, op. cit., p. 56.

8   A Medical Practitioner of Several Years' Experience in India, *A Domestic Guide to Mothers in India Containing Particular Instructions on the Management of Themselves and Their Children,* Bombay American Mission Press, Bombay, 1856, p. 178.

9   *Madras Almanac and Compendium of Intelligence for 1839,* Edmund Marsden, Madras, 1839, p. 140.

10   C.E. Buckland, CIE, *Dictionary of Indian Biography,* Swan Sonnenschein & Co, London, 1906, p. 78.

11   Eneas Mackenzie, *Memoirs,* p. 10.

12   Ibid., p. 8.

13   Ibid., p. 17.

14   The first British "School of Industry" was set up in 1799 in the Lake District. There were not many such schools for girls. Apart from basic reading and writing, they taught vocational subjects, such as knitting, sewing and spinning. Caroline may have fashioned her school upon this style of institution.

15   A Medical Practitioner of Several Years' Experience, op. cit., p. 22.

16   Ibid., p. 33.

17   Ibid., p. 57.

18   *The Asiatic Journal and Monthly Miscellany,* vol. 25, January to April 1838, Wm. H Allen & Co, London, 1838, p. 114.

19   *Madras Almanac, 1839,* , op. cit., p. 140.

20   *The Asiatic Journal,* op. cit., p. 259.

Chapter 5: The Bounty Girls

1   The description of Sydney is based on sources including: *The Rocks, History and Heritage,* www.therocks.com/history-and-heritage; Sydney Military Hospital, http://thedirton.therocks.com/2012/03/first-hospital. htm; Grace Karskens, "The Rocks", *Dictionary of Sydney,* 2008, http:// dictionaryofsydney.org/entry/the_rocks. For Robert Campbell, see Margaret Steven, "Campbell, Robert (1769–1846)", *Australian Dictionary of Biography,* National Centre of Biography, Australian National University, http://adb.anu.edu.au/biography/campbell-robert-1876/ text2197, published first in hard copy 1966, accessed online 15 June 2017.

2   David Mackenzie, MA, *The Emigrant's Guide, or, Ten Years' Practical Experience in Australia,* W.S. Orr & Co, London, 1845, p. 57.

3   In 1838 New South Wales made up most of the continent of Australia: to the west it bordered present-day Western Australia. South Australia had been proclaimed an independent colony in 1836; Tasmania too was separate, ruled by a lieutenant governor, but New South Wales comprised the rest of the mainland, including modern-day Victoria and Queensland, as well as New Zealand (until 1840).

4   Mrs Charles Meredith (Louisa Ann Meredith), *Notes and Sketches of New South Wales during a Residence in that Colony from 1839 to 1844*, John Murray, London, 1844, p. 34. Louisa Ann Meredith sailed into Sydney Harbour in September 1839, almost exactly one year after Caroline.

5   Roger Therry, Esq., *Reminiscences of Thirty Years' Residence in New South Wales and Victoria*, Sampson Low and Son and Co., London, 1863, p. 68. Barrister, judge, acting Attorney-General of New South Wales and a politician, Therry maintained that members of the lower social classes, either children of emancipists or working-class immigrants, should be given the opportunity, through education, to improve their standing in society.

6   James Maclehose, *Picture of Sydney and Strangers' Guide in NSW for 1839*, J. Maclehose, Sydney, 1839, p. 59.

7   David Mackenzie, op. cit., p. 150.

8   Meredith, op. cit., p. 38.

9   *The Australian*, advertising columns, Thursday, 27 November 1845, p. 2.

10 Meredith, op. cit., p. 39.

11 Maclehose, op. cit., p. 72.

12 The foundation stone for the original church was laid in 1820. The church was described by Maclehose as "an architectural ornament to the town" and it included "an excellent organ". The building was ruined by fire in 1865. The foundation stone of the present St Mary's Cathedral was laid in 1868.

13 David Mackenzie, op. cit., p. 32.

14 Callaghan, op. cit., p. 116.

15 *The Sydney Gazette*, 11 December 1838, p. 2.

16 Ibid, 29 December 1838, p. 2.

17 Therry, op. cit., p. 286.

18 Caroline Chisholm to Earl Grey, London, 27 January 1847, C.O.
    201/390. F. 225 Public Record Office, London; copy in the Mitchell
    Library, Sydney.

19 David Mackenzie, op. cit., p. 105.

20 Ibid., p. 106.

21 Ibid., pp. 34–36.

22 Meredith, op. cit., p. 36.

23 Garry Wotherspoon, "Economy", *Dictionary of Sydney*, 2008; see http://
    dictionaryofsydney.org/entry/economy, viewed 17 May 2017.

24 Australian Data Archive. According to the census of 2 March 1841
    of the Police Districts of New South Wales, there were 87,290 men
    compared to 43,550 women in the colony.

25 Kiddle, op. cit., p. 12.

26 Eneas Mackenzie, *Memoirs,* op. cit., p. 23.

27 History of the Parishes in the Catholic Diocese of Parramatta, at
    www.parra.catholic.org.au/about-your-diocese/history/history-of-the-
    parishes/history-of-the-parishes-in-the-catholic-diocese-of-parramatta.
    aspx/histories-of-the-parishes-of-the-catholic-diocese-of-parramatta/
    windsor---st-matthew-s-parish--est-1832-.aspx

28 Boating History of the Hawkesbury, at www.hawkesbury.net.au/
    memorial/wisemans_ferry_convicts/wfcm7.html

29 Kiddle, op. cit., p. 13.

30 Sidney, *Three Colonies of Australia*, p. 134.

Chapter 6: Flora's Story

1   Although the narrative at the start of this chapter is fictionalised, it
    is essentially true: part of it comes directly from Caroline's own pen,
    in her first published work, *Female Immigration Considered*. Caroline
    incorporated Flora's story into her account of the events that led to her
    establishing her home.

2   *The Australasian Chronicle*, Tuesday, 27 April 1841, p. 3; *The Australasian
    Chronicle*, Tuesday, 4 May 1841, p. 3.

3   Sidney, *Three Colonies of Australia*, p. 134.

4   Ibid.

5   Chisholm, *Female Immigration Considered*, p. 2.

6   Ibid.

7   Ibid.

8   Ibid.

9   Ibid.

10   Ibid.

11   Ibid., p. 4.

12   Eneas Mackenzie, *Memoirs*, p. 39; and Therry, op. cit., p. 423.

13   Chisholm, *Female Immigration Considered*, p. 3.

14   Ibid., p. 5.

15   Ibid., p. 4.

16   Ibid., p. 6.

17   *The Australasian Chronicle*, Saturday, 18 September 1841, p. 2.

18   Chisholm, *Female Immigration Considered*, p. 7.

19   Ibid.

20   Ibid., p. 9

Chapter 7: The Immigrants' Home

1   According to Caroline's pamphlet *Female Immigration Considered*, she asked
     two women friends to accompany her to *The Sydney Herald* (soon to be
     The Sydney Morning Herald) offices. They refused and she went alone.
     She asked the new proprietors, Fairfax and Kemp, to publish ten letters
     from bounty girls but they refused for the reasons given in this account.
     The letters no longer exist; the ones quoted at the start of the story are
     fictitious. Fairfax and Kemp did, however, support the establishment of
     the home and, when it began, gave Caroline a £2 donation. Some of
     the details regarding John Fairfax and Charles Kemp are drawn from
     their entries in the *Australian Dictionary of Biography*. See J. O. Fairfax,
     "Fairfax. John (1804–1877)", *Australian Dictionary of Biography*, National
     Centre of Biography, Australian National University, http://adb.anu.
     edu.au/biography/fairfax-john-3493/text5357, published first in hard
     copy 1972; and Charles Kemp, G. J. Abbott, "Kemp, Charles (1813–
     1864)", *Australian Dictionary of Biography*, National Centre of Biography,
     Australian National University, http://adb.anu.edu.au/biography/kemp-
     charles-2295/text2963, published first in hard copy 1967.

2   "Mrs. Chisholm on the Land Question", *The Empire*, Saturday, 9 July
     1859.

3   *The Australasian Chronicle*, Saturday, 11 September 1841, p. 2.

4   *The Australasian Chronicle*, Tuesday, 14 September 1841, p. 2.

5   *The Sydney Herald*, Friday, 24 September 1841, p. 2.

6   *The Australasian Chronicle,* Tuesday, 26 October 1841, p. 2.

7   Stinson, op. cit., pp. 82–83.

8   Hoban, op. cit., p. 56.

9   Ibid., p. 109.

10 Chisholm, *Female Immigration Considered,* pp. 10–11.

11 Ibid.

12 Amongst the lawyers who helped Caroline was her friend Thomas
    Callaghan; see Callaghan, op. cit., p. 116. Another well-known friend,
    colonial lawyer, judge and politician Sir Roger Therry, asserted that
    none of her contracts were ever questioned; see Therry, op. cit., p. 423.

13 *Report of the Select Committee of the House of Lords on Colonization from
    Ireland; together with the Minutes of Evidence. Session 1847,* ordered by the
    House of Commons to be printed 23 July 1847, p. 413.

14 Ibid., p. 414.

15 Chisholm, *Female Immigration Considered,* pp. 11–12.

Chapter 8: Going Bush

1   This fictional account is designed only to give a view of how Caroline
    and her protégées travelled from Sydney and through the bush, and of
    the dangers they faced. There is no record of Caroline being stopped
    by bushrangers. This bushranger is loosely based on Teddy "Jewboy"
    Davis, who roamed with his gang throughout the Lower Hunter Valley
    up until March 1841, when they were caught and hung. Until the end
    of 1840 they avoided killing anyone, but during an armed robbery in
    Scone in December that year one of the gang shot and killed a man.
    Teddy Davis and his gang had something of a Robin Hood reputation.
    Their stash of stolen goods has never been discovered. See www.
    jenwilletts.com/jewboygang.htm

2   Chisholm, *Female Immigration Considered,* p. 12.

3   Sidney, *Three Colonies of Australia,* p. 150.

4   With thanks to Richard Stafford for lending me his report, prepared
    for the University of NSW and Heritage Council of Australia in
    1985, *Conservation Plan of Caroline Chisholm's Barracks.* The building in
    Maitland is now known as Caroline Chisholm Cottage.

5   *Report of Select Committee of the House of Lords on Colonization from Ireland,*
    op. cit., p. 410.

6   Therry, op. cit., pp. 421–22.

7   Chisholm, *Female Immigration Considered*, p. 62.

8   Ibid., p. 36

9   Ibid., pp. 20–21.

10 Ibid., pp. 44–45.

11 Ibid., pp. 41–42.

12 Caroline Chisholm, *Prospectus of a Work to be Entitled "Voluntary Information from the People of New South Wales Respecting the Social Condition of the Middle and Working Classes in the Colony"*, Introduction, with quote about flockmasters published in W.A. Duncan's *The Weekly Register of Politics, Facts, and General Literature,* vol. V, Saturday, 30 August 1845, no. 110, p. 98. It was also published the following year in, bizarrely, *The Bengal Catholic Herald,* 10 January, 1846, p. 24. Extracts were included seven years later in Sidney, *Three Colonies of Australia*, p. 152.

13 Caroline Chisholm, *Emigration and Transportation Relatively Considered; In a Letter, Dedicated, by Permission, to Earl Grey. By Mrs Chisholm*, John Olliver, London, 1847, p. 21.

14 Summers, op. cit., p. 51.

15 Chisholm, *Emigration and Transportation Relatively Considered*, pp. 7–8.

16 Chisholm, *Female Immigration Considered*, p. 37.

17 *ACTU Worksite*, History of the Gender pay gap, http://worksite.actu. org.au/equal-pay-equal-value/

18 David Mackenzie, op. cit., p. 93.

19 *The Argus,* Saturday, 17 February 1855, p. 5.

20 Walker, op. cit., p. 144.

21 Margaret Alic, *Hypatia's Heritage: A History of Women in Science from Antiquity to the Late Nineteenth Century,* The Women's Press, 1986, p. 182.

22 Chisholm, *Female Immigration Considered*, pp. 45–48.

23 Ibid., pp. 45–48.

24 Ibid., p. 48.

Chapter 9: The Trouble with Men

1   Thomas Callaghan was an impecunious Dublin lawyer who landed in Sydney in 1839, being admitted to the Bar within six days of arriving. From early 1840 until mid-1845 he kept a diary, which gives a fascinating insight into not just the legal world but also the social world of Sydney at that time. Callaghan and Caroline moved in much

the same circles and had many friends and acquaintances in common. The diary reveals that Callaghan first met Caroline at the home of Ann and Roger Therry, and that he was greatly attracted to her. See Callaghan, op. cit, especially the entry for Tuesday, 22 February 1842.

2   *The Sydney Herald,* Tuesday, 19 April 1842, p. 2.

3   Ibid.

4   Sidney, *Three Colonies of Australia,* p. 140; also Matthew French, "Private Criminal Prosecutions: Caroline Chisholm: The Carthaginian Case and Private Prosecutions in Mid-Nineteenth Century New South Wales", University of Notre Dame, Sydney, https://mrschisholmdotcom.files. wordpress.com/2016/02/private-criminal-prosecutions_-matthew-french1.pdf

5   *The Australasian Chronicle,* Saturday, 23 April 1842, p. 2.

6   Therry, op. cit., p. 222.

7   Ibid., p. 223.

8   Callaghan, op. cit., p. 116.

9   Ibid., p. 116.

10   Ibid., p. 117.

11   Ibid., p. 117.

12   Ibid., pp. 123–24.

13   Ibid., p. 151.

14   Ibid., p. 156.

15   Hoban, op. cit., pp. 81–82.

16   John Molony, *The Native-Born: The First White Australians*, Melbourne University Press, Melbourne, 2000, p. 61.

17   Eneas Mackenzie, *Memoirs*, p. v.

18   Ibid., p. 143.

19   Sidney, *Emigrants' Journal*, p. 271.

20   Thanks to Mrs Don (Judith) Chisholm for the family story, told during an interview in Sydney in 2016.

21   Callaghan, op. cit., p. 169.

22   Sidney, *Emigrants' Journal*, p. 21.

23   J.M. Bennett AM, "Biographical Notes", in Callaghan, op. cit., p. ix.

24   Chisholm, *Female Immigration Considered,* preface, p. viii.

25   Patricia Clarke, "Barton, Charlotte (1796–1867)", *Australian Dictionary of Biography*, National Centre of Biography, Australian National

University, http://adb.anu.edu.au/barton-charlotte-12787/text23073, published first in hard copy 2005.

26 Hoban, op. cit., p. 111.

27 David Clune, "1843: The Year It All Began", *Australasian Parliamentary Review,* vol. 26, no. 1, autumn, 2011, pp. 23–40.

28 This was called the Committee on Petition from Distressed Mechanics and Labourers; see R.F. Doust (ed.), *New South Wales Legislative Council 1824–1856, The Select Committees,* from the Parliament of New South Wales Parliamentary Library, pp. 100–01.

29 D. Shineberg, "Towns, Robert (1794–1873)", *Australian Dictionary of Biography,* National Centre of Biography, Australian National University, http://adb.anu.edu.au/biography/towns-robert-4741/text7873, published first in hard copy 1976, accessed online 14 November 2016.

30 Neroli Blakeman, "To Live and Have Land: Caroline Chisholm in Illawarra", *Illawarra Historical Society Bulletin,* June 1996, pp. 46–48.

31 Arthur Cousins, *The Gardens of New South Wales — A History of Illawarra and Shoalhaven Districts, 1770–1900,* Illawarra Historical Society, Wollongong, 1994, p. 102; and *The Sydney Morning Herald,* 6 December 1849, p. 2.

32 Doust, op. cit., p. 122.

33 Kiddle, op. cit., p. 47.

34 Ibid., p. 48.

Chapter 10: On the Move

1 *The Australian,* Monday, 18 November 1844, p. 2.

2 It's not known whether Caroline met Archibald at Circular Quay when he arrived, or whether he did indeed have to go looking for her. Whatever the case, it is likely that he would have found that his wife's name was very well known in Sydney. The Customs House building was started in 1844 and opened for business in 1845. There were two camels in the grounds of Old Government House; Governor Gipps had purchased them in 1842 at a cost of £225 as an experiment in whether to introduce them into the colony. The pub where Archie ate lunch, the Bull's Head, did exist on the eastern side of George Street, between Market and Parks streets, and it had a large window looking out onto

George Street. The first David Jones shop was established on the corner of George and Barrack streets in 1838.

3   The *Coringa Packet* was a 237-ton barque, which departed Calcutta on 11 December 1844 and arrived in Sydney via Hobart on 11 March 1845.

4   British National Archives, held by the British Library: Asian and African Studies: Reference: IOR/L/AG/23/10/1 no. 1355.

5   Walker, op. cit., p. 219.

6   *The Sydney Morning Herald,* Tuesday, 18 April 1854, p. 3.

7   Chisholm, *Emigration and Transportation*, p. 8.

8   Kiddle, op. cit., p. 55.

9   *The Bengal Catholic Herald*, op. cit., p. 42.

10 Pearson, op. cit., p. 173.

11 Sidney, *Three Colonies of Australi*a, p. 151.

12 First published in part in W.A. Duncan's *The Weekly Register of Politics, Facts, and General Literature,* vol. V, Saturday, 30 August, 1845, no. 110, pp. v, 98; also part published in *The Bengal Catholic Herald*, Saturday, 10 January 1846, pp. 24–25, 41–42, probably through Archibald, who corresponded with the newspaper about his wife's activities. See also Sidney, *Three Colonies of Australia,* p. 151.

13 Sidney, *Three Colonies of Australia,* p. 152.

14 Ibid., p. 151.

15 Chisholm, *Emigration and Transportation*, pp. 32, 36–37.

16 *Report of the Select Committee of the House of Lords on Colonization from Ireland; together with the Minutes of Evidence. Session 1847,* ordered, by the House of Commons, to be printed, 23 July 1847, p. 410.

17 Hoban, op. cit., p. 172.

18 J.D. Heydon, "Macarthur, James (1798–1867)", *Australian Dictionary of Biography*, National Centre of Biography, Australian National University, http://adb.anu.edu.au/biography/macarthur-james-2389/text3151; published first in hardcopy 1967, accessed online 2 December 2016.

19 *Design & Art Australia Online,* www.daao.org.au/bio/emily-macarthur/biography/

20 Herminie Chavanne, *Une Jeune Suisse en Australie,* Emile Beroud, Genève, 1852, p. 172.

21 *The Sydney Morning Herald,* Saturday, 14 March 1846, p. 3.

22 *The Sydney Morning Herald,* Friday, 20 March 1846, p. 3.

23 Hoban, op. cit., p. 182.

24 *The Sydney Morning Herald*, Monday, 13 April 1846, p. 2.

Chapter 11: Back Home

1 Edith Pearson, "Caroline Chisholm, 'The Emigrant's Friend', 1808–1877", in *Ideals and Realities*, R. & T. Washborne Ltd, London, 1914; also Stinson, op. cit., p. 176. Sydney, Caroline's fourth son, was born at sea on 6 August 1846. Caroline was unable to feed the baby. According to Pearson (who wrote her account after interviewing Caroline's daughter), goat milk kept the infant alive until the boat docked in Hull a few days later. Pearson also wrote that the passengers on board decorated the goat and cheered it and Caroline ashore. However, her account appears to be rather confused, as she suggests that Caroline gave birth whilst taking some 600 immigrants to Sydney. Caroline did not personally take any immigrants to Sydney; she also only gave birth once at sea and that was in 1846, just before she arrived in Hull. Other biographers, such as Mary Hoban (op. cit., pp. 185–86), have also told the goat story, including the claim that it was decorated in recognition of the part it played in saving Sydney. It's reasonable to suppose that goat's milk was used to feed Sydney, but it is difficult to substantiate the rest of the tale.

2 Joel Mokyr, "Great Famine", *Encyclopaedia Britannica*, 19 April, 2017, www.britannica.com/event/Great-Famine-Irish-history

3 *British Almanac and Companion 1868,* Knight and Co., London, p. 12.

4 Henry Mayhew, *Morning Chronicle*, January 1850.

5 F.C. Husenbeth, *The History of Sedgley Park School, Staffordshire,* Richardson and Son, London, 1856, p. 243.

6 Walker, op. cit., p. 116.

7 Her letter was reprinted in *The Sydney Morning Herald* on Monday, 5 April 1847, p. 2, but originally dated and sent on 29 October 1846.

8 Ibid.

9 Ibid.

10 *The Empire,* Friday, 13 June 1862, Letter to the Editor, pp. 2–3.

11 *The Sydney Morning Herald*, Monday, 5 April 1847, p. 2.

12 Ibid., from the letter dated 16 November 1846.

13 Ibid., from the letter dated 30 November 1846.

14 *The Empire*, Friday 13 June 1862, p. 2.

15 Ibid.

16 *The Sydney Morning Herald*, Tuesday, 7 April 1846, p. 3.

17 Colonial Land and Emigration Commissioners, *Seventh General Report of the Colonial Land and Emigration Commissioners, 1847*, Charles Knight and Co., London, 1847, p. 16.

18 Ibid., p. 17.

19 Ibid., p. 3.

20 Ibid.

21 Caroline Chisholm, *The A.B.C. of Colonization: In a Series of Letters by Mrs Chisholm No. I. Addressed to the Gentlemen Forming the Committee of the Family Colonization Loan Society, Viz. Lord Ashley, M.P., The Right Hon. Sydney Herbert, M.P., The Hon. Vernon Smith, M.P., John Tidd Pratt, Esq., F.G.P. Nelson, Esq., M. Monsell, Esk., M.P, having Appended A Letter to Lord Ashley and the Rules of the Family Colonization Loan Society,* John Ollivier, London, 1850, p. 8.

22 Caroline Chisholm, letter to Earl Grey, 27 January 1847, C.O. 201/390. F. 225, Public Record Office, London; copy in the Mitchell Library, Sydney.

23 Ibid.

24 *The First Report from the Select Committee of the House of Lords Appointed to Inquire into the Execution of the Criminal Law, especially respecting Juvenile Offenders and Transportation; together with The Minutes of Evidence taken before the said committee and An Appendix. Session 1847,* ordered to be printed 1847; and *Report of the Select Committee of the House of Lords on Colonization from Ireland; together with the Minutes of Evidence. Session 1847,* ordered, by the House of Commons, to be printed, 23 July 1847.

25 Hoban, op. cit., p. 204.

26 Caroline Chisholm, letter to Earl Grey, 27 January 1847.

27 Lucy Hughes Turnbull, "The End of Transportation", *Dictionary of Sydney*, 2008, http://dictionaryofsydney.org/entry/the_end_of_transportation.

28 Chisholm, *Emigration and Transportation*, p. 5.

29 Ibid., p. 7.

30 Ibid., p. 9.

Chapter 12: Cultivating Fame

1 This is a direct quote from Charles Dickens, *Bleak House,* Chapter IV. The character of Mrs Jellyby in the novel was modelled, to some degree, on Caroline Chisholm.

2   Now 32 Charlton Place, Islington, London. The building is marked by
    a blue plaque identifying it as Caroline's home in London.

3   Lady Herbert was a strong supporter of Caroline and also of emigration
    to Australia, but, proving that there was still considerable anti-Catholic
    feeling and that even wealthy well-connected women were vulnerable,
    she had a sad life in her later years. After her husband died in 1861,
    Lady Herbert converted to Roman Catholicism, but lost control of her
    children when her husband's family, staunch Protestants, ensured that
    they became wards in Chancery, insisting that they be brought up in the
    Church of England.

4   Letter from Elizabeth Herbert to Caroline Chisholm, 24 February
    1850.

5   Baroness Angela Burdett-Coutts did finally marry. In 1881, when
    she was sixty-seven years old, she married her twenty-nine-year-old
    American-born secretary, William Lehman Ashmead-Bartlett, who
    took his wife's surname after they married.

6   Letter from Charles Dickens to Angela Burdett-Coutts, 4 March 1850.

7   *Bleak House*, Chapter IV.

8   Walker, op. cit., p. 95.

9   For example, the British Parliament Passenger Act 1849 and 1852
    improved steerage passengers' rations, and sanitary and health
    conditions.

10 John Wolffe, "Cooper, Anthony Ashley, Seventh Earl of Shaftesbury
    (1801–1885)", *Oxford Dictionary of National Biography*, Oxford University
    Press, 2004.

11 Arthur L. Bowley, *Wages in the United Kingdom in the Nineteenth Century*,
    Cambridge University Press, Cambridge, 1900, p. 35.

12 Chisholm, *The A.B.C. of Colonization*, p. 39.

13 Ibid., p. 18.

14 Ibid., p. 17.

15 Ibid., pp. 32–36.

16 Charles Dickens, "Better Ties than Red Tape Ties", *Household Words*,
    no. 101, Saturday, 28 February 1852, pp. 529–34.

17 The British Newspaper Archive. A partnership between the British
    Library and findmypast, the archive already contains most of the runs of
    newspapers published in the UK since 1800.

18 Eneas Mackenzie, *Memoirs*, pp.175–76.

19 Ibid., p. 181.

20 Ibid., p. 182.

21 A.L. Whitby, "An 1850 Voyage to Melbourne: Log of Voyage from London to Port Phillip per Barque 'Slains Castle'", contributed by Allan Hillier and published in *The Genealogist,* the official journal of the Australian Institute of Genealogical Studies (AIGS), vol. III, no. 8, December 1981. Thanks to Tricia Parnell at the AIGS for her assistance.

22 Eneas Mackenzie, *Memoirs*, p. 183.

23 R.F. Doust (ed.), *New South Wales Legislative Council 1824–1856, The Select Committees*, from the Parliament of New South Wales Parliamentary Library, Committee on Immigration, p. 238.

24 *The Illustrated London News,* 17 April 1852.

25 Walker, op. cit., p 95.

26 Eneas Mackenzie, *Memoirs*, pp.183–34.

27 *The Illustrated London News,* 30 July 1853.

28 Australian Data Archive, Historical, NSW 1856 Census, table showing the percentage of each Religion to the Total Population 1851 & 1856, http://hccda.ada.edu.au/pages/NSW-1856-census-02_xxii

29 *The Adelaide Observer,* Saturday, 9 August 1851, p. 6.

30 *The Argus,* Monday, 26 April 1852, p. 6.

31 *The Argus,* Friday, 30 April 1852, p. 2.

32 Kiddle, op. cit., p. 142.

33 Ibid., p. 148.

34 Chisholm, *The A.B.C. of Colonization*, p. 36.

35 *John O'Groat Journal,* 9 December 1853.

36 Caroline Chisholm's Scrapbook, Museum of Victoria.

37 *The Adelaide Observer,* Saturday, 2 August 1851, p. 6.

38 Walker, op. cit., p. 114.

39 Ibid.

40 Ibid., pp. 114–15.

41 *The Argus,* Thursday. 1 July 1852, p. 4.

42 *The Connaught Watchman,* Wednesday, 2 March 1853.

43 Hoban, op. cit., p. 282.

44 Eneas Mackenzie, *The Emigrant's Guide to Australia,* p. 112.

45 Jabez Hogg, *The Domestic Medical and Surgical Guide, for the Nursery, the Cottage, and the Bush; Giving the Best Advice in the Absence of a Physician or Surgeon, in Cases of Accident or Sudden Illness; Useful to Families, Emigrants,*

Travellers, Missionaries, Village Clergymen, and Sea Captains, second edition, Ingram, Cook and Co., London, 1853, p. v.

46 Ibid., pp. 14–15.

47 John Dunmore Lang, open letter to Earl Grey, 14 November 1849, written aboard the ship *Clifton,* off Gravesend, and published in *The Spectator* on 17 November 1849, p. 6; also published in other newspapers, including *The British Banner.*

48 Ibid.

49 Australian Data Archive, Historical, NSW 1856 Census, http://hccda. ada.edu.au/pages/NSW-1856-census-02_xxii.

50 *Freeman's Journal,* Saturday, 15 June 1861, p. 5.

51 Ibid.

52 *Punch,* 20 August 1853.

53 Walker, op. cit., p. 128.

Chapter 13: A Golden Land

1 Caroline and her eldest son, Archibald, visited the goldfields about three months after she arrived in Melbourne. Their trip to Bendigo took them through what was then called the Black Forest, situated between Macedon and Woodend, a well-known hideout for bushrangers. After heavy rain, the dirt tracks through the forest were almost impassable. Caroline's trip came almost on the eve of the Eureka Stockade rebellion.

2 *The Argus,* Saturday, 15 July 1854, p. 5.

3 Australian Data Archive, Historical, Vic-1854-Census, p. vii.

4 From Van Diemen's Land, i.e. from Tasmania.

5 Mrs Charles (Ellen) Clacy, *A Lady's Visit to the Gold Diggings of Australia in 1852–53,* Hurst and Blackett, 1853, pp. 6–7.

6 Hoban, op. cit., p. 331.

7 *The Argus,* Tuesday, 25 July 1854, p. 5.

8 *The Argus,* Saturday, 2 September 1854, p. 4.

9 *The Argus,* Tuesday, 26 September 1854, p. 5.

10 *The Argus,* Saturday, 4 April 1855, p. 4.

11 Hoban, op. cit., p. 329.

12 *The Argus,* Saturday, 4 April 1855, p. 4.

13 Hoban, op. cit., p. 354.

14 Mary L. Shannon, *Dickens, Reynolds, and Mayhew on Wellington Street: The Print Culture of a Victorian Street,* Routledge, London, 2016, p. 189.

15 William Howitt, *Land, Labour, and Gold; or, Two Years in Victoria: with Visits to Sydney and Van Diemen's Land*, Longman, Brown, Green and Longmans, London, 1855, pp. 195–205.

16 Ibid.

17 *The Age,* Tuesday, 7 November 1854, p. 5.

18 Hoban, op. cit., p. 331.

19 *The Argus,* Saturday, 11 November 1854, p. 5.

20 Ibid.

21 Ibid.

22 Howitt, op. cit., p. 205.

23 *The Argus,* Saturday, 11 November 1854. p. 5.

24 *The Age,* Tuesday, 7 November 1854, p. 6.

25 *The Argus,* Monday, 6 November 1854, p. 6.

26 *The Argus,* Saturday, 9 December 1854, p. 5.

27 Kiddle, op. cit., p. 177.

28 *Civil Establishment of the Colony of Victoria for the Year 1864*, Compiled from Official Records in the Registrar-General's Office, p. 3.

29 Brenda Stevens-Chambers, *Caroline Chisholm: Her Friends and Foes 1840–2004,* Springfield & Hart, Kyneton, 2004.

30 *The Argus,* Monday, 31 December 1855, p. 6.

31 Stevens-Chambers, op. cit.

32 *The Argus,* Monday, 31 December 1855, p. 6.

33 *The Argus,* Friday, 16 January 1857, p. 6

34 Stevens-Chambers, op. cit.

35 John Hirst, *Making Voting Secret, Victoria's Introduction of a New Method of Voting that has Spread Around the World,* Victorian Electoral Commission publication, pp. 34–35; www.vec.vic.gov.au/files/Book-MakingVotingSecret.pdf

36 To be eligible to vote, a man over twenty-one years of age had to own land worth in excess of £1000 or lease property at an annual rental value of £100. It is unlikely that the Chisholms would have been in that position. See the Victorian Government website: www.parliament.vic.gov.au/council/publications-a-research/information-sheets/17-electoral-system-1851-2003.

37 Stevens-Chambers, op. cit.

38 Ibid.

39 Ibid.

40 *The Age*, Friday, 10 October 1856, p. 5.

41 *The Argus*, Tuesday, 28 August 1855, p. 8.

42 Stevens-Chambers, op. cit.

43 *The Argus*, Wednesday, 22 April 1857, p. 4. St Francis was Bishop Goold's Cathedral Church until the diocesan seat was moved to St Patrick's Cathedral in 1868.

44 Hoban, op. cit., p. 378.

45 *The Bendigo Advertiser*, Wednesday, 21 January 1857, p. 3.

46 *Census of Victoria, 1857, Population Tables 1. Inhabitants and Houses. Population Enumerated 29th March, 1857, Presented to Both Houses of Parliament by His Excellency's Command*, by Authority John Ferres, Government Printer, p. 34, table VII, Report, 5 November 1857.

47 *The Argus*, Saturday, 13 June 1857, p. 5.

48 *The Age*, Thursday, 26 November 1857; and *The Argus*, Thursday, 26 November 1857, p. 5.

Chapter 14: The Female Radical

1 This is a reimagining of Caroline's second public lecture in Sydney, held at the Temperance Hall in Pitt Street, Sydney, which seated four hundred people. The fact that Caroline invited the women onto the stage suggests not only that there was a huge crowd, but also, and unusually for the era, that many women had attended the lecture. It was a point that Caroline obviously wanted to highlight. The talk was held in the middle of the 1860 New South Wales election campaign, and Caroline was supporting the Cowper–Robertson side, which was in favour of freeing up land so that it could be bought in small lots by less wealthy farmers, in direct opposition to the powerful squatters. See John Moran (ed.), *Radical, in Bonnet and Shawl: Four Political Lectures by Caroline Chisholm*, Preferential Publications, Ashgrove, 1994, p. 63.

2 Hoban, op. cit., p. 387.

3 *The Empire*, Friday, 13 June 1862, p. 3.

4 Ibid.

5 Kiddle, op. cit., p. 176.

6 Hoban, op. cit., p. 390.

7 Cleveland Street Intensive English High School, NSW Government website, www.clevelandi-h.schools.nsw.edu.au/school-history

8   Memorandum of Mrs Munro, wife of Donald Munro, first secretary of the Victorian Agricultural Society, quoted in Hoban, op. cit., p. 390.

9   All Nuns website, http://web.stbedes.catholic.edu.au/Other/nuns/down/AllNuns.pdf

10 John Askew, *A Voyage to Australia and New Zealand,* Simpkin Marshall, London, 1857, p. 214.

11 Ibid., p. 185.

12 Ibid., p. 212.

13 Ibid., p. 221.

14 Letter from publisher of the Sydney *Freeman's Journal,* J. K. Heydon, to Father Therry, May 1859; see Kiddle, op. cit., p. 177.

15 NSW Office of Environment & Heritage, Chinese Market Gardens website: www.environment.nsw.gov.au/Heritage/aboutheritage/chinesemktgarden.htm

16 *The Sydney Morning Herald,* Tuesday, 26 November 1861, p. 3.

17 Kiddle, op. cit., p. 177.

18 Hoban, op. cit., p. 392.

19 Winifred Holtby, *Women and a Changing Civilisation,* John Lane, 1934, p. 48.

20 *The Empire,* Saturday, 9 July 1859, p. 8.

21 Ibid.

22 Walker, op. cit., p. 101.

23 Bede Nairn, "Robertson, Sir John (1816–1891)", *Australian Dictionary of Biography,* National Centre of Biography, Australian National University, http://adb.anu.edu.au/biography/robertson-sir-john-4490/text7337, published first in hard copy 1976; and John M. Ward, "Cowper, Sir Charles (1807–1875)", *Australian Dictionary of Biography,* National Centre of Biography, Australian National University, http://adb.anu.edu.au/biography/cowper-sir-charles-3275/text4967, published first in hard copy 1969.

24 *Freeman's Journal,* Saturday, 23 February 1861, p. 3.

25 *The Sydney Morning Herald,* Friday, 22 February 1861, p. 4.

26 *The Empire,* Friday, 14 June 1861, p. 5.

27 Ibid. "Crinoline" referred to the massive hooped skirts that were fashionable throughout much of the Victorian era.

28 Ibid.

29 *The Empire,* Monday, 15 August 1859, p. 4.

30 *The Empire,* Saturday, 24 May 1862, p. 1.

31 Catherine Bishop, *Minding Her Own Business: Colonial Businesswomen in Sydney,* New South Publishing, Sydney, 2015.

32 *The Empire,* Saturday, 24 May 1862, p. 1.

33 *The Empire,* Thursday, 14 May 1863, p. 8.

34 The Rathbone's Liverpool home was called "Greenbank" without the hyphen. There is no obvious reason why Caroline chose the different spelling.

35 *The Empire,* Thursday, 14 May 1863, p. 8.

36 *The Sydney Morning Herald,* Saturday, 20 February 1864, p. 9.

37 Dating from the 1830s, the building that housed the school still stands on the Cooks River at Arncliffe and is known as Tempe House. It has been largely restored and is open a few times a year to the public.

38 Opening couplet from William Wordsworth, "She was a Phantom of Delight", 1804.

39 *The Empire,* Tuesday, 14 October 1862, p. 5.

40 *The Sydney Morning Herald,* Thursday, 8 November 1866, p. 2.

41 *The Tumut and Adelong Times,* Thursday, 5 April 1866, p. 2.

42 *Freeman's Journal,* Saturday, 7 April 1866, p. 209.

43 Walker, op. cit., p. 146.

44 *The Sydney Morning Herald,* Monday, 21 November 1864, p. 9.

45 Caroline Chisholm, letter to Elizabeth Rathbone, 22 September 1865, held by the University of Liverpool (RP VI 1).

46 Ibid.

47 Ibid.

Chapter 15: The Final Journey

1 Caroline spent her final days bedridden in a sunlit room in Fulham. According to a letter from her daughter, Monica, the street was a cul-de-sac and had a common at the end. Caroline's death certificate stated that she had been suffering from senile softening of the brain, possibly a type of oedema, or cerebral oedema for the past six years. She was also, near the end, suffering from bronchitis. One imagines that she did think back over the success of her work.

2 *The Daily Mail,* Saturday, 15 December 1866, p. 3.

3 Walker, op. cit., p. 150.

4 Caroline Chisholm, letter to Elizabeth Rathbone, 22 September 1865, held by the University of Liverpool (RP VI 1).

5   Ibid.

6   Walker, op. cit., p. 147; and Kiddle, op. cit., p. 181.

7   *The Illustrated London News,* Saturday, 2 February 1867, p. 103.

8   *The Daily News,* Saturday, 15 December 1866, p. 3.

9   *The Standard,* Monday, 13 May 1867, p. 2.

10 *Lloyd's Weekly London Newspaper,* 19 May 1867, p. 6.

11 *The Northampton Mercury,* Saturday, 18 May 1867, p. 3.

12 Hoban, op. cit., p. 414.

13 Ibid., p. 413.

14 *The Sydney Morning Herald,* Saturday, 9 July 1870, p. 1.

15 *The Sydney Morning Herald,* Friday, November 1871, p. 8.

16 Hoban, op. cit., p. 413.

17 Ibid., p. 416.

18 Pearson, in Stinson, op. cit., p. 179.

19 Certified Copy of an Entry of Death Given at the General Register
    Office, Somerset House, London. State Library of New South Wales,
    Papers relating to Caroline Chisholm, ca. 1853–ca. 1953, Call Number
    Ac19/Folder2, item II, copy of 1877 death certificate for Caroline
    Chisholm, issued 12 February 1924.

20 *The Argus,* Saturday, 9 June 1877, p. 10.

Afterword

1   Walker, op. cit., p. 151.

2   *The Illustrated London News,* 3 August 1878, p. 102.

3   Monica Gruggen, letter to Mr Thomas, an Australian researcher who
    had contacted Monica in Canada through contacts in Northampton,
    regarding information about Caroline's artefacts, including her
    painting. State Library of New South Wales, Papers relating to Caroline
    Chisholm, ca. 1853–ca. 1953, Call Number Ac19/Folder2, holograph
    letters (2) from Monica Gruggen, Canada, to J.F. Thomas.

4   *National Library of Ireland News,* Number 19, Spring 2005.

5   Monica Gruggen, letter to Mr Thomas, op. cit.

6   R.P. Davis, "Dwyer-Gray, Edmund John (1870–1945)", *Australian
    Dictionary of Biography*, National Centre of Biography, Australian
    National University, http://abd.anu.au/biography/dwyer-gray-edmund-
    john-6068/text10385, published first in hard copy 1981.

Bibliography

Books

A Medical Practitioner of Several Years' Experience in India, *A Domestic Guide to Mothers in India containing Particular Instructions on the Management of themselves and their Children*, Bombay American Mission Press, Bombay, 1856.

William Acton, MRCS, *Functions and Disorders of the Reproductive Organs in Childhood, Youth, Adult Age and Advanced Life Considered in the Physiological, Social and Moral Relations*, John Churchill, London, 1857.

Anonymous or Plain Observations, *Plain Observations on the Management of Children during the First Month, Particularly Addressed to Mothers*, Underwood, London, 1828.

Raymond Apple, "The Jewish Emigrants from Britain: Australia and New Zealand", in Gabriel A. Sivan (ed.), *The Jewish Emigrant from Britain 1700–2000: Essays in Memory of Lloyd p. Gartner*, Jewish Historical Society of England, Israel Branch, Jerusalem, 2013.

John Askew, *A Voyage to Australia and New Zealand*, Simpkin Marshall, London, 1857.

Australian Dictionary of Biography, Australian National University.

Catherine Bishop, *Minding Her Own Business: Colonial Businesswomen in Sydney*, New South Publishing, Sydney, 2015.

Arthur L. Bowley, *Wages in the United Kingdom in the Nineteenth Century*, Cambridge, University Press, Cambridge, 1900.

C.E. Buckland, CIE, *Dictionary of Indian Biography*, Swan Sonnenschein & Co, London, 1906.

Thomas Callaghan, *Callaghan's Diary: The 1840s Sydney Diary of Thomas Callaghan of the King's Inns, Dublin, Barrister at Law,* transcribed, edited and introduced by J.M. Bennett, Francis Forbes Society for Australian Legal History, Dream Weaver Publishing, Sydney, 2005.

Robert Cecil, Marquess of Salisbury, *Lord Robert Cecil's Gold Fields Diary,* introduction and notes by Sir Ernest Scott, Melbourne University Press, Melbourne, 1945.

Herminie Chavanne, *Une Jeune Suisse en Australie,* Emile Beroud, Genève, 1852.

Caroline Chisholm, *The A.B.C. of Colonization. In a Series of Letters by Mrs. Chisholm. No. I. Addressed to the Gentlemen Forming the Committee of the Family Colonization Loan Society, Viz. Lord Ashley, M.P., The Right Hon. Sydney Herbert, M.P., The Hon. Vernon Smith, M.P., John Tidd Pratt, Esq., F.G.P. Nelson, Esq., M. Monsell, Esq., M.P., having Appended A Letter to Lord Ashley, and the Rules of the Family Colonization Loan Society,* John Ollivier, London, 1850.

Caroline Chisholm, *Emigration and Transportation Relatively Considered; In a Letter, Dedicated, by Permission, to Earl Grey,* John Ollivier, London, 1847.

Caroline Chisholm, *Female Immigration Considered, in a Brief Account of the Sydney Immigrants' Home,* James Tegg, Sydney, 1842.

Caroline Chisholm, *Little Joe,* First published in *The Empire* 1859, 1991 edition introduced and edited by John Moran, Preferential Publications, Ashgrove, Australia.

Caroline Chisholm, *Prospectus of a Work to be Entitled "Voluntary Information from the People of New South Wales Respecting the Social Condition of the Middle and Working Classes in the Colony",* 1845, W. A. Duncan, Sydney.

Mrs Charles (Ellen) Clacy, *A Lady's Visit to the Gold Diggings of Australia in 1852–53,* Hurst and Blackett, London, 1853.

Arthur Cousins, *The Gardens of New South Wales — A History of Illawarra and Shoalhaven Districts, 1770–1900,* Illawarra Historical Society, Wollongong, 1994.

Faramerz Dabhoiwala, *The Origins of Sex: A History of the First Sexual Revolution,* Oxford University Press, New York, 2012.

Charles Dickens, *Bleak House*, London, 1853.

R.F. Doust (ed.), *New South Wales Legislative Council 1824–1856, The Select Committees*, Parliament of New South Wales Parliamentary Library, Sydney, 2011.

Sarah Stickney Ellis, *The Daughters of England, their Position in Society, Character and Responsibilities*, D. Appleton and Co. New York, 1843.

Sarah Stickney Ellis, *The Wives of England, their Relative Duties, Domestic Influence, and Social Obligations*, D. Appleton & Co, London, 1843.

James Fordyce DD, *Sermons to Young Women: Two Volumes in One*, Third American Edition from the Twelfth London Edition, M. Carey, Philadelphia, 1809.

Deborah Gorham, *The Victorian Girl and Feminine Ideal*, Croom Helm, London, 1982.

Robert Harris (attributed), *What has Mrs Chisholm Done for the Colony of New South Wales?*, James Cole, Sydney, 1862.

Mary Hoban, *Fifty-one Pieces of Wedding Cake: A Biography of Caroline Chisholm*, Lowden Publishing Co., Kilmore, Victoria, 1973.

Jabez Hogg, *The Domestic Medical and Surgical Guide, for the Nursery, the Cottage, and the Bush; Giving the best Advice in the Absence of a Physician or Surgeon, in Cases of Accident or Sudden Illness; Useful to Families, Emigrants, Travellers, Missionaries, Village Clergymen, and Sea Captains*, second edition, Ingram, Cook and Co., London, 1853.

Winifred Holtby, *Women and a Changing Civilisation*, John Lane, London, 1934.

William Howitt, *Land, Labour, and Gold; or, Two Years in Victoria: with Visits to Sydney and Van Diemen's Land*, Longman, Brown, Green and Longmans, London, 1855.

F.C. Husenbeth, *The History of Sedgley Park School, Staffordshire*, Richardson and Son, London, 1856.

Margaret Kiddle, *Caroline Chisholm*, Melbourne University Press, Melbourne, 1996.

David Mackenzie, MA, *The Emigrant's Guide, or, Ten Years' Practical Experience in Australia*, W.S. Orr & Co, London, 1845.

Eneas Mackenzie, *The Emigrant's Guide to Australia with a Memoir of Mrs Chisholm*, Clarke, Beeton & Co., London, 1853.

Eneas Mackenzie, *Memoirs of Mrs Caroline Chisholm, with an Account of Her Philanthropic Labours in India, Australia, and England; To which is added a History of the Family Colonization Loan Society; also the Question, Who Ought to Emigrate? Answered,* Webb, Millington and Co., London, second edition, 1852.

James Maclehose, *Picture of Sydney and Strangers' Guide in N.S.W. for 1839,* John Ferguson Pty Ltd, Sydney, 1977.

Madras Almanac and Compendium of Intelligence for 1839, Edmund Marsden, Madras, 1839.

Julia Maitland, *Letters from Madras. By a Lady During the Years 1836– 1839,* John Murray, London, 1846.

Mrs Charles Meredith (Louisa Ann Meredith), *Notes and Sketches of New South Wales during a Residence in that Colony from 1839 to 1844,* John Murray, London, 1844.

Helena Michie, *Victorian Honeymoons: Journeys to the Conjugal,* Cambridge University Press, Cambridge, 2006.

John Molony, *The Native-Born: The First White Australians,* Melbourne University Press, Melbourne, 2000.

John Moran (ed.), introduction to *Little Joe,* by Caroline Chisholm, Preferential Publications, Ashgrove, 1991.

John Moran (ed.), *Radical, in Bonnet and Shawl: Four Political Lectures by Caroline Chisholm,* Preferential Publications, Ashgrove, 1994.

Artemas Bowers Muzzey, *The English Maiden, Her Moral and Domestic Duties,* Tallboys, Clark & Wilson, London, 1942.

Renton Nicholson, *The Swell's Night Guide; or, a Peep Through the Great Metropolis, under the Dominion of Nox: Displaying the Various Attractive Places of Amusement by Night,* H. Smith, London, 1846.

Mrs William Parkes (Fanny Parkes, née Byerly), *Domestic Duties; or, Instructions to Young Married Ladies, on the Management of their Households, and the Regulation of their Conduct in the Various Relations and Duties of Married Life,* Longman, Rees, Orme, Brown and Green, London, 1828.

Edith Pearson, "Caroline Chisholm, 'The Emigrant's Friend', 1808– 1877", in *Ideals and Realities,* R. & T. Washborne Ltd, London, 1914

Joan Perkin, *Women and Marriage in Nineteenth-Century England,* Routledge, London, 1989.

Sir John Philippart, KGV and KPS (ed.), *General Index to the First and Second Series of Hansard's Parliamentary Debates forming A Digest of the Recorded Proceedings of Parliament, from 1803 to 1830,* Baldwin & Cradock, London, 1834, "Petition from Northampton, against any further Concession to the Catholics, the object of the Petitioners being to secure as completely as possible, the Integrity and Safety of the Protestant Establishment in Church and State, 1829".

"Philogamus", *The Present State of Matrimony: Or, the Real Causes of Conjugal Infidelity and Unhappy Marriages,* John Hawkins, London, 1739

F.K. Prochaska, *Women and Philanthropy in Nineteenth-Century England,* Oxford University Press, New York, 1980.

Jane Randall, *Women in an Industrializing Society: England 1750–1880,* Basil Blackwell Ltd, Oxford, 1990.

Penny Russell (ed.), *This Errant Lady, Jane Franklin's Overland Journey to Port Phillip and Sydney, 1839,* National Library of Australia, Canberra, 2002.

Mary L. Shannon, *Dickens, Reynolds, and Mayhew on Wellington Street: The Print Culture of a Victorian Street,* Routledge, London, 2016.

Samuel Sidney, *The Three Colonies of Australia: New South Wales, Victoria, South Australia; Their Pastures, Copper Mines and Gold Fields,* Ingram, Cooke and Co., London, 1853.

Monica-Maria Stapelberg, *Through the Darkness: Glimpses into the History of Western Medicine,* Crux Publishing, London, 2016.

Brenda Stevens-Chambers, *Caroline Chisholm: Her Friends and Foes 1840–2004,* Springfield & Hart, Kyneton, 2004.

Rodney Stinson (ed.), *Unfeigned Love,* Yorkcross Pty Ltd., 2008.

Anne Summers, *Damned Whores and God's Police,* Penguin Books Australia Ltd, Camberwell, Victoria, revised edition, 2002.

Roger Therry, Esq., *Reminiscences of Thirty Years' Residence in New South Wales and Victoria,* Sampson Low and Son and Co., London, 1863.

Henry Venn, *The Complete Duty of Man or, a System of Doctrinal and Practical Christianity. With Prayers for Families and Individuals,* William Collins, London, 1829.

Carole Walker, *A Saviour of Living Cargoes: The Life and Works of Caroline Chisholm,* Wolds Publishing Limited, Leicester, UK, 2010.

James Welsh, *Military Reminiscences; Extracted from a Journal of Nearly Forty Years' Active Service in the East Indies,* Smith, Elder and Co, London, 1820.

William Whellan and Co., *History, Gazetteer, and Directory of Northamptonshire; Comprising A General Survey of the Country and a History of the Diocese of Peterborough: with Separate Historical, Statistical and Topographical Descriptions of all the Towns, Parishes, Townships, and manors. To which is Subjoined a List of the Seats of the Nobility, Clergy and Gentry.* Whittaker and Co., 1849.

Elizabeth Windschuttle (ed.), *Women, Class and History Feminist Perspectives on Australia 1788–1978,* Fontana/Collins, Melbourne, 1980.

Mary Wollstonecraft, *A Vindication of the Rights of Woman, with Strictures on Political and Moral Subjects. With a Biographical Sketch of the Author.* A.J. Matsell, New York, 1833.

Anand A. Yang, *Markets, Society, and the Colonial State in Gangetic Bihar,* University of California Press, Berkeley, 1998.

Journals and reports

The Asiatic Journal and Monthly Miscellany, vol. 25, January to April 1838, Wm. H Allen & Co, London, 1838.

The Bengal Catholic Herald, no. 2, Calcutta, Saturday, January 10, 1846.

Neroli Blakeman, "To Live and Have Land: Caroline Chisholm in Illawarra", *Illawarra Historical Society Bulletin,* June 1966.

British Almanac and Companion 1868, Knight and Co., London.

British National Archives held by the British Library: Asian and African Studies: Reference: IOR/L/AG/23/10/1 no. 1355.

Census of Victoria, 1857 Population Tables 1. Inhabitants and Houses. Population Enumerated 29th March, 1857, Presented to both Houses of Parliament by his Excellency's Command, by Authority: John Ferres, Government Printer, p. 34, table VII Report, 5 November 1857.

Geoffrey Chamberlain, "British Maternal Mortality in the 19th and Early 20th Centuries", *The Journal of the Royal Society of Medicine*, vol. 99, November 2006.

Civil Establishment of the Colony of Victoria for the Year 1864, compiled from Official Records in the Registrar-General's Office.

David Clune, "The Year It All Began", *Australasian Parliamentary Review*, vol. 26, no. 1, autumn 2011, http://search.informit.com.au/documentSummary;dn=201213910;res=IELAPA, ISSN: 1447-9125.

Charles Dickens, *Household Words, A Weekly Journal, Conducted by Charles Dickens*, no. 1, Saturday, March 30 1850, and no. 22, Saturday, August 24 1850.

W.A. Duncan's *The Weekly Register of Politics, Facts, and General Literature*, vol. V, Saturday, 30 August 1845.

First Report from the Select Committee of the House of Lords Appointed to Inquire into the Execution of the Criminal Law, Especially Respecting Juvenile Offenders and Transportation; together with The Minutes of Evidence Taken Before the Said Committee, and An Appendix, Session 1847, ordered to be printed 12 March 1847.

John Hirst, "Making Voting Secret, Victoria's Introduction of a New Method of Voting that has Spread Around the World", Victorian Electoral Commission publication, www.vec.vic.gov.au/files/Book-MakingVotingSecret.pdf

Loudon I., "Deaths in Childbed from the Eighteenth Century to 1935", *Medical History*, Cambridge Journals of Medical History, vol. 30, issue 1, 1986, https://www.ncbi.nlm.nih.gov/pmc/articles/PMC1139579/pdf/medhist00072-0005.pdf

The Old Limerick Journal, vol. 40, 2004.

T.M. Parssinen, "Popular Science and Society: The Phrenology Movement in Early Victorian Britain", *Journal of Social History*, vol. 8, no. 1, 1974, www.jstor.org/stable/3786523

Report of the Select Committee of the House of Lords on Colonization from Ireland; together with the Minutes of Evidence. Session 1847, ordered by the House of Commons to be printed 23 July 1847.

D.K. Shearing, *Education in the Peterborough Dioceses in the Century Following the "Glorious Revolution" 1688*, PhD Thesis, Institute of Education, University of London, 1990.

Samuel Sidney, *Sidney's Emigrant's Journal and Traveller's Magazine, Second Series,* Wm. S. Orr and Co., London, 1850.

Richard Stafford, *Conservation Plan of Caroline Chisholm's Barracks, Prepared for the University of NSW and Heritage Council of Australia, 1985.*

A.L. Whitby, "An 1850 Voyage to Melbourne, Log of Voyage from London to Port Philip per Barque 'Slains Castle'", contributed by Allan Hillier, published in *The Genealogist,* the official journal of the Australian Institute of Genealogical Studies, vol. III, no. 8, December 1981.

Online

All Nuns website: http://web.stbedes.catholic.edu.au/Other/nuns/down/AllNuns.pdf

Australian Data Archive, Historical, *Table showing the percentage of each Religion to the Total Population 1851 & 1856*, http://hccda.ada.edu.au/pages/NSW-1856-census-02

Boating History of the Hawkesbury: www.hawkesbury.net.au/memorial/wisemans_ferry_convicts/wfcm7.html

Bushranger History online: Free Settler or Felon, http://www.jenwilletts.com/index.htm

Archibald Chisholm, Military Record: http://discovery.nationalarchives.gov.uk/details/rd/9b2fc886-0822-4ea0-96f5-2cec9bdef5f9

Family Planning Association, London, "Contraception: Past, Present and Future", www.fpa.org.uk/sites/default/files/contraception-past-present-and-future-factsheet-november-2010.pdf

Farm Wages and Living Standards in the Industrial Revolution: England, 1670–1850, by Gregory Clark, Dept. of Economics, UC-Davis, CA 95616, gclark@ucdavis.edu: www.econ.ucdavis.edu/faculty/gclark/papers/farm_wages_&_living_standards.pdf

Historic Hawkesbury – Australia's Third Settlement: www.hawkesburyaustralia.com.au/information/area_history.asp

History of the Catholic Church in England (16th–19th Century): www.thepapalvisit.org.uk/The-Catholic-Faith/History-of-the-Catholic-Church-in-England-16th-19th-Century

History of the Parishes in the Catholic Diocese of Parramatta, at www.parra.catholic.org.au/about-your-diocese/history/history-of-the-parishes/history-of-the-parishes-in-the-catholic-diocese-of-parramatta.aspx/histories-of-the-parishes-of-the-catholic-diocese-of-parramatta/windsor---st-matthew-s-parish--est-1832-.aspx

International Clan Chisholm Society: www.rampantscotland.com/clans/blclanchisholm.htm

Myall Creek Massacre: www.creativespirits.info/aboriginalculture/history/myall-creek-massacre-1838#axzz4kFQZqgmm

NSW Office of Environment & Heritage, Chinese Market Gardens website: www.environment.nsw.gov.au/Heritage/aboutheritage/chinesemktgarden.htm

Max Roser, "Life Expectancy", OurWorldInData.org: https://ourworldindata.org/life-expectancy

Lucy Hughes Turnbull, "The End of Transportation", *Dictionary of Sydney*, 2008, http://dictionaryofsydney.org/entry/the_end_of_transportation

Garry Wotherspoon, "Economy", *Dictionary of Sydney*, 2008, http://dictionaryofsydney.org/entry/economy

Acknowledgements

A book like this is only possible with the assistance of many people. I am greatly indebted to Caroline's descendants, primarily her great-great grandson, Professor Don Chisholm, and his wife, Judith, who have been incredibly generous with their time and information, inviting me into their home for interviews and allowing me access to Caroline's personal artefacts and pictures. Similarly, I am very grateful to Don and Judith's daughter, Sarah, who gave up her time to talk to me and is living proof, along with the rest of her family, that Caroline's desire to aid the less fortunate has been passed down through the generations. I would like to thank the Australian Catholic University at North Sydney and particularly Anne Foubister and Dean Smith for making it possible for me to view and photograph a number of Caroline's objects held there on permanent loan.

Many of the staff at the State Library of New South Wales have been extremely helpful during my research, aiding me in finding and retrieving important information. On the other side of the world, Anna Towlson, the Archives and Special Collections Manager at the London School of Economics Library in London, was invaluable in sourcing and copying some rare original letters; also helpful were Charlotte Dunne and Elizabeth Williams,

Library Assistants at the Special Collections and Archives at Liverpool University Library, England.

My thanks also go to Tricia Parnell, Office Manager at the Australian Institute of Genealogical Studies Inc., for making it possible for me to use the wonderful 1850 journal of A.L. Whitby, who travelled on the Slains Castle. Such a document helps bring history to life. Richard Stafford was very kind in letting me borrow (for a number of years) his 1985 conservation plan of Caroline's Maitland Barracks; thank you also to Matenia Mandalidis for following through initially, and putting me in touch with Richard.

Both the Australian Society of Authors (ASA) and the NSW Writers' Centre are invaluable resources for writers and I would like to acknowledge the opportunities both organisations provide for writers and their vital support; in particular, I would like to mention Jane Coulcher at the ASA and, from the Writers' Centre, Richard Brookton, Derek Mortimer, Loretta Re, Jenny Hale, K-J Eyre, Maddy Oliver and Angeles Galvez. Their comments have been insightful and hugely helpful. I would also like to very much thank historian Paul Brunton for his review of my manuscript and his highly constructive comments.

I am indebted to publisher Catherine Milne for her faith in the project and for being so supportive and confident throughout. I am also grateful to Catherine for suggesting that Scott Forbes should edit the book. He has been unremittingly professional, positive and patient; I have been very fortunate to have such a brilliant editor. It goes without saying, though, that any mistakes are my own.

On a personal note, I want to thank my close girlfriends who, when my mother died during the writing of this book, helped me at that very difficult time by ringing me and just letting me know that they were there for me. They kept me on track.

Thanks to Alice, who has taken me on long walks and sat at my feet whilst I worked, and has ears large enough to hear everything I say yet has never argued with me. Finally, thank you to my three men, who have given me unconditional love and support: Steven, who has encouraged me from the very start of the project and known when to make me laugh; Charles, who understood the need for drama as well as IT skills; and Rupert, who, despite being on the other side of the world, spent hours discussing the book and helping me to clarify ideas. I could not have completed this without them.

Index